THE ROLE OF THE STATE
IN DEVELOPMENT PROCESSES

EADI BOOK SERIES 15

THE ROLE OF THE STATE
IN DEVELOPMENT PROCESSES

edited by
CLAUDE AUROI

FRANK CASS • LONDON

Published in collaboration with
The European Association of Development Research
and Training Institutes (EADI), Geneva

First published in 1992 in Great Britain by
FRANK CASS & CO. LTD.
Gainsborough House, Gainsborough Road,
London E11 1RS, England

and in the United States of America by
FRANK CASS
c/o International Specialized Book Services, Inc.
5602 N.E. Hassalo Street
Portland, Oregon 97213

British Library Cataloguing in Publication Data

Role of the State in Development
Processes – (EADI Book Series; Vol. 15)
I. Auroi, Claude   II. Series
320.1

ISBN 0-7146-3493-X

Library of Congress Cataloging-in-Publication Data

The role of the state in development processes / edited by Claude
Auroi.
    p.   cm. — (EADI-book series ; 15)
    Includes bibliographical references.
    ISBN 0-7146-3493-X (U.S.)
    1. Economic development—Political aspects. 2. State, The.
3. Industry and state. I. Auroi, Claude, 1944-   II. Series.
HD87.R65   1992
338.9–dc20   92-26250
                                                        CIP

Printed in Great Britain by
Antony Rowe Ltd, Chippenham, Wilts.

CONTENTS

IV. CHALLENGES FOR RESEARCH AND EDUCATION IN SOCIAL SCIENCES

Introduction

CLAUDE AUROI

In the 1970s, the state was already the subject of an ongoing debate, but one which focused on different aspects to those which would be discussed two decades later. Today, the form of government is questioned and the withdrawal of the state is on the agenda, whereas 20 years ago the debate centred on the nature of the state and the state building process. The concerns, especially among young nations, focused on which type of state system would best guarantee the coming into being of an organised nation, socially integrated and with an economic structure capable of ensuring rapid development.

The ideological debate was relatively simple since two major currents dominated the world and corresponded to a reality which had as symbols the Western type of state and the Marxist state.

Admittedly, each current encompassed various tendencies which, in their analysis, emphasised different elements and even reached diverging conclusions. But the fundamental debate did focus on socialist state versus 'bourgeois' state.

Though the dichotomy appeared irreducible, the two ideologies of the state had nevertheless several points in common. The main one was the will to build a 'strong' state. The qualifying adjective meant that the entity called 'state' took over the responsibility for a multitude of activities or services, whether as a Welfare state - the most accomplished example being the Swedish model - or as a state modelled on the neo-Stalinist pattern where the productive machinery itself was planned and controlled by the state. Henri Lefebvre said:

> The importance of Stalinism in the World does not stem from the fact that it is a specific Russo-Soviet phenomenon but that its development has influenced and has been followed not only by socialist countries but also in so-called capitalist countries. Everywhere the state assumes the management of the entire society even under a liberal system.[1]

Although this affirmation may seem extreme, it was not without foundation for the *authoritarianism* a state was supposed to display to exercise its power.

1

Several reasons were put forward to justify the real and symbolic violence exercised by the state. On the one hand the needs of the class struggle, of the fight against imperialism, and on the other those of institutional building, social integration and the defense against communism.

On the periphery, the paths to state building proved to be surprisingly converging despite some apparent ideological differences. To build a new state, neither the 'liberation movements' in countries still under colonial domination nor the political parties struggling to overthrow established governments had any alternative to offer to centralism and authority.

However, some authors warned against the transfer of concepts developed under other latitudes. The notion of 'authenticity', though subsequently hackneyed by some states, had appeared earlier than the 1960s. Its origins have been more typically African and are linked to a concern for the recognition and rehabilitation of the History of that continent. Cheik Anta Diop and Joseph Ki-Zerbo[2] among French-speakers as well as English-speaking historians and politicians such as Azikiwe, Nkruma, Nyerere, Jomo Kenyatta etc. had raised the question of borrowing external modes of institutional and economic functioning.

But the voices which asked for models different from those proposed by Western or Eastern Europe, or the United States, did not get much echo at the time. Though one can wonder at the speed at which the nation-state collapsed at the end of the 1980s, the reasons for such collapse cannot be considered surprising. Yves Person had properly perceived the fragile nature of these new states when writing in 1977:

> Then, the nation-state became the favoured framework for this phenomenon (the building of a social structure of domination) though it had lost the role of market creation which it performed in the 18th century ideology. But the ideology of the absolute sovereignty of the state - of the state as absolute subject - and of the contract between abstract citizens is faithfully reproduced, because it justifies the marginalisation of the masses, which are the bearers of the national culture, and their exploitation with the view of sustaining the whole system. Physical violence not being enough, ideology and education impress upon those masses the violence of symbols which consider them with spite. Domination requires that dominated people live in a culture of dominated.[3]

On every aspect of state intervention in the field of social life action was based on open or hidden use of violence.

The concept of 'civil society' was little referred to by the generation of the 1960s and 1970s to whom its true relevance was not obvious since efforts were exclusively devoted to state building. On the contrary, nowadays it is perhaps the newest element in the debate on the role of the state in the development process. The failure of the state results from its inability to solve the crisis it had to face and thus alternative models must be sought. As Paulin J. Houtondji writes 'people have become bolder and are no longer afraid of crying out their demand for liberty'. Everywhere, civil society has become a determinant of great weight to be reckoned with in development strategies, and not merely to be considered in a perspective of manipulation. *Nolens volens* it will be highly improbable to do away with the state, but its nature will need to be redefined so as to be reconciled with the usurped authenticity. Only to this condition will a consensus be able to emerge from the civil society/institutions dialectic, and the state capable of functioning again in a climate of acceptance of its role as coordinator and a strong support in the development drive, but no longer as the only leading force.

After the first section which briefly recalls the theories which marked the advent of the notion of state [*Hegel-Marx*] the papers presented in this volume[4] touch upon the problematique of the role of the state in relation to the emergence of civil society and the loss of institutional legitimacy. While it appears difficult to ascertain whether any correlation exists between form of government (i.e. authoritarian or democratic), pace of development and income distribution, the emergence of social movements, especially in Latin America, is a new parameter which has not yet reached its full expression. But the unsolved economic crisis could set back the role these movements might play in the future. The case of India provides a good illustration of substantial grass-root development efforts undertaken by a state which stayed, however, fundamentally authoritarian and in a country where the proportion of the poor remained desperately at the same level over the years.

The third section treats the effects of reforms such as structural adjustment programmes and the change of export strategies on African economies, Latin America and Arab countries in the context of the internationalisation of the economic relations. The success story of Taiwan is analysed through its different development phases which allows an understanding of internal mechanisms in detail, and in par-ticular the decisive role played by the state.

In the debate on the state and its role in the development process, the social sciences have a leading part to play and this book which brings together papers from analysts from all the continents offers a

3

good example. But researchers are often in a difficult situation, either because the means at their disposal are too small, or because their role is merely instrumental. The social sciences are not yet fully integrated in the newly emerging state/civil society relations as most examples show. We can only hope for this integration to take place because socio-political processes could be much improved if they were submitted to independent and publicly tested analysis.

We would like to thank all the authors for their readiness to revise the papers they presented at the IVth ICCDA Conference. We also extend our thanks to Marina Leybourne for correcting the texts and to Janine Rodgers for her contribution to the editing.

NOTES

1. Round-Table on the phenomenon of state in the periphery. In 'Les Espaces du Prince. L'Etat et son expansion dans les formations sociales dépendantes', *Cahiers de l'IUED*, No 6 (Geneva). Paris, Presses universitaires de France, 1977, pp.179.
2. Cheikh Anta Diop, 1978, *Black Africa*. New York, Westport: Lawrence Hill & Co.; Also: *Precolonial Black Africa*. New York, Westport: Lawrence Hill & Co.; 1987, Ki-Zerbo, Joseph (ed), 1990, *Methodology and African Prehistory*. London: James Currey.
3. Round Table on the phenomenon of state control in the periphery, op. cit.: 202.
4. All the texts (except one) were presented at the ICCDA conference on 'The Role of the State in Development Processes' organised with the help of UNESCO in Paris in April 1990. Mr Bassem Serhan's paper was presented at the SID Conference in New Delhi in 1987. ICCDA is the Inter-regional Coordinating Committee of Development Associations, which comprises five associations: AICARDES (Association of Arab Research Institutes and Centres for Economic and Social Development), ADIPA (Association of Development Research and Training Institutes of Asia and the Pacific), CLACSO (Latin America Social Science Council), CODESRIA (Council for the Development and Economic and Social Research in Africa) and EADI (European Association of Development Research and Training Institutes).

PART I

THE GENERAL PROBLEMATIQUE

1

State and Civil Society: Prospects for the Theme

ABDELLATIF BENACHENHOU

In this chapter we will consider, in three parts, the general theme of this book. Firstly, there is the idea under the theme 'The Role of the State in Development Processes' that there are very different questions and effects in the different regions of the world: the interest of the theme proposed in this book can be found in this variation.

Secondly, we will examine the market, as often when we talk of the state and the development process, we make reference to the possibility of the market replacing the state during this development process. However, the market must be considered as being both economic and political, and it is the place where competition supposedly occurs. Finally, the third point covered will be the action to take, once the questions concerning the first two points have been cleared.

I. THE DIVERSITY OF SITUATIONS

In order to understand the diversity of situations when talking about the state and the development process, three general areas of confusion must be avoided:

(1) The difference between a producer state and a regulator state. When we speak of state intervention in economic terms, it is not known whether the state in question has a productive public sector, or if it is like a regulating agent in its global economic activity. These two situations create very different analyses.
(2) The economic and political forms, as generally only rapid and practical evaluations are made between the public sector, planning and political authoritarianism on the one hand, and the private sector, the market and democracy on the other. History has shown that there is not necessarily a link between the private sector and democracy, and examples in Asia and Latin America prove that this general evaluation is too superficial. Moreover, the public

7

sector, in Europe for example, is able to function democratically.
(3) The meaning of the word, 'state' itself, as normally, as soon as something is called a 'state', it is thought that everyone is talking about the same thing. In fact, there are many varieties of state; the Latin American state is not at all like an African or an Asian one, for example. The same problem occurs when western European states are compared with those in eastern Europe.

We can only start discussing the relations between the state and the development process when these three areas of confusion have been cleared up. It is only at that moment that the important working hypothesis - that the problems of relationship between the state and the development process are radically different in the West, in eastern Europe and in the Third World - can be considered.

If we start with the situation in the West, no-one would now seriously contest the existence of democracy, and everyone knows that developed country states have a social base which has been created by the normal functioning and historical importance of democratic institutions. The producer state has been accepted in the public sector for a long time and market regulation has not been questioned. However, what is questioned is the acceptable dose of regulation in a state with regard to the internationalisation of the economy. How can the state lighten fiscal pressure so that enterprise can recover market resources? How can the state participate, in one way or another, in the reduction of work-related production costs in an enterprise? This is the whole debate on the social costs, health and other work-related expenses. But no-one really questions the intervention of the state when it is important for the internationalisation of capital in the original country, or the intervention of the state in education. In fact, the opposite is the case.

In addition, no-one seriously contests the intervention of the state in research and the development of technology, even when it concerns the arms industry, or the state's role in international commerce, particularly because this profits enterprise of rich countries. In fact, the debate in the West on the state and the development process is not a political one on democracy, but rather a debate which centres more on the amount of regulation desired by the population, and accepted or required of the state.

In eastern European countries, the debate has emerged during a production and social creativity crisis, and has essentially developed due to the necessity of transforming the political base of the states. In this area, planning and the autonomy of public enterprise compared to

8

central planning systems has obviously been questioned. However, there is no question of a state producer or state regulator, but more the state as the determiner of the different forms of production and regulation within the country. Democracy is more the requirement than economic organisation and regulation which are only the consequences.

Despite the diversity of the debate in different regions of the Third World, it is the performance of the producer state which is at the centre of the debate. Whether we take the Latin American case, where there is a long discussion on import substitution, or the case in Africa where the discussion is directed more at structural adjustment policies, or even the comparison of performances between India and south-east Asia, we can see that it is fundamentally the question of the performance shown by producer states: in other words the capacity of the states to advantageously utilise development strategies which have been built on structural transformations of the economies.

This does not mean that the question of democracy has not emerged in the Third World, but this question does not totally cover the debate on the producer state. The experiences in democracy that we have observed, in Latin America in particular, do not seem to have really changed the terms of the debate on economic development and another question is now being posed: how are the democracies which are being born, for example in Latin America, going to positively transform the development strategies and actors? There is no definite response to this at the moment.

In conclusion, it is necessary to understand that if the debate remains at a very general level, we will not get very far in the analysis. It would be better to try to find some elements of analysis which review the most important debates and, in particular, to separate the essential and the information of secondary importance in this analysis of the state in the development process. We must start with the market.

II. THE MARKET CONCEPT

The second major interrogation actually concerns both the political and the economic markets. We could start with the economic market by considering the hypothesis that the massive substitution of the market in a number of states, whilst not being clearly defined, cannot normally regulate all the problems posed. Fukuyama, in his writing, has clearly affirmed that the market is presently structuring the world and that all the ingredients necessary to place the market throughout the world are now together. It is these affirmations which must be discussed.

In fact, there are four questions concerning the economic market:

(1) The uncertain functioning of the market, as if we observe the world as it stands at present rather than as economic ideologists, we can see that all the markets of produce, capital and technology are uncertain as to their future. In other words, we cannot state with certainty how these markets will evolve, and it appears impossible to be able to identify what decisions to take and when to take them. For economists, the major question seems to be: 'what to do with this uncertainty?' What will happen to the theory of comparative advantage which depends on certainties, not uncertainties? This theory stipulates that each country has, at a certain moment, certain comparative advantages in international commerce, and that the country can utilise these to develop itself. All the literature at present supposes that each country has a comparative advantage; but due to the uncertainty that reigns at present, no country can really clearly identify what are its comparative advantages.

(2) The second question concerns the actors in the market. In all regions, there are actors who ensure the functioning of the market; being either private local enterprise or foreign enterprise. The market is actually an abstraction of the enterprise, as the market as a *sui generis* entity does not exist. What exists are the enterprises which produce for the market. In other words, there is no certainty which can be stated about the actors in the market, national actors or international actors.

When considering national actors, we should look at the policies of structural adjustment in Africa, which include policies of market restoration, and which have been struck with difficulties precisely due to insufficient numbers of national actors. Where success stories exist, it has principally been due to minority groups, generally non-African, who had installed themselves in Africa and through privatisation had monopolised the economic market.

This observation becomes even more serious when we observe the case in Latin America, particularly during the process of privatisation. In these countries, privatisation has not really created or developed a competitive market; rather it has led to a heavy monopolisation of the economy, for example in Mexico

10

and Chile. Another example is Argentina, and other countries, where a shortage of foreign currency has pushed private local enterprise into exporting capital and not investing it locally.

The situation concerning international actors has created a hypothesis which states that direct international investment is not presently being oriented towards developing countries, despite all efforts being made to encourage this investment. We also need to know if the actors are in fact present in the market or not, as this creates a question which is central to the analysis of the links between the state and the development process. Otherwise, the debate is only ideological.

(3) The third question is the future evolution of the world market, and also the problem of whether we should start thinking more in terms of several world markets, rather than a single market. At present, the world market is developing its techniques towards the restruc-turing of the economy of only a fraction of the developing countries, and for only a fraction of the society in these particular countries. Even in the developed countries, the logic of the functioning of the world market has produced, and continues to expand, a dualistic society where a fraction of the society follows international modernisation whilst the rest remains at a lower level of production and revenue. At present, the unemployment rate in EC countries is between eight and ten per cent. How can we imagine that an international logic - which produces a dualistic system in developed countries - could produce anything else other than a heavy dualistic system in developing countries?

(4) The final question concerns the political market. Generally, democracy and the political market are associated with the existence of a multiparty system. A prenatal crisis of a multiparty system can be seen in developing countries and in the countries of eastern Europe where the political parties lack sociological depth. In the case of Latin America, there exists the central question of the functioning of political parties in relation to the whole society. In the Arab region and in Africa, this social crisis of parties can also be observed. What can be thought of the political market where political parties cannot function correctly? What analysis can be made on this political market in order to guarantee the democratisation of economic life and the state while it acts as a producer and a regulator? Can we imagine democratic development in the context of limited political culture?

III. CERTAINTIES AND IMPERATIVES

The general sentiment is that in five or six years the debate on the state, the market and development will no longer be fashionable. What will be retained will be a diversified economy, both in its actors and in its process of development. The illusion of anti-statism and of the market as a transcendental entity producing new societies will be abandoned, as the illusion of the state being omnipresent in the economy of a country has already been abandoned. However, it is evident that the state cannot be absent any more than the market; and there are five elements with which we should construct the future:

(1) In all the developing regions, including the eastern bloc countries, ideas are still being generated on what new structures should be built, and the market is still incapable of realising the necessary structural transformations in these regions. We could consider the technical crisis in African agriculture, scientific and technical under-development in the developing regions and the eastern block, and the uncertainty in capital markets as three examples of structural problems. They show that the state should probably not remove itself from the development process, as there are still structural transformations which must be realised. International saving is going to become rarer, therefore the state will become more involved in this process of transformation than other social actors.

(2) The second element concerns the actors. In fact, private actors do not necessarily generate a process of sustainable development, therefore it is important to consider the articulation between the private national actor, the private international actor and the public actor who must encourage development. At present, there is less privatisation of developing economies than massive export of capital, which is contrary to successful privatisation. The best combination of actors - private and public - must be found in order to regulate the structural problems, and it is necessary to reconstruct the market rather than to accept it as it already is. This reconstruction could take place on an international scale, but this proposition leads to the debate on whether the market should open its doors to all the products coming from developing countries, thereby removing protectionist and discriminatory practices (The work done by the OCDE should be referred to in this case). Developing country markets should also be recon-structed to avoid a market monopoly, and also to make them competitive, creative and dynamic.

12

(3) The depoliticization of enterprise will also be necessary. In most parts of the world, the question concerning the autonomy of enterprise compared to the bureaucratic sphere and political influence is often posed. But this does not mean that the enterprise should be left to itself, and it must not become involved in illegal activities. Corrupt practices exist almost everywhere, and the debate on the privatisation or the autonomy of the public sector hinges on the fundamental question of preservation of the enterprise from illegal political influence. Privatisation is occurring in the Philippines, for example, where the sector is already considered 'private', in that illegal interests to the profit of private oligarchies are already prevailing in the public sector.

(4) It is important to accept the concept of economic equilibrium. When an economy is in disequilibrium, a situation which occurred in many countries during the 1970s, policies of increasing indebtedness towards the exterior were followed. Research on economic equilibrium is equivalent to research on indicators of public action, as no-one will be convinced that economic equilibrium of a state is necessary without these indicators.

(5) The final element concerns political analysis. The previous four elements cannot be put into practice without any research towards new social pacts, in other words research pertaining to the opposition between capitalism and socialism which will help prevent illegal acts, protect legitimate interests and create political instruments capable of solving the problem of economic action of the state and of other actors in the market.

IV. CONCLUSION

The relationship between the state and development poses a fundamental question on the new contemporary social pact. This is not just an internal social pact, but also an international one, as no serious economic reform within a country can be sustained without a solid transformation of the international environment and equilibrium within the market. Rather than thinking in terms of opposition between the market and planning and between the East and the South, we should consider both internal and international conditions of regulation of any new economic and social tensions which may develop.

2

Conceptualising State and Civil Society Relations: Towards a Methodological Critique of Contemporary Africanism

MAHMOOD MAMDANI

I. STATE AND CIVIL SOCIETY: CONTRADICTORY PERSPECTIVES

For much of the contemporary debate on social movements and the process of democratisation, the starting point is the distinction between state and civil society. Whilst the state/civil society distinction first came to life in Euro-American political theory, there is no consensus - either now or historically - as to its meaning. It is no surprise that different strands in the current debate take their points of departure as different and even contradictory conceptions of what constitutes the distinction between state and civil society. It should thus be useful to begin our discussion on social movements and the democratic struggle by describing the two major contenders in this debate.

The dominant tendency today is for the state and civil society to stand in a diametric and one-sided opposition. The process of democratisation is considered as synonymous with the coming to life of civil society. In turn, civil society is itself conceptualised as existing as a force against the state. This perspective was first put forth by Thomas Paine, who saw civil society as a natural condition of freedom,[1] and a legitimate arena of defence against the state. This dominant tendency involves nothing less than a one-sided anti-state romanticism of civil society.[2]

In sharp contrast to Paine stands the conception advanced by Hegel which was partially revised by Marx. Hegel's perspective stands out in two important respects, and was revised by Marx in a third. These three aspects need to be emphasised as a starting point for a discussion of social movements and the democratic struggle in contemporary Africa.

First and foremost, civil society for Hegel was not a natural condition of freedom but an historically produced sphere of life.
Sandwiched between the patriarchal family and the universal state,
civil society was the historical product of a multi-dimensional process.
This was a process whose first dimension was the spread of commodity relations and the emergence of a market, freeing the sphere of
economic relations from the weight of extra-economic relations, and
thus the economy from the sphere of politics. Another dimension involved the formulation of civil law which regulated contractual
relations amongst free and autonomous individuals. Yet another
dimension was reflected in the depersonalisation of violence and the
centralisation of the absolutist state in what contemporaries have
termed the advent of civilisation.

Historically, the birth of civil society was the product of a transition
to capitalism. In both Hegel and Marx, there is a tendency to equate
civil society with bourgeois society: Hegel often used the two terms
interchangeably. In Marx and Engels,[3] the descriptive historical material
tends to equate the rise of civil society with that of the bourgeoisie.

Given this tendency, it is vital to emphasise that the relationship
between civil society and capitalism is contingent, not necessary; the
birth of civil society cannot just be turned into a unique aspect of that
transition only. Like other historical constructs - democracy and
nation[4] - civil society has been able to rise under different historical
conditions.

From this perspective arise a number of questions. To what extent
can we speak of the existence of civil society in contemporary African
countries? What is the expression of its coming into being? And what
is the significance of this process, particularly from the point of view
of the democratic struggle?

Hegel's second major contribution put him squarely at odds with
the theses advanced by Paine, de Tocqueville and the entire Weberian
tradition that followed. In sharp opposition to the view that saw civil
society as the realm of freedom against the state as institutional des-
potism, Hegel conceptualised civil society as a contradictory
construct. For him, the state does not act against civil society, but in
continuous conflict with it.[5] Rather than the picture of a harmonious
and noncontradictory sphere, civil society is seen as a contradictory
combination with constant conflict between classes and groups.

The implication is clear: neither civil society nor movements that
arise from within it can be idealised in such a conception. In contrast,
movements within civil society demand concrete understanding for
they harbour contradictory possibilities.

16

An analysis anchored in such a theoretical perspective cannot accept such demands - as those for democracy or human rights - as the general demands of civil society against the state. It must penetrate every general formulation to highlight the concrete meaning of any general demand to form several different and particular points of view. Such a perspective gives rise to an entirely new and fruitful series of questions: what is the meaning of democracy from the point of view of different classes and social groups? What specific interests are organising the general demand for democracy? What is the political significance of different types of democratic transitions, for example a transition from above where the tendency is to freeze property and class relations (Senegal), as opposed to a transition effected through sharp struggles from below which calls into question precisely these relations (South Africa)?

Hegel's third thesis, his conception of the state, tended towards its idealisation. While he underlined conflicts within civil society, Hegel tended to see the state as a noncontradictory formation, and as the embodiment of the universal interest which kept particular interests in civil society from blowing it apart. It is this idealisation of the state that Marx challenged. For Marx, contradictions within civil society are reproduced within the state; at the same time, the state reinforces certain interests in civil society and undermines others. Civil society is not just external to the state; rather, various and even contradictory groups in civil society differentially penetrate the state.

From this Marx derives a conception of the state that is radically at variance with that of Hegel. For the state is no longer a force that just confronts civil society as something external to it, it is simultaneously an arena of struggle for forces whose springboard is none other than civil society.

Such a conception raises yet another series of analytical questions. While it calls for a linking of state policy to interests in civil society, it sees the relationship between them as reciprocal, and not just one-sided. While it conceptualises a state interest, it does not see this as either uniform or just shaped by a contradiction between institutional (state) and individual (corruption) interests. Rather, it directs attention to the very process of decision-making as a struggle between apparatuses of the state as potentially contradictory. It thus raises the question of both consistency and contradiction within state policy, and as a result, it poses the twin possibility of the state power as being both coherent and internally fractured, as both reflecting the balance of interests in civil society and shaping them. Finally, it raises the question of the historical development of the state and of its changing and diverse forms.

II. AFRICAN STUDIES

The state/society distinction has become the analytical focus of contemporary writings on African studies in North America. It is the single methodological thread that unites writers as distinct as Tom Callaghy and Richard Sklar, Richard Joseph and Richard Sandbrook, Goran Hyden and Crawford Young.

The purpose of this section is to highlight and criticise this common methodological thread and to abstract from them the differences that mark the analysis put forth by each of these writers.

Contemporary Africanism's methodological premise is best summed up in Tom Callaghy's works, given that he is also the most conscious of the significance of the method. This shared perspective can be summed up in three broad statements. One, the central feature of contemporary African reality is the process of state formation. This process is a slow and uneven consolidation of central political and economic authority out of dispersed power conditions internally and dependent conditions externally [*Callaghy, 1987*].

So conceived, the African State is described in various terms: as a 'weak Leviathan' by Callaghy,[6] as undergoing 'decline' and 'decay' by Crawford Young and Thomas Turner,[7] as 'weak' and 'suspended above society 'by Goran Hyden,[8] as 'soft' by Rothschild[9] and Keller,[10] and as 'omnipresent but ... hardly omnipotent' by Naomi Chazan.[11] In short, all agree that the centrepiece in the drama of contemporary African politics is the struggle for the consolidation of political (state) power.

Second, this centralisation is being achieved through the revival and consolidation of a centralist and corporatist colonial tradition and authoritarian practices. The result is a colonial-type state, an 'organic-statist' authority, which is characterised by varying degrees of patrimonialism (corruption by the political aristocracy), and by highly personalised forms of rulership, both political and administrative.

A theory of 'patrimonialism' is sketched by Callaghy,[12] a theory of the African 'aristocracy' by Jackson and Roseberg,[13] and a theory of 'prebendalism' by Richard Joseph in his study of Nigeria.[14;15] This same clientalist network is christened by Goran Hyden as 'the politics of affection'.[16]

Finally, the theoretical conclusion: this form of state power - variously called early modern authoritarian state or early modern absolutist State, 'the patrimonial administrative state' or 'the patri-monial autocratic state'[17] - is likened to its earlier expressions in 17th century Europe or early post-colonial Latin America, and in both instances is considered a political feature of the transition to capitalism.

The above conceptualisation suffers from three major problems. It is part of a long-standing, at times implicit but quite often explicit, consensus in development theory marked by a unilinear evolutionist perspective that has tended to mar writings on both sides of the ideological divide.

Its most caricatured presentation in Marxist theory has been Stalin's formulation on the various stages in historical development:[18] from primitive communalism through to slavery, feudalism, capitalism, socialism and finally to communism. In spite of Marx's renunciation of this form of formula-making as a supra-historical mental exercise substituting a concrete historical analysis, this formulation has been the central feature of economics in Marxist thinking. Unilinear evolutionism was also the sum and substance of the modernisation school, whose various theorists tried to cull various essential features from the concrete historical process of modernisation in European history that were supposed to mark a similar transition in the post-colonial countries.[19]

The result is that an historical process, unfolding under concrete conditions - in this case, of 16th to 18th century Europe - is presented as a universal path that all subsequent social development is fated to tread, resulting in history by analogy rather than history as a process. The Africanist is akin to a person learning a foreign language who must translate every new word back into his/her mother tongue, in the process missing precisely what is new.

From such a perspective, the most intense controversies dwell on what is indeed the most appropriate translation, the most adequate fit, or the most appropriate analogy that will capture the meaning of the phenomenon under observation. In Africanist writings, the debate ranges over whether contemporary African reality most closely resembles the transition to capitalism under the 17th century European absolutism or that under other Third World experiences [*Hyden*], or whether the post-colonial State in Africa should be labelled Bonapartist or absolutist [*Callaghy*].

Whatever their differences, all are agreed that African reality has meaning only in so far as it can be seen to reflect a particular stage in the development of European history. The central tendency of such a methodological orientation is to lift a phenomenon out of context and process it. The resulting bias lends itself more to description and speculation than to concrete analysis.

In as much as it privileges the European historical experience as its touch-stone, contemporary unilinear evolutionism should be characterised more concretely and appropriately as Eurocentrism. Obviously Eurocentrism has a double aspect, as it also presents the European historical experience in an idealised, mythologised and non-contradictory form. The conceptualisation of human rights as a result of the French Revolution expunges the perspective of the Sans-Culotte from the historical record. Similarly, contradictory perspectives on democracy and socialism are also dissolved in a single chorus that privileges the perspective of a particular class or group at a particular conjuncture with a Universalist claim.

Just as it holds up European history and society as a mirror in which to gauge the significance of all other human development, Eurocentrism also has the tendency to view non-European people as lacking in capacity to comprehend their own history as a step in taking the initiative towards making it. It is this Eurocentrism that dependency theory challenged under the political impetus of the Cuban Revolution, summed up in the call of its leader to the intellectuals and the working people of Latin America to 'break into history'.[20] We must not forget that dependency theory was at once a critique of both developmentalism and a mechanical Marxism, both being variants of unilinear evolutionism that dependency theory succumbed to when it collapsed, thus denying the possibility of a capitalist transition in any and every dependent country no matter what the historical circumstance.

The second weakness that contemporary Africanist analysis suffers from is that its methodological thrust is basically anti-democratic. Like much of neo-Weberian and neo-Marxist thinking from which it draws inspiration, the key issues for the Africanists are state autonomy and state capacity. At its strictest, state autonomy must mean the capacity to implement and enforce policies in the face of opposition from civil society. Their categories are the 'soft state' and the 'hard state', and their problem is that of 'state decay' and 'state incompetence'.

The state itself is conceptualised as exclusively an institutional category, with its own coherence, logic and capacity; it is not at all seen as a condensation of social relations and a relatively autonomous arena of struggle which shapes the same relations. The state interest is actually seen as purely the interest of its managers; it is not put in the context of a wider galaxy or struggles within civil society. The problem of state decay is summed up by a single conflict between the institutional in-terest of the state (governance) and the individual interest of its managers (corruption).

Here, finally, is the triumph of Huntington, for at the centre of our theorist's concern is the problem of institutional efficiency and order. Within the parameters of this type of conceptualisation of the state, there is no room for the question of democracy: the only problem that can be raised is that of efficiency. No wonder its proponents are increasingly apt to describe their own preoccupation as that of how to get African states to govern efficiently; in other words, governance.

Finally, this perspective involves a single-minded focus on one aspect of the historical process: that of state formation. Since the 1960s when Africanism had a strong tendency to caricature the object of its analysis in anthropological terms, contemporary Africanism has moved away from its one-sided preoccupation with 'tribalism' and 'ethnicity'; its best practitioners have successfully integrated both a political economy approach [*Callaghy; Joseph; Hyden*] and the language of class analysis [*Callaghy; Schatzberg; Young*] in their endeavours.[21]

However, the real abstraction that spoils the writings of the whole corpus of Africanist theory is its side-stepping of the process of popular resistance. A marked tendency in Africanism is to consider its object as incapable of making history or of comprehending it. As Jomo Kenyatta recognised almost three decades ago, for the Africanist to concede that the object of his/her analysis could possibly emerge as the subject of history is to imagine 'a rabbit turned poacher!'[22] Thus, the process of state formation is reconstructed in abstraction from the history of popular struggles; it is either seen as the realisation of the will of state managers or as a supra-historical realisation of some universal ethical Idea, Hegel-fashion. Because they sidestep real struggles for democracy, their democratic professions appear as so many postures and so many prescriptions.

III. CONCLUSION

A discussion of social transformation needs to be simultaneously that of structure and agency. At the core of such an analysis, there needs to be a focus on the actual process of the coming to life of various social forces, of their self-consciousness and self-organisation, their vision and their capacities, their demands and their struggles to realise these. The point is not to treat Africa as an exception in world history, nor to see it as a simple mirror reflection, nor a replay of an earlier and more authentic history. Neither is it to impose a solution from without on the African people, no matter how democratic its claim and formulation. For any neatly packaged recipe on what constitutes democracy that does not arise from the very history of democratic struggles on the continent must inevitably be an arbitrary imposition on it.

The fact is that no solution which sidesteps the creativity of a people can claim to be democratic. For the realisation of democracy in any country, whether in Africa or elsewhere, cannot be without the simultaneous constitution of a democratic subject. Moreover, this democratic subject cannot be exported to Africa in the form of technical aid; it can only be the outcome of actual struggles for democracy within Africa. For those who claim to be interested in the democratis-ation of the continent, there is no escape from coming to terms with the experience of popular movements in Africa.

NOTES

1. The 18th century saw a decisive shift in the conceptualisation of civil society in European political theory. Pre-18th century conceptions, on the other hand, were part of an older European tradition that can be traced from modern natural law back through Cicero to classical political philosophy. For Aristotle, civil society simply equalled the polis (the state). As carefully and amply documented by John Keene in the opening chapter of his 'State and Civil Society', civil society in pre-18th century European political theory referred in general to 'a type of political association which placed its members under the influence of laws and ensured peaceful order and good government'.
2. Its careful bibliographical spadework not withstanding, most contributions in John Keene's edited work cited above fall squarely within this framework.
3. 'Civil society comprises the entire material interaction among individuals at a particular evolutionary stage of the productive forces. ... The term 'civil society' emerged in the 18th century when property relations had already evolved from the community of antiquity and medieval times. Civil society as such only develops with the bourgeoisie'. Marx and Engels, *The German Ideology*, quoted in Keene (ed.), op. cit., pp.63-64.
4. In his more recent writings, Samir Amin has moved away from the capital-centred definition of a nation. He no longer sees nation formation as necessarily con-comitant with the rise of capitalism, but a 'social phenomenon which can appear at every stage of history'. Amin argues that the class which controls the state apparatus and ensures economic, political and cultural unity may be other than a bourgeoisie. Further, he contends that nation formation is not necessarily an irreversible stage on the road of social development, or a moment in a unilinear process, but is a historical development that is reversible under certain conditions. See Amin, Samir, 1980, *Class and Nation, Historically and in the Current Crisis*, New York: Monthly Review Press.
5. With the obvious exception of colonialism and the partial exception of revolution.
6. Callaghy, Thomas, 1987, 'The State as Lame Leviathan: The Patrimonial-Administrative State in Africa,' in Ergas (ed.), *African State in Transition*, London: Macmillan Press.

7. Young, Crawford and Thomas Turner, 1985, *The Rise and Decline of the Zairean State*, Madison: University of Wisconsin Press.
8. Hyden, Goran, 1983, *Beyond Ujamaa in Tanzania*, London: Heinemann; and 1983, No Shortcuts to Progress, London: Heinemann.
9. Rothchild, Donald, 'Hegemony and State Softness: Some Variations in Elite Responses', in Zaki Ergas (ed.), *The African State in Transition*, pp.117-148.
10. Keller, Edmond J., 'Beyond Autocracy: Prospects for Progressive Statecraft'.
11. Chazan, Naomi, 1988 'State and Society in Africa: Images and Challenges', in Donald Rothchild and Naomi Chazan, *The Precarious Balance: State and Society in Africa*, Westview: Boulder Co., p.327.
12. Callaghy, Thomas, 1984, *The State-Society Struggle: Zaire in Contemporary Perspective*, New York: Columbia University Press. See also Boyle, Patrick M., 1988, 'View from Zaire', *World Politics*, Vol.XL, no. 2, pp.268-87.
13. Jackson and Roseberg, 1982, *Personal Rule in Black Africa. Prince, Autocrat, Prophet, Tyrant*, Berkeley: University of California Press.
14. See *Perestroika Without Glasnost*, Report of the Inaugural Seminar of the Governance in Africa Programme of the Carter Centre, Emory University, February 17-18, 1989, p.12.
15. Class, Richard Joseph, 1984, 'State and Prebendal Politics in Nigeria', in N. Kasfir (ed.), *State and Class in Africa*, London: Frank Cass, p.25.
16. Hyden, Goran, *Perestroika Without Glasnost*, op. cit., p.12.
17. See Callaghy, Thomas, 'The State as Lame Leviathan', op. cit.; and Young, Crawford, *Perestroika Without Glasnost*, op. cit., pp.8 and 41.
18. Stalin, Joseph, 'Dialectical and Historical Materialism', in Bruce Franklin (ed.), 1973, *The Essential Stalin*, London: Croom Helm, pp.300-34.
19. For a critique, see Mamdani, Mahmood, Thandika Mkandawire and Wamba-dia Wamba, 'Social Movements, Social Transformation and the Struggle for Democracy in Africa', Dakar: CODESRIA, Working Paper 1/88.
20. Fidel Castro as cited in Frank, Andre Gunder, 1969, *Latin America: Underdevelopment or Revolution?*, New York, p.407; see also Jimenez, Michael F., 1988, ''Citizens of the Kingdom': Toward a Social History of Radical Christianity in Latin America', *International Labour and Working Class History*, No.34, pp.3-21.
21. This point is made by Young in his review article. Young, Crawford, 1986, 'Nationalism, Ethnicity and Class in Africa: A Retrospective', *Cahiers d'Etudes Africaines*, xxvi (3), 103, pp.421-95.
22. Kenyatta, Jomo, 1962, *Facing Mt. Kenya: The Tribal Life of the Gikuyu*, New York: Vintage, p.xvi.

The Nation-State as the Main Factor of Social Destabilisation in the Periphery. The Gordian Knot of Development

FARHAD AFSHAR

In any discussion on development there is an analytical taboo: the nation-state. It is an axiom of developmental theory. Economic models are specially designed monoaxiomatically, and they require the nation-state and its national market as a basis for foreign trade. This axiom, the nation-state, can be compared to a Janus face. One side is temptation and the other is oppression. The nation-state is the false axiom of a possibly correct theory which would like to solve the problem of disparate development.

The nation-state, however, is not only the axiom but the problem itself. The nation-state is disparity, as it is not ethnic groups and populations who are in worldwide conflict with each other but the countries themselves. State borders often divide people who are related to each other, cutting whole ethnic groups in two as well as their traditional social and economic relations.

This analysis is additionally complicated by a curious social fact:[1] Man constructs ideas which become more real and dense than physical reality. He comes up with institutions which all of a sudden subjugate their creator and become a threat to him. A dangerous construction of this kind is the 'nation'.

Heinrich von Kleist records in a historical analysis in literary form the moment of emergence of this *topos*, the birth of a nation:

> Mirabeau's thunderbolt comes to my mind with which he dealt with the master of ceremonies who, after the dissolution of the last monarchic conference of the king on June 23rd, during which the king had ordered the professions to break up, came back to the conference hall where the professions were still present, and asked them if they had heard the king's order.
>
> 'Yes', Mirabeau answered, 'we have heard the king's order' - I am

sure that at this human beginning he did not yet think of the bayonets
with which he concluded.

'Yes Sir', he repeated, 'we have heard it' - one notices that he did not
really know what he wanted. 'But what gives you the right' - he
continued, and suddenly outrageous ideas came to his mind - 'to men-
tion orders to us? We are the representatives of a nation.' That was
what he (Mirabeau) needed!

'The nation gives orders but does not receive any ' - and bursting out
in utter boldness, he said: 'and in order to make myself clear to you,' -
and only then he found the words to express the opposition for which
his soul was armed: 'so tell your king that we cannot be forced from
our places in any other way than by the force of bayonets.'[2]

This word, being up to that moment without content, filled itself with
meaning, involving a socially experienced contradiction. The nation
became a category of political order: before it had been only a word,
now it was a topos.

This topos, this 'nation', established itself; it became institutional;
it put itself on concrete terms with the nation-state. It was in Europe
that this nation-state first became effective. Later on, through the
newly emerged industrial nations, it was spread world-wide.

According to Montesquieu, the nation-state is based on the theory
of separation of powers. This theory accepts the principle of divided
power in order to achieve equivalence between legislative, executive,
and judicial branches of a government. The inherent contradiction
between the representatives of a nation-state, the parties, has been left
out of consideration.

In fact historically, different parties emerged only after the creation
of a nation-state. Their organisation is entirely different to the ideal of
separation of powers. They are structured after the principle of
monopolisation of power. Hence, the principal question concerning
parties is not how to divide power but how to get hold of it, as parties
who win elections want to have legislative, executive, and judiciary
control. Parties monopolise the claim for power within the nation-
state, thus, creating two opposing principles: Montesquieu's ideal of
separation of powers and the actual monopolisation of power by the
parties.

We have to face a major problem with the nation-state being
applied worldwide as a category of political order. In the Third World,
parties and organisations of the nation-state meet societies which are
not built after a bourgeois model. This clash leads to a time-lag which
is absurd in its consequences, as in Third World societies it is not the
development of a bourgeoisie that leads to the creation of the nation-
state and the formation of parties, but the transferred nation-state

which creates bourgeois parties and decrees the bourgeois society as the sovereign political power. The labour movement is a similar case, however in the Third World it is not the workers who organise themselves into unions, but the other way around. First the trade unions come into being and then they look for workers as members. In the political field the exported labour party arises, looking for its proletariat in the Third World (e.g. Afghanistan).

All these organisations have one thing in common: They contradict the traditional political culture of the countries in which they make their claim for power. The nation-state and the parties are industrial nation implants, shifted in space and time, which meet with vehement defensive reactions in the Third World. The conflict caused by this has become a deciding factor in any development programme, due to the fact that the intensive fusion of the Third World with ethnocentric categories of industrial nations leads to a point where neither the traditional categories of political order nor any new ones adapted from industrial nations have any validity. During acculturation very specific forms of order emerge, being: (i) weak, (ii) strongly adaptive, (iii) intensely aggressive.

CULTURAL CONFRONTATION DURING ACCULTURATION

1. ACCULTURATION

The expansion of a culture is in no way a sign of its high quality, as it merely indicates its great potential for social energy. Greece, for instance, was a much more highly-developed and richer culture than the expansive ancient Rome. Nevertheless, the Hellenic people submitted to the order of a military Pax Romana.

Societies who have an imaginary similarity to their original emerge by means of acculturation, although they tend to build their own identity after entirely different patterns. The similarity at first sight is amazing. It is like the monkey looking into a mirror and getting a lot of pleasure from looking at the other monkey who actually does not exist. This illusion is called the 'Gordian knot of development'.

Industrial nations are only able to form an idea of the Third World within the political frame of the nation-state. It is important to point out that these nation-states do have some international legality but cannot claim any national legitimacy. It is therefore rather pointless to carry out economic plans for development within the context of the nation-state, if this context fails to be socially accepted by the population for which it is intended. Those projects which have failed are a sign that, despite the contradictory reality, an idealistic axiom of developmental economy dating from the 19th century has been maintained to the point of losing all relevance. The question to ask is: Do nation-states fulfil the expectations of being able to establish useful social orders in Third World societies?

The result of acculturation is that the established order of the Third World collapses and that a new order, which has been established by force, fails to represent the people. Empirically it is evident that in the Third World the nation-state as an institution loses its effectiveness just a few kilometres outside the city centres and can hardly be found at all in rural areas.

It is not actually the nation-state that represents reality but the dual system of economy and society, or of citizen and inhabitant. In fact, a new mixture of reality develops in the centre of these states, with two logical systems simultaneously claiming validity. The nation-state raises expectations far beyond anything the government could provide, such as independent justice, land reform, emancipation of women, nationalisation of resources, industrialisation and the building up of a modern society while at the same time guarding traditions. Eventually everyone becomes disappointed and unhappy and people's experiences and their behaviour within acculturation become, according to the circumstances, contradictory. The society becomes divided in the dual system between the state, communities and the nation. The Iranian writer Dschalal Ale Ahmad describes this situation in a literary way in his book 'Gharbzadeghi':

> I think Gharbzadeghi[3] (that is the way he calls this split culture)[4] is just like cholera or frostbite. But no, it is at least as bad as sawflies in a wheat field. Have my readers seen the way they infest the wheat? From the inside out. Sometimes one can see a perfect husk, but it is only the husk, just like the skin of a cicada on a tree. Iranian cities are like flea markets, where Europeans can get rid of their industrial products. In no time we will have mountains of clapped-out machines all over the country, instead of towns and cities. Each one of them will be the size of an American junkyard, just as big as Teheran. The greed (of the split people and) of this consumerism seizes the country. Every day the cities want more western goods as their food, and every day

28

they become more alike in their decay, their rootlessness, and their ugliness. In these cities live the Euromaniacs. These are the villagers who have fled to the city and who will never return to their villages again, because the hairdresser in the village does not have any hair-cream, because there is no cinema, and because you cannot buy any sandwiches there. The Euromaniac is inwardly indifferent to everything, especially his own cultural heritage. The Euromaniac is someone who has no real origin. He is afraid of the discovery that the shimmering bubble of air, which he calls his own instead of any thoughts, might be empty.[5]

Euromania is, sociologically speaking, a cultural obsession, which leads to the destruction of collective identity.[6] This destruction accumulates and accelerates, creating a collective obsession for an intensification of sequences of events. Everything that is fast is experienced as something which is sensible. The slow traditional life, however, is thought of as antiquated and obsolete. The past is seen as something that has fallen behind.

CULTURAL CONFRONTATION DURING ACCULTURATION

2. EUROMANIA

PARCEL REALITY WITH HIGH POTENTIAL OF AGGRESSION

This obsession is transmitted by means of cultural relations, in particular by intellectuals. It is like a meteor of destruction that appears whenever a country is reduced to rubble. Euromania causes wars and revolutions in the Third World, and the revolutions that break out do not ask the scientific theories for permission and they do not go by the diaries of the managers.[7] They erupt into meaninglessness when the identity of a society is shattered by Euromania.

Euromania has a form of dissemination like a diabolic trinity. It justifies itself through the ideology of 'freedom, progress, and democracy'. Euromania is the main problem in the transmission of the nation-state to societies in the Third World, this basis for transmission being social and economic interdependence which is founded on accumulation.

The disintegrated collective identity leads to an increased potential for aggression, which would be aimed internally, after the collapse of the established order, against the population in the form of a revolution, and externally would be aimed against the neighbours in the form of wars.

One example of this internal aggression, which is not comprehensible without the concept of Euromania - the cultural disintegration of identity - is the Polpot regime in Cambodia, which annihilated about one third of its population. The regime wanted to establish an original type of communist state in order to develop the country. Other examples, just as striking, are the displacements in Ethiopia, where hundreds of thousands of people have been driven into misery, or the airs and graces of Bokassa who, in an imitation of Napoleon, declared himself Emperor of the Central African monarchy.

From an historical point of view we can see that wars have continuously broken out in the Third World since the end of World War II. Why has this occurred?

This cannot be explained by approaching each individual case in an historical-descriptive manner. There is one essential question: What is the reason for these outbursts of aggression? A possible answer is Euromania. Local conflicts or contradictions within society would not develop such a destructive power if they did not have a powerful instrument at hand. This instrument is the nation-state which provides, by monopolisation of power, a potential for destruction by the Euromaniac elites, which does not seem able to be controlled by the ethics and traditions of the respective culture. Thus, the nation-state in the Third World is under an obligation not to its own people but to the ideologies of progress of its acculturated elites.

Euromania is not only a problem of the acculturated elites, however, as it is exported by the industrial nations just as are technology, science and weapons. Euromania is exported not as a finished product but in the form of components such as the Eurocentric international law, the scientific screen of perception, or economic doctrines such as 'everything has its price' or 'private property is a natural thing'.

A possible misconception should be avoided here. It is not the nation-state in an industrial society[8] which is being considered here, but the nation-state which has been transmitted to the Third World, and the effects of this thoughtless transferral of European categories of order. These categories of order fit into a society on an industrial basis, and are presently just as impossible in the Third World as they would have been in Europe during the time of feudalism or in ancient times. Transferring the nation-state to the Third World is of comparable absurdity as transferring the development plan for New York City to the rural Swiss Emmental region.

The deciding factor in the clash of cultures is the emergence of a specific reality, which is neither based on traditional order nor on the transmitted one. It can be clearly observed that there is a situation of conflictual acculturation in the peripheral societies, as in its dual construction it shows a specific form of social order. Tradition and eclipse develop complex forms of being related to reality, as any kind of action takes place in a double context, which is where the decisive difference can be found when comparing with the simple order of industrial society.

Of course, action takes place within the bounds of physical experience in acculturation as well, but this sphere of physical experience is confronted with two symbolic levels of meaning at the same time, instead of being confronted with only one. Any action is integrated into a double context of meanings, which are often conflictingly opposed to each other.

A trivial example is the following: a beverage such as beer has got a sphere of physical experience - a consistency, a nutritional value and an alcoholic content - but at the same time it has a double symbolic meaning. The action of drinking beer in an Islamic society is related to two symbolic levels: on the one hand, beer is an indication of status and is associated with being open-minded about the modern way of life. On the other hand, the drinking of alcohol is connected to a traditional meaning which declares that the consumption of beer is reprehensible.[9] From a sociological point of view this is not a matter of the - often misunderstood - question of value systems, but a matter of acculturative formation of identity. Values are intrinsically divisible and revocable, however identity is not subject to free changeability.

If we can recognise the conflictory actions and the complexity of a dual reality in acculturation by the trivial example given above, how much more do these facts apply to actions on a higher social level. For example, what happens when a category of order like the nation-state is transmitted from one culture to another which already has categories of order that are historically opposed to categories like the nation-state? If development projects are carried out in the context of this acculturative nation-state, they are subject to a different attribution of meaning right from the start.

Thus, the developing reality is like a sea of mist, out of which jut fragments of the traditional categories of order. They are largely invisible, but they have a devastating effect on the development projects which shatter, rather like ships on a reef. Development projects are therefore carried out in a reality which is only partly understood and which basically has a conflictory structure.

CULTURAL CONFRONTATION DURING ACCULTURATION

3. CONFLICTUAL ACCULTURATION

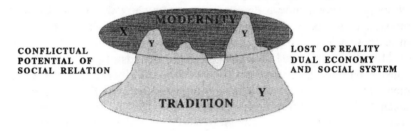

CONFLICTUAL
POTENTIAL OF
SOCIAL RELATION

LOST OF REALITY
DUAL ECONOMY
AND SOCIAL SYSTEM

Many nation-states in the Third World have their roots in resistance or liberation movements. The irony of history is that the resistance movements, which were the basis for the formation of these new states, later organised themselves politically into one-party systems. In the form of nation-states, established liberation movements have often wound up being the oppressors of their own people. Examples include Cambodia, Ethiopia and Afghanistan. No development today can avoid the nation-state, but this is the biggest problem restricting development, as in its function the nation-state encounters a triple opposition. It contradicts regional culture and the ethnic groups who live there, and it also stands in contradiction to the claims of leadership of other nation-states.

We can show the complexity of cultural construction of acting and meaning with a sociological demonstration. If one burns a banknote, Sfr.100 for instance, what can anyone, observing this action, actually see? Some would answer in amazement that some money has gone up in smoke and they would be affected by that. Why is this so? From a physical point of view the observation is in no way one of money being destroyed, as money has a symbolic barter relation and this cannot be burned. It is just the paper that has been physically burned.

Why then does the burning of this piece of paper cause so much agitation? Paper is often burned without causing a similar reaction. The agitation develops because of the social attribution of meaning which befalls this special piece of paper - the banknote. This piece of paper shows symbols; stamps, coats of arms, signatures etc., which attribute a collectively accepted significance to the paper and which exceed its value to a large degree.

From an economical point of view the burning of the banknote does not destroy the money, as it is a quantitative reduction in the money supply, albeit in a rather peculiar way. Ironically this action even contributes to the reduction of inflation. Nevertheless, the agitated feeling remains, indicating that reality is primarily constructed symbolically and internalised mentally. To reduce reality to the physical components of supposed data and facts is the dangerous error of economic theories of modernisation. Therefore, categories of order of other cultures, which do not become apparent at first sight, are considered to be nonexistent or traditionally without any further meaning, and are neglected in an inappropriate manner.

In fact, development projects regularly fail because the effect of conflictory acculturation is neglected. The reality in which societies come into being is constructed mentally as well as physically. The failure of projects is therefore a regular consequence of the economically reduced view of the acculturative reality.

A solution could be found by surveying the categories of order in the Third World and by eventually accepting them in their effectiveness as alternatives to the setting up of a new system of order. Three alternative concepts from the Islamic area to the ideas of nation, proletariat, and property are listed as examples:

(1) The *umma*, the Islam religious community/nation. For Islams, the umma is not merely a religious community as for Christians, but a cultural way of life that integrally arranges religion, economy, and politics. This religious community accepts neither race, class, nor national territory. After the Iranian revolution for example, the Lebanese Mussa Sadre was supposed to become President of Iran, but he was killed in Libya. Iran absorbed two million Afghan refugees who were not treated as refugees but as members of the umma who had been staying in another country for some time.[10]

(2) *Mostasafin*, those who have been deprived of their rights/ proletariat. This category suggests solidarity with anyone who has been deprived of his rights, no matter what his religious beliefs and his nationality may be. There is a practical duty to support

33

him. Iran, for instance, actively supports Nicaragua, the Philippines, and the anti-apartheid movement in South Africa.[11]

(3) *Tohid*, usufruct/property. This category implies that only the creator of an object can be its owner. Since man did not create the earth, he can only borrow it, as he is not the owner of the earth but its usufructuary. However, he is the owner of the products he produces.[12] Acculturation leads to the fact that in the modern nation-state, traditional forms of usufruct were lost and cancelled in favour of the private right of ownership. In Switzerland, for example, a similar residential law is preserved by which the usufruct of common land and the use of water is laid down in a traditional way (in the Canton of Valais, for instance).

Only a few analytical categories of order have been mentioned in this chapter. All the cultures of the Third World have their own specific categories of order with regard to their territories, their economy, and their politics. These should be dug up among the ideological debris of the nation-state, before we, confronted with an imaginary reality, give up by means of a theoretical rash action. What currently exists is not a justification of itself but a challenge to judge it rationally, and if the nation-state as a category is found to be useless, it should be put aside without any further consideration.

As far as the countries of the Third World are concerned, the nation-state of acculturation remains the 'Gordian knot of development' - to go back to the metaphor - as long as the monkey looks into the mirror!

NOTES

1. For the concept of social fact see: Durkheim, Emile, 1895, *Regeln der soziologischen Methode*, Luchterhand, 1961.
2. Von Kleist, Heinrich, 1989, 'Kunst und Weltbetrachtung, Gesamtausgabe', in Henrik Kreutz: Das Ende der 'General Linear Reality'!, in the report from the fourth International Symposium on Sociological Computer Simulation, München, Vol.5, pp.53-58.
3. The concept of Gharbzadeghi has been well translated by Roy Mottahedeh as 'Euromania'.
4. For cultural schizophrenia: Daryush, Shayegan, 1989, *Le regard mutilé*, Schizophrénie culturelle, Paris.
5. Dschalal, Ale Ahmad, 1962, Gharbzadeghi, Teheran. Summarised after Roy Mottahedeh, 1988, *Der Mantel des Propheten oder Leben eines persischen Mullahs in Religion und Politik*, Beck, pp.260-63.
6. For the sociological concept of Euromania, see. Afshar, F., 1989, 'Das Problem der sozialen Beschleunigung', in W. Kälin and R. Moser, *Migration und Akkulturation*, Bern, p.51.
7. Economic theory normally starts out from the assumption that situations of short supply are responsible for upheavals. Not taken into account so far is the fact that economic growth also threatens stability. The Iranian revolution was a growth-related revolution of that kind, which grew out of anomy. For the connection between economic prosperity and anomy, see: Durkheim, Emile, 1897, *Der Selbstmord*, Neuwied und Berlin 1983, p.273.
8. Nevertheless it is worth thinking that, as a consequence of the nation-state, Europe was reduced to rubble by two world wars in this century alone. Meanwhile there has been a fundamental rejection of the nation-state as a category of order in Europe, which expresses itself in the dissolution of national markets and borders and in the movement towards a European Community. Nonetheless the validity of the nation-state for the Third World is maintained analogous to the export of old production machinery and antiquated weapon systems.
9. For the importance of mental development of causality in the construction of reality see: Afshar F., E. Gerber and P. Schädelin, 1990, *Der Kampf mit dem Drachen*, Anleitung zur Sozio-Logie, Stuttgart, p.163.
10. For the importance of the umma see: Rodinson, Maxim, 1986, *Islam und Kapitalismus*, Frankfurt.
11. For the political work of the Islam with European categories of order, see: Shariati, Ali, 1980, *Marxism and Other Western Fallacies, An Islamic Critique*, Berkeley. Particularly for sociology see: Shariati, Ali, 1979, *On the Sociology of Islam*, Berkeley.
12. For Islamic economic theory see: Homyaoun, Katouzian, 1981, 'Shiah und moderne islamische Wirtschaftslehre', in Berliner Institut für vergleichende Sozialforschung: *Religion und Politik im Islam*, Frankfurt.

PART II
PARTICIPATION AND THE STATE

4

Democracy, Dictatorship and Development. Consequences for Economic Development of Different Forms of Regime in the Third World

GEORG SØRENSEN

In this chapter we will consider the ways in which democratic and authoritarian regimes are contributing (or not contributing) to economic development in Third World countries. Firstly, we will consider the following question: What are the consequences, for democratic and authoritarian regimes respectively, of economic development in the Third World?

It is clear that the question is both relevant and interesting; but is it also 'researchable': in other words, can it be analysed? The answer to this is less straightforward, as it is impossible to weigh the relative importance of regime form for economic development against the role of all the other relevant causal factors. But this is a problem which any inquiry of this type in social science faces [*Pye 1985: 13*]. If this stopped us, it would also stop any other attempt at causal explanation in social science.

There is another, perhaps more serious, objection to the question. It has to do with the fact that we can point to some authoritarian regimes that have progressed rather well in terms of economic development and others with no such success. The same goes for democracies: some do well economically, some do not. The immediate conclusion is that the form of the regime is not a very important factor in explaining economic development, and some observers have already drawn that conclusion [*e.g. La Palombara/Weiner 1966: 1-7; Pye 1966; Martinussen 1977: 35-61*].

But it may not be wise to discard our question on such a superficial and general level. When the question is backed up with conceptual refinement which discriminates between types of democracies and authoritarian systems as well as aspects of economic development, it may be the rejection of the question that turns out to be spurious, not the question itself. In any case, this is not something that can be proved in any strict sense other than by demonstrating the validity of the question through concrete analysis. Before moving on to this, we may note that a large number of contributions continue to find the question sufficiently meaningful to make attempts at answering it. At the same time, there has been further consensus about the way in which the question should be transformed into research hypotheses, but for the present it is enough to state the two dominant hypotheses in the field, as follows:

(1) Authoritarian rule is much better suited than democracy for promoting economic growth, as Lowenthal has stated: 'Every increase in freedom takes place at the cost of a slowdown of development; every acceleration of development involves less freedom' [*Lowenthal 1963*].

(2) Democracy is better equipped to take care of the welfare aspect of economic development. Several observers have found that democracies promote welfare at the expense of growth and investment, because, 'Under a system in which lawmakers ... seek the approval of the electorate, the politician cannot afford .. to follow any policies which will not produce tangible benefits for the electorate by the time the next election comes around' [*Nehru 1979: 57n*]. In other words, unlike authoritarian systems, democracies are unable to curb consumption to the benefit of investment and growth.

There is also, however, a more optimistic variant of the latter hypothesis, which claims that 'All good things go together' [*Packenham 1973: 123-29*], meaning that development in the economic sphere (growth and welfare) could and should go hand in hand with development towards democracy in the political sphere [*Schwartzmann 1977: 89; Huntington 1987: 6*]. At the same time, justified scepticism has been shown towards the possible economic blessings of authoritarian rule. Jack Donelly has noted that '... economic returns to the masses (from the suspension of civil and political rights) are not automatic. Unless inequality is addressed first, it is likely to combine with political exclusion to prevent the poor from receiving a reasonable return for their sacrifices' [*1984: 281*]. So what are we to think?

The attempt to answer this question constitutes a somewhat unorthodox approach to the theme of 'Participation and new relationships in State-Civil Society', yet the objective is that of trying to provide a macro-foundation for the debate on the developmental consequences of participation, through the analysis of the consequences for economic development (growth and welfare) of some long-standing democracies and authoritarian regimes. Increased popular participation and influence should be noted at all levels of society, but at the same time, we should not cheat ourselves. The mode of participation called democracy (meaning simply a political system with participation in the selection of leaders, competition for major positions of government, and a number of civil and political liberties) has failed to solve fundamental problems of economic development. On the other hand, it will also appear from what follows that this is not necessarily an argument in favour of authoritarian rule.

I. FIRST APPROACH: DATA COLLECTION AND CORRELATIONS SEARCH

We should begin with the contributions which collect data on economic results from a number of countries and attempt to relate these results to the form of regime as the independent variable. By and large, such investigations seem to confirm the dominant hypotheses about authoritarian regimes performing well in economic growth while democracies are better when it comes to welfare. Perhaps the most comprehensive study, a survey of 98 countries for the period 1955-70, has been made by Robert Marsh. He concludes that:

> Political competition/democracy does have a significant effect on later rates of economic development; its influence is to retard the development rate, rather than to facilitate it. In short, among the poor nations, an authoritarian political system increases the rate of economic development, while a democratic political system appears to be a luxury which hinders development. [*Marsh 1979: 244*]

A similar conclusion is reached in Cohen's study of economic growth in a number of Latin American countries [*1985: 123-36*]. Berg-Schlosser's analysis of African regimes finds that authoritarian systems have a 'strong positive effect on the overall rate of GNP growth' [*1984: 143*], but he also emphasises that democratic (polyarchic) regimes have done better than should be expected:

> Thus polyarchic systems fare quite well both in terms of GNP growth and the improvement in the basic quality of life. They also have the best record concerning normative standards (protection of civil liberties and freedom from political repression. [*1984: 121*]

41

Dwight Y. King reaches a similar conclusion in his study covering six Asian countries:

> If performance is evaluated in terms of material equality and welfare rather than growth, and is examined diachronically over the past decade and within differentiated population groups (rural landless, and near landless), democratic-type regimes (Malaysia, Sri Lanka) have performed better than bureaucratic-authoritarian ones (Indonesia, Philippines, Thailand). [*1981: 477*]

At the same time, G. William Dick has examined the growth record of 72 countries between 1959 and 1968. He uses a classification with three different forms of government: authoritarian, semi-competitive, and competitive. Although the data are not, as the article readily admits, unambiguous, it is maintained that: 'these results certainly do not support, and tend to refute, the view that authoritarian countries are universally capable of achieving faster economic growth in the early stages of development than countries having competitive political systems...' [*Dick 1974: 823*].

Dick's contribution is a good example of the problems involved in attempting to answer our question on the basis of a relationship between data on economic performance from many countries covering a limited period of time, and a questionable classification in terms of the forms of regimes. Firstly, it does not seem reasonable to base such an analysis on a period covering less than 10 years. Secondly, a very large number of countries invariably give problems in regime classification. The best growth performers in Dick's analysis were the 'semi-competitive' countries, which were defined as follows: 'there is either one major and several minor political parties, with the major winning all elections, or one political party which conducts legitimising elections from time to time. Also control over the population is not extensive' [*Dick 1974: 818*].

This definition means that countries such as Algeria, Ethiopia, South Africa, all the Francophone countries in Africa, and Nicaragua under Somoza are classified, not as authoritarian, but as 'semi-competitive', using 1970 data. However, it would be easy to argue that such regimes could be considered authoritarian, and the basis for Dick's whole conclusion disappears. This might be taken to mean that the only analysis casting some doubt over the dominant hypotheses, namely Dick's, can be disregarded, thereby making these hypotheses even stronger. But this is not the case, because the contributions supporting the dominant hypotheses are plagued by problems similar to those identified in Dick's analysis. Thus, we have a large number of countries which are either not clearly identifiable as democratic or authoritarian, and/or they move very fast between the categories - semi-democratic yesterday, authoritarian today and semi democratic tomorrow. Each time they make a stop in one of the categories, they lend their economic performance data, often covering only a few years, to a different argument in these investigations.

How much can we learn from this? Does it really make us able to grasp the nuances in the economic development efforts of different types of regime? The answer is obvious. We have to change the approach in order to get a more satisfactory answer to our question.

II. SECOND APPROACH: THE POLITICAL ECONOMY OF TRANSITION

Early investigations on democracy in the Third World were quite optimistic, supporting the notion of 'all good things go together' and thus seeing the chances for democracy increase with economic development [*Diamond, Linz and Lipset 1986 and Berg-Schlosser 1985*]. This notion was seriously questioned with O'Donnell's study on Bureaucratic-Authoritarianism [*1973*]. Pointing to Brazil he argued that economic development contained contradictions which headed towards non-democratic, authoritarian rule rather than towards democracy [see also *Collier (ed.) 1979*]. Thus the frequent changes in regime form in many Third World countries have paved the way for any amount of literature on transition, analysing the actual transition processes and their determinants, initially in order to understand the large number of democratic breakdowns in the late 1960s and early 1970s [*e.g. Mueller 1985*].

In the 1980s, the focus has been on movements towards democracy in several countries [*e.g. O'Donnell, Schmitter and Whitehead 1986*]. Are studies in this tradition able to provide an answer to our question? We must first note that they analyse the reverse relationship: the form of regime is treated as the dependent variable, and economic development as the independent one. The arguments may or may not come out in support of the notion that economic development and democracy go together, but it does not deal directly with the problem we are concerned with here; that is, the effects of various regime forms on economic development. Some recent efforts have tended to focus on 'the broader issue of the political economy of delayed and dependent industrialisation, which leaves open the question of the type of regime under which it may be pursued' [*Cammack 1985: 6*].

At the same time, however, it can be argued that 'we must abandon the search for a general model which explicitly seeks to abstract away from the structurally and historically determined specificities and internal logic of individual cases' [*Cammack 1985: 5*]. Rather, the aim should be 'theoretically informed accounts of particular cases, respecting their internal logic, specific dynamics, and unique patterns of causality' [*Cammack 1985: 13*]. These starting points lead towards very detailed analyses of the interplay of politics and economics covering rather short periods of time [*Cammack and O'Brien 1985*]. What we then get are highly sophisticated analyses of both political and economic aspects of single administrations, including their relations with classes and other social forces. It provides a general understanding, for example of 'the retreat of the generals' in a specific historical conjuncture in a number of important Latin American countries [*Cammack and O'Brien 1985*], but it does not provide an answer to the question asked about the economic consequences of the form of the regime.

Thus, the choice of optional approaches is being progressively reduced. We have rejected 'quantitative' approaches based on large-scale comparisons of aggregate economic performance data from many countries, as well as approaches zooming in on detailed, qualitative analysis of the political economy of transition. There is one option left, however, but even this has two variants.

III. THIRD APPROACH: THE CASE STUDY WITH A COMPARATIVE PERSPECTIVE

A case-study approach would have to start by readily admitting that many Third World countries are not really relevant to our question, either because they have see-sawed between different forms of regime (e.g. Bolivia, Ghana, Nigeria), or because they are not clearly identifiable as either democratic or authoritarian (e.g. Kenya, Egypt, Côte d'Ivoire). Even with rather tolerant definitions of the two regime forms, there is obviously a wide grey area when it comes to Third World countries [*Sklar 1983; Berg-Schlosser 1985*].

Thus, a country which cannot, with a reasonable degree of certainty, be classified as either democratic or authoritarian, a country which has had only a brief experience with democratic or authoritarian rule, or a country with frequent changes of regime form, is much less relevant for the analysis of economic consequences of regime form than is a country with a long, stable period of either a democratic or an authoritarian regime.

Clearly, significant economic consequences of certain forms of regime should be expected to take time to manifest themselves. We will therefore proceed with an in-depth investigation of a few relevant cases which are analysed on the basis of hypotheses concerning the economic consequences of regime form. On the basis of a discussion of concepts and definitions, we will consider four cases: two long-standing democracies, Costa Rica and India, and two long-standing authoritarian systems, China and Taiwan. Several hypotheses will be examined, but the two main ones are those which were called 'dominant', as shown earlier.

Thus, 'economic development' is seen as containing two aspects: autocentric growth (growth of the variety involving structural change which strengthens the economy) and welfare (material well-being of the population). Democracy is expected to be conducive to the latter, not the former. Welfare has been the aspect of economic development where democratic regimes are expected to perform well; the argument has been that democratic regimes are answerable to an electorate at regular intervals, and will tend, therefore, to produce tangible benefits to this end. Such policies could also be found in India and Costa Rica, but in the Indian case they had an impact which never made a serious difference in improving the lot of the poorer half of the population. The percentage of the population living in absolute poverty (around 40 per cent) has remained nearly unchanged since independence.

In the case of both Costa Rica and India, it can be argued that political, economic and social power is at the core of the definition of the possibilities for welfare improvement. A dominant coalition of industrial bourgeoisie, rich landowners and bureaucrats could be identified in the Indian case, and is not very different to the 'masked hegemony of competing elites' seen in the Costa Rican context. In fact, the policies of the two democracies remain within the limits of what is acceptable to the dominant coalition, thus constraining the extent to which the policies of welfare improvement are possible.

The other side of this picture is the relative weakness, not only in economic, but also in social and political terms, of the poorest sections of the population in both countries. Against this background, it is perhaps not too surprising that there is a tendency for welfare measures to aid the middle sectors of the population rather than those at the bottom. At the same time, it is clear that the general welfare situation is much better in Costa Rica than in India, and this can only be partly explained by the existence of different levels of general welfare at the starting points of the analysis, around 1950.

Two elements go a long way in explaining this difference; one is

45

the higher level of organisational strength and political influence of the popular forces in Costa Rica, and the other is the strength of social democratic ideology of social justice in the dominant coalition. In both cases, it is worth emphasising that there is a dynamic element of change; it is possible, within the framework of democracy, to success-fully organise and push policies which produce welfare improvement for the poor. Such efforts have appeared much more often in Costa Rica, but there are also a number of examples of this in India.

On the basis of these results, it is possible to reformulate the original hypothesis concerning the relationship between a democratic form of regime and the welfare aspect of economic development. The new hypothesis runs as follows:

There is no automatic link between a democratic form of regime and measures improving welfare for the people. Democracy contains a potential in this regard, which may or may not unfold, depending on a number of circumstances; the most important among these being the resources and the strength, in terms of consciousness, organisation and political influence, of the popular forces. This should be seen in relation to the character and strength of the elite forces, who often cooperate in a dominant coalition. The position of the agrarian elite is of particular importance because it may block reform measures in the countryside which are often vital for overall welfare improvement.

We should now turn to the other aspect of economic development - autocentric growth, where no great performance has been expected from democratic regimes. The original argument was that democratic regimes were less able to curb consumption to the benefit of accumulation and economic growth, but the case studies reveal a somewhat more complicated picture. If the focus is on the overall rate of growth, both countries have performed rather well compared to many other countries, even if it cannot be overlooked that growth in per capita terms has been very modest in India, and progress in terms of autocentric growth has not been impressive in Costa Rica.

However, it seems out of place to blame the democratic regime for being unable to curb popular consumption in a country like India, where some forty per cent of the population lives in absolute poverty. Moreover, democratic governments in both Costa Rica and India have, on several occasions, proven capable of taking unpopular measures which have meant cut-backs in consumption possibilities for large popular groups.

These case studies point to other types of problems as being the most important impediments to economic growth, the most important probably being an insufficient ability to mobilise resources for economic growth from other sources than the curbing of mass consumption. For example, in India there has been an unrealised potential for productivity increases in agriculture.

In both cases, the contributions from agriculture in terms of resources for industrial growth have been much too small. In Costa Rica, a high degree of external dependence, with foreign investors dominating many areas of industry and a rapidly increasing foreign debt, has limited the resources available for growth. Behind the failure of sufficient resource mobilisation lies the fact that economic policies which could pose a serious threat to any elite faction have been consistently avoided.

Thus, the new hypothesis concerning the relationship between a democratic form of regime and the autocentric growth aspect of economic development may be formulated as follows:

There is a tendency for democratic governments to respect elite interests to such a degree that it impedes their capacity for mobilising resources for autocentric growth. This does not necessarily mean, however, that the autocentric growth performance of democratic regimes is consistently poorer than that of authoritarian regimes. The authoritarian regimes, China and Taiwan, were expected to perform well in terms of autocentric growth, and the reason given was the capacity of such regimes to curb consumption to the benefit of accumulation and economic growth. Whilst it is true that such measures were taken in both cases, especially in agriculture where the states took out a sizeable surplus for the promotion of industrialisation, this was neither the only nor the most important reason for the fast process of autocentric growth in both cases, as there were other elements involved.

Firstly, agrarian reform produced a surplus for investment which did not have to be taken out of mass consumption, mostly that which had earlier accrued to large landowners, middlemen and money-lenders. Secondly, mass consumption was curbed in a way which, in most cases, did not take it below earlier levels: redistributive measures and support for faster growth made the entire 'cake grow larger'which paved the way towards the production of a surplus for investment without cutting back on consumption.

In summary, authoritarian developmentalist regimes do curb consumption for the benefit of autocentric growth, but this does not necessarily mean that consumption is taken below previous levels, and neither is it the most important reason for their success in pushing autocentric growth. In fact, reform measures are taken which provide an investible surplus from other sources than the squeezing of mass consumption.

With this in mind, part of the reason why these regimes have also performed rather well on the welfare dimension has already been given. The restructuring of the economy has made room for improved welfare as well as for autocentric growth. In Taiwan, the labour-intensive growth process in industry has gone hand in hand with extraordinarily high productivity increases, giving an element of improved welfare built into the growth process itself, as improved productivity could contribute to accumulation as well as to welfare.

In China, at least until the late 1970s, industrial growth did not contain a similar mechanism. There was little labour absorption in the industrial strategy which gave priority to heavy industry. This, together with a much lower level of welfare from the outset, meant that China had to rely on specific measures, especially in the areas of public health and education, to improve welfare, and even then progress was significantly slower than in Taiwan.

While it is true that authoritarian developmentalist regimes do not concern themselves with the provision of tangible benefits for an electorate, they may well promote welfare through a combination of measures restructuring the economy on the one hand and improving specific dimensions of welfare on the other. There has been behind these processes, in both cases, a strong regime in the sense that it has not faced internal opposition and has had no ties with established elites in industry or agriculture. This has made radical reforms possible.

At the same time, both regimes have been highly committed to promoting economic development, partly for ideological reasons and partly due to a combination of internal and external pressures. Yet it is also clear that Taiwan has been substantially more successful than China in the promotion of both aspects of economic development. This is only partly explained by Taiwan's more advantageous starting point, although this should not be underestimated. China was engaged in a vicious civil war during the first half of the twentieth century. During the same period, Japanese rule in Taiwan provided a basis for further advances in economic development.

But there are other reasons also. Taiwan has had a smooth process of growth and increases in productivity, both in agriculture (with the system of family farms), and in industry (with light, labour-intensive manufacturing supported by public enterprises in basic industries). The whole process has been supported by significant U.S. economic aid.

China, on the other hand, imitated a Stalinist model of industrial accumulation which overemphasised heavy industry, and left very narrow room for growth in light industry and agriculture up to the late 1970s. In addition, China was internationally isolated for a long period, and its ties with the Soviet Union during the 1950s did not provide much economic assistance compared to the assistance Taiwan received from the United States. Moreover, whenever Mao attempted to correct the problematic elements of this strategy of development, the result was a situation which created more problems rather than removing existing ones. In fact, there were policy failures which harmed economic development without seriously providing gains in non-economic development aspects. Policy failures which affected economic development were by and large avoided in Taiwan, mainly due to advice from the United States.

IV. DEMOCRACY VERSUS AUTHORITARIANISM: COMPARING DIFFERENT SYSTEMS

We shall now look at the comparable cases of India and China, and Costa Rica and Taiwan.

Authoritarian China has done better than democratic India in economic development, in growth as well as in welfare. Yet in some respects the difference is not dramatic and there are areas where the similarities are more striking than the differences. Both countries gave much attention to agriculture in the early years; China completed an agrarian reform and India took measures against the Zamindar system and pushed the Community Development Programme. A long period followed where both countries gave top priority to industrial growth, with emphasis on heavy industries, providing little opportunity for labour absorption in industry. There were also tendencies of stagnation in agriculture, which still held the large majority of the labour force. India's answer was the Green Revolution whilst China took 'the Great Leap Forward' and later underwent the Deng reforms.

The overall result in agricultural growth and welfare improvement again puts China first, but, with such information alone, we cannot decide whether the social and human cost involved in the process of rapid social change in China is justified. However, there is no reason to lower this issue to the level of a grizzly body-count debate. The core of the matter is that radical reforms in China have paved the way for economic development and a number of non-economic changes which have benefited the population and provided a decent level of living for the large majority. This could not have been done without strong leadership bent on pushing such policies, perhaps even to the point of employing coercion against opponents.

At the same time, these radical reforms have involved conflicts and mistaken policies which have led to human suffering and loss of life. Moreover, the other side of the strong, determined leadership has been the blatant lack of basic human and civil rights and, of course, the complete absence of democracy. In India democracy has, by and large, meant the protection of basic civil and human rights. Policy excesses have been avoided, as have human catastrophes such as large-scale famines, but democracy has also maintained a highly unequal social structure headed by a dominant elite, which resists any structural change benefiting the poor.

For some years now, raising the income levels of the rural poor in India has been a prime objective of the nation's development policy. But when it comes to the practical implementation of the programme, very limited success has been achieved. The ruling classes are able - within the democratic structure - to resist real change in this area, thus leading to human suffering and loss of life; not through spectacular disasters and catastrophes as in China, but through the quiet, continuous suffering of the 40 per cent absolute poor.

In comparing economic development achievements of democratic Costa Rica and authoritarian Taiwan, we may first note that they have both done very well on the question of welfare. By the early 1980s, these two countries had achieved similar results in the general welfare indicators (PQLI; Infant Mortality; Life Expectancy; Calorie Supply). Whilst there was a higher percentage of poor in Costa Rica, it should be remembered that the country's wealth in terms of GNP per capita was only about half of that of Taiwan.

In Costa Rica, social achievements are based on state expenditure, the larger part of which is devoted to welfare, including education and health. In Taiwan, the family unit takes basic responsibility for this provision, and the state plays a much smaller role, primarily in the areas of education and health. Welfare progress in Taiwan could be combined with a limited role in state expenditure because the growth model pursued by the state contained employment and entrepreneurial possibilities which could be transformed into welfare progress. At the same time, the state consciously and consistently pursued autocentric growth through industrialisation and the upgrading of the economy.

It is this consistent pursuit of autocentric growth which marks the most important difference when compared with Costa Rica, where the formulation and implementation of a consistent strategy of economic development under democratic conditions has proved much more difficult.

There have been some differences to Taiwan's advantage, the most important among these being the different stands taken by the United States in the two cases. The United States provided significant assistance to help encourage economic development in Taiwan during the 1950s and 1960s, but no such assistance was given to Costa Rica. Although the U.S. role has changed over time, it is fair to say that concern for U.S. economic interests has consistently held a higher priority in policies towards Costa Rica. Aid to locally controlled industries or the encouragement of an agrarian reform has not been high on the agenda.

In both Taiwan and Costa Rica, the process of economic development has involved a comparatively low level of human and social cost. The difference in economic growth between the two countries lies elsewhere. It is tempting to claim that Taiwan has achieved much more in terms of autocentric growth and has 'paid' with the absence of democracy, and that the 'price' of a highly developed democracy in Costa Rica has been the lack of significant autocentric growth. But it has been demonstrated that other factors have also been involved. In addition, there is no guarantee that authoritarian rule in Costa Rica would have produced the same results as in Taiwan.

V. CONCLUSION: THE CASE STUDIES IN PERSPECTIVE

What is the general relevance of the conclusions reached on the basis of these case studies regarding democratic and authoritarian regimes for economic development? The argument that each of these four cases are really *sui generis* should be rejected, but do the four cases have features in common which make them stand out, as a group, against other groups of Third World countries?

The only reservation that is going to be made in this respect has to do with very weak states. All four countries studied here have had a comparatively high 'degree of government' [*Huntington 1968: 1*] meaning, among other things, that they are nation-states with regimes which had the capacity to exercise authority, to mobilise their populations towards development goals, and which could count on back-up from, if not necessarily efficient, reasonably functioning administrative apparatuses. Therefore the states studied here have all been comparatively strong states. A 'typical' Black African state, would appear to be much weaker in all these respects [*Jackson and*

Rosberg 1982; Sandbrook 1985 and Hyden 1983], and it is necessary to consider this before applying any conclusion to such weak states.

There is no specification here of the states which may belong to this category. Instead, a positive identification is attempted of democracies and authoritarian regimes relevant to the results of the analysis.

Beginning with the democratic states, we could state that there are not many in the Third World. Defining democracy in a similar way to that described here, Sklar [*1987: 692*] has listed 31 [*1986*]. If very small countries with populations of less than one million are omitted, there are 16 countries left, namely: Egypt, India, Turkey, Papua New Guinea, Argentina, Bolivia, Brazil, Colombia, Costa Rica, Dominican Republic, Ecuador, Jamaica, Peru, Trinidad and Tobago, Uruguay and Venezuela. However, there also has to be a measure of stability over time before the results from the above analysis can be claimed relevant. Even without being very demanding, we are left with only a handful of countries, all of which are in the Western Hemisphere, except for India and Papua New Guinea, namely Colombia, Costa Rica, Jamaica, Trinidad and Tobago, and Venezuela.

In other words, there are only five countries where the above results concerning the democracies' consequences for economic development have relevance.

Given the broad and negative way in which authoritarianism is defined here, there are many more of them than of democracies, and it is not possible to formulate categories which can exhaustively classify the broad range of very different types of authoritarian regimes. However, the type of authoritarian regime analysed in the case studies could be called the Authoritarian Developmentalist regime. This regime is looked upon as an ideal type and is compared with two others: the Authoritarian Growth regime and the Authoritarian State Elite Enrichment regime.

The central feature of the Authoritarian Developmentalist, the AD-regime, is its capability of promoting growth as well as welfare. Authoritarian rule can be combined with certain other features, such as a reform-oriented regime which is strong and independent vis-a-vis vast elite interests, an ideological commitment to the promotion of economic development, and a regime being pushed in the same direction by internal and external pressures.

When these features of an AD-regime are combined with the demand for stability in regime form in a time dimension, there are only two other countries which can be clearly regarded as AD-regimes, namely North and South Korea. Both cases have received comprehensive treatment [*Halliday 1983: 114-55; Foster-Carter 1987; Menzel 1985; Asche 1984*] and there is no reason for going into a lengthy description here. It is clear that South Korea has many traits in common with Taiwan, while North Korea is a case of a socialist AD-regime which has taken the centralisation of political and economic control even further than has been seen in China.

There will be some borderline cases which share only some of the features of AD-regimes or have been AD-regimes for a shorter period. Examples are Singapore [*Hamilton 1983, Luther 1980*] on the capitalist side and Cuba and Vietnam [*Carciofi 1983; White 1983*] on the socialist side. The two latter cases have had significant problems with policy failures and over-centralisation of political and economic power. Furthermore, U.S. hostility towards both has constituted a much more serious threat than it did in the case of China, and it has severely limited their possibilities for economic development.

It is clear when we look at the broader development context of the most successful AD-regimes analysed here, that Taiwan experienced conditions which were very different to the typical situation of many Third World countries, such as significant economic aid and advice from the most powerful country in the world, and internal preconditions which were a good starting point for economic development, both in terms of the 'groundwork' done by the Japanese and in terms of a relatively high competence level of the population. In addition, the regime could draw on bureaucratic expertise which, in turn, was given a high degree of autonomy in forming efficient and competent institutions for the promotion of economic development. Finally, the regime succeeded in creating an environment where the Chinese work ethic could flourish. In other words, there were also cultural elements in Taiwan which were highly conducive to economic development.

The only other AD-regime coming close to having a similar pattern of factors helpful to the promotion of economic development is South Korea.

Turning to the two other main types of authoritarian regimes, we see firstly a regime which strives to promote growth, but not welfare, called the Authoritarian Growth, AG-regime. Brazil during military rule could be an example of this type of regime, being regarded as an ideal-type AG-regime due to these characteristics: autocentric growth objectives are pursued with the aim of building a strong national economy (which, in turn, can provide the basis for a strong military power); and the long term interests (but not necessarily the immediate interests) of the dominant social forces are respected while the economic surplus to get growth underway is set to come from workers and peasants of the poor majority.

The military regimes which imposed authoritarian rule in Uruguay, Chile and Argentina in the mid-1970s attempted to push growth models with similar features [*Nohlen and Waldmann 1982: 81-139, 334-58*]. In contrast to Brazil, they had much less success as they opened their economies to external shocks which, before corrective measures were taken, led to a decrease in industrialisation [*Ominami 1988*].

Thus, in relation to the overall distinction between main types of authoritarian regimes presented here, these Latin American cases meet the expectation that authoritarian regimes will curb popular consumption to the benefit of growth. This is done by attempting to consider the long term interests of the dominant social forces. The regimes pursue their growth objectives through an alliance with elite interests. However, at the same time, it is also necessary to consider the specific features of each of these cases in order to understand why Brazil's relatively successful growth record was not replicated.

The last main type of authoritarian regime was the one which promoted neither growth nor welfare, but functioned mainly for the self-enrichment of the elite which controlled the state, called an Authoritarian State Elite Enrichment, ASEE-regime. It is often based on autocratic rule by a supreme leader whose actions may not be understandable from any formal economic development point of view, but perfectly rational through the lens of patronage and clan politics. The clan is a political faction, operating within the institutions of the state and the governing party: Above all, it exists to promote the interests of its members through political competition, and its first unifying principle is the prospect of the material rewards of political success.

Political office and the spoils of office are the very definition of success, and loot is the clan's totem [*Cruise O'Brien 1975: 149*, quoted in *Hyden 1983: 37*]. The surplus which falls into the hands of the leadership through its control of the state is distributed among the clan or a coalition of clans which in turn provide political support for the leader. It is not, of course, an equal pattern of distribution; the lion's share of the benefits accrues to the supreme leader and to a small elite surrounding him. There is no clear distinction between politicians and civil servants; the latter are actively involved in efforts to gain personal advantage from their public posts.

Thus, despite official claims to the contrary, the ruling elite takes no real interest in economic development, be it in terms of growth or welfare. The main aim is self-enrichment. This requires a balancing act against potential opponents and a measure of distribution of spoils which may have side-effects in terms of promoting either welfare or growth, but this is not the main aim.

Zaire [*Nour 1982: 468-522; Gould 1980*] under Mobutu may be the clearest example of an ASEE-regime. The inner circle of the Mobutu clan comprises his 'fraternity', numbering several hundred people. The lucrative positions in 'state, diplomatic corps, party, army, secret police and the Presidency' [*Nour 1982: 512*] are reserved for clan members. The latter directly claim some 20 per cent of the national budget, and the income is complemented through smuggling (diamonds and gold) and 'private' sales of copper. Mobutu himself has a personal share in all foreign undertakings operating in Zaire, and his family controls sixty per cent of the domestic trade net. He has accumulated enormous wealth abroad and is recognised to be one of the three richest men in the world.

Thus the defining characteristic of the ASEE-regime is simply that the elite which controls the state is preoccupied with enriching itself. Other examples from Africa which fit this description are the Central African Republic under Jean Bedel Bokassa and Uganda under Idi Amin.

There are also authoritarian regimes outside Africa which have much in common with the ASEE type of regime: Haiti under Duvalier Senior and Junior (Papa and Baby Doc); Nicaragua under Somoza, and Paraguay under Alfredo Stroessner.

In closing this brief survey on the main types of authoritarian regimes and their consequences for economic development, we may conclude that there is no automatic link between an authoritarian form of regime and economic development, not even when development is defined only in terms of autocentric growth.

In conclusion, has our question been answered? The response is both yes and no. Yes, insofar as the dominant hypotheses set out in the beginning have been rejected and a number of more nuanced for-mulations have taken their place, and no insofar as we have not, and cannot expect to, reach a point where we can say that as a particular regime is democratic (or authoritarian), we can expect so and so in terms of economic development. The form of regime is not definitely decisive for economic development outcomes, and it is impossible to identify any single factor which alone determines economic development.

REFERENCES

Asche, H., 1984, *Industrialisierte Welt? Ein Vergleich von Gesellschaftsstrukturen in Taiwan, Hongkong und Sudkorea*, Hamburg: VSA Verlag.

Berg-Schlosser, D., 1984, 'African Political Systems. Typology and Performance', *Comparative Political Studies*, Vol. 17, No. 1.

Berg-Schlosser, D., 1985, 'Zu den Bedingungen von Demokratie in der Dritten Welt'. *Politische Vierteljahresschrift*, Sonderheft 16.

Cammack, P., 1985, 'The Political Economy of Contemporary Military Regimes in Latin America: From Bureaucratic Authoritarianism to Restructuring', in P. O'Brien and P. Cammack (eds.), *Generals in Retreat. The Crisis of Military Rule in Latin America*, Manchester: Manchester University Press.

Carciofi, R., 1983, 'Cuba in the Seventies' in G. White et al. (eds.), *Revolutionary Socialist Development in the Third World*, Brighton: Harvester Wheatsheaf.

Cohen, Y., 1985, 'The Impact of Bureaucratic-Authoritarian Rule on Economic Growth', *Comparative Political Studies*, Vol.18, No.1, pp.123-36.

Diamond, L. et al., 1986, 'Developing and Sustaining Democratic Government in the Third World'. Paper for the 1986 Annual Meeting of APSA, Washington, Aug. 28-31.

Dick, G.W., 1974, 'Authoritarian versus Non-authoritarian Approach to Economic Development', *Journal of Political Economy*, Vol. 82, No. 4.

Donelly, J., 1984, 'Human Rights and Development. Complementary or Competing Concerns?', *World Politics*, Vol. 36, No. 2.

Foster-Carter, A., 1987, *North Korea. The End of the Beginning*, Leeds: Leeds University Korean Project.

Gould, D.J., 1980, *Bureaucratic Corruption and Underdevelopment in the Third World. The Case of Zaire*, New York: Pergamon Press.

Halliday, J., 1983, 'The North Korean Enigma', in G. White et al. (eds.), *Revolutionary Socialist Development in the Third World*, Brighton: Harvester Wheatsheaf.

Hamilton, C., 1983, 'Capitalist Industrialisation in East Asia's Four Little Tigers', *Journal of Contemporary Asia*, Vol. 13, No. 1.

Huntington, S.P., 1968, *Political Order in Changing Societies*, New Haven and London.

Huntington, S.P., 1987, 'The Goals of Development', in M. Weiner and S.P. Huntington (eds.), *Understanding Political Development,* Boston: Little, Brown.

Hyden, G., 1983, No Shortcuts to Progress. *African Development Management in Perspective*, London: Heinemann.

Jackson, R.H. and C.G. Rosberg, 1982, *Personal Rule in Black Africa. Prince, Autocrat, Prophet, Tyrant*, Berkeley: University of California Press.

King, D.Y., 1981, 'Regime Type and Performance. Authoritarian Rule, Semi-Capitalist Development and Rural Inequality in Asia', *Comparative Political Studies*, Vol. 13, No. 4.

La Palombara, J. and M. Weiner, 1966, 'Political Parties and Political Development', *Items*, No. 20, pp.1-7.

Löewenthal, R., 1963, 'Staatsfunktion und Staatsform in den Entwicklungslandern', in R. Loewenthal (ed.), *Die Demokratie im Wandel der Gesellschaft*, Berlin: Colloquium Verlag, pp.164-92.

Luther, H.U., 1980, *Okonomie, Klassen und Staat in Singapur*, Frankfuram Main: Metzner.

Marsh, R.M., 1979, 'Does Democracy Hinder Economic Development in the Latecomer Nations', *Comparative Social Research*, Vol. 2, pp.215-48.

Martinussen, J., 1977, 'Styreformen og de sociale klasser', *Den Ny Verden*, Vol. 11, No. 3, pp.35-61.

Menzel, U., 1985, *In der Nachfolge Europas. Autozentrierte Entwicklung in den ostasiatischen Schwellenlandern, Sudkorea und Taiwan*, Munchen: Simon and Magiera.

Müller, E.N., 1985, 'Dependent Economic Development, Aid Dependence on the United States and Democratic Breakdown in the Third World', *International Studies Quarterly*, No. 29, pp.445-69.

Nohlen, D. et al., 1982, *Handbuch der Dritten Welt*, Vols. 1-8, Hamburg: Hoffmann and Campe.

Nour, S., 1982, 'Zaire', in D. Nohlen et al. 1982, *Handbuch der Dritten Welt*, Vols. 1-8, Hamburg.

O'Brien, P. and P. Cammack (eds.), 1985, *Generals in Retreat. The Crisis of Military Rule in Latin America*, Manchester: Manchester University Press.

O'Donnell, G., 1973, *Modernisation and Bureaucratic-Authoritarianism. Studies in South American Politics*, Berkeley: University of California Press.

O'Donnell, G. et al., 1986. *Transitions from Authoritarian Rule*, Baltimore and London: John Hopkins Press.

Ominami, C., 1988, 'L'industrialisation et la restructuration industrielle en Argentine, au Brésil et au Chile', *Problèmes d'Amérique Latine*, No. 89, pp.55-79.

Packenham, R., 1973, *Liberal America and the Third World*, Princeton: Princeton University Press.

Pye, Lucian W., 1966, *Aspects of Political Development*, Boston: Little, Brown.

Pye, Lucian W., 1985, *Asian Power and Politics: The Cultural Dimensions of Authority*, Cambridge, Mass: Belknap Press.

Sandbrook, R., 1985, *The Politics of Africa's Economic Stagnation*, Cambridge: Cambridge University Press.

Schwartzmann, S., 1977, 'Back to Weber: Corporatism and Patrimonialism in the Seventies', in J.M. Malloy (ed.), *Authoritarianism and Corporatism in Latin America*, Pittsburgh.

Sklar, R.L., 1983, 'Democracy in Africa', *African Studies Review*, Vol. 26, Nos. 3-4, pp.11-25.

Sklar, R.L., 1987, 'Developmental Democracy', *Comparative Studies in Society and History*, Vol. 29, No. 4, pp.686-714.

Sørensen, Georg, 1990, Democracy, Dictatorship and Development, in *Selected Development Forms of Regime in the Third World*, London: Macmillan, New York: St Martin's Press.

White, G., 1983, 'Recent Debates in Vietnamese Development Policy' in G. White et al. (eds.), *Revolutionary Socialist Development in the Third World*, Brighton: Harvester Wheatsheaf.

White, G., 1984, 'Developmental States and Socialist Industrialisation in the Third World', *Journal of Development Studies*, Vol. 21, No. 1.

5

Social Movements and Processes of Democratisation in Latin America

FERNANDO CALDERON and
MARIO DOS SANTOS

This chapter focuses on the current changes that are taking place in the relationships between the state, society and the economy in a region, with emphasis on the role of social actors and movements. An attempt will be made to answer two basic questions; first, why can traditional patterns of articulation between the state, society and the economy no longer reproduce themselves, and second, what are the chances and conditions for a new democratic scene?

What we are really concerned with is the future of democracy in Latin America, and what the likelihood is of an historical arena in which social actors and political institutions can interact with each other. A key issue is the idea of development in a new perspective.

To begin with, Latin America is currently undergoing a very paradoxical and challenging historical stage, including the pressure of the most serious economic crisis ever to be experienced in the region, since it is currently undermining the social tissue which has been constructed over the past four decades by industrialisation and modernisation.

At the same time, never has such a global process of revalorisation of democracy been experienced. Whilst this process is taking place in a variety of ways, such as development differences between Chile and Mexico, society right through Latin America is demanding democratisation at different levels, from the functioning of the institutional system to issues in daily life.

The state has organised development in Latin America since the 1930s. The executive branches of the states have been key actors in the economic, social and political scenes. These actors have led the process of modernisation and industrialisation in Latin American society, whilst the democratic political system - in other words the political parties, congress and other representative institutions - have played secondary roles. In some cases the democratic political system has been absorbed into the system and in others it has simply been absent. Different examples can be seen in the region, from the National Popular states built during revolutionary processes in Bolivia and Mexico, to the neocolonial state of Puerto Rico. However, in nearly every case the state has dealt the cards and called the game.

Even the main movements during this period have had an orientation towards the state, towards power and towards control of the historical process through the control of the bureaucratic institutions. This has not only occurred during populist movements, such as Peronism in Argentina or Aprismo in Peru, but also in class-oriented movements like the revolutionary unions of the miners in Bolivia (the Sindicalismo Revolucionario). This type of orientation can also be seen in other types of forces, such as the Che Guevara guerrillas or even in 'The Alliance for Progress'.

It appears that this historical orientation is over, as the state cannot continue to play the role of articulator between society and the economy, but paradoxically a kind of populist revival is now taking place in Latin America (for example in Argentina, Ecuador and Mexico). Cesar Vallejo was right when he said: 'in fact everything is gone, but in truth everything is still here.'

'Here' is precisely where the topic of populist transgression lies, as the historical chances of the populist model - the model of the state as the core of development - are gone, but the social impulse is still here and quite alive.

To understand the crisis of the state, two phenomena are crucial: On the one hand, there are internal limitations for the reproduction of the relationship between the state, society and economy. There are three basic trends:

(1) The growing inability of the state to satisfy essential demands such as housing, health, nutrition, etc. The criticisms of society towards the state and the demands for autonomy from social movements must be taken into account.
(2) The impossibility of maintaining a permanent expansion of the state, both as a bureaucracy and as a development investor. The state cannot keep pace with the irrational increase of its network of clients whilst at the same time trying to invest in production and development.
(3) The strong demands for privatisation from the new right.

On the other hand, there are also external constraints, in particular constraints from the international economy which are unequal in terms of trade, the external debt problem, the new international division of labour, etc. The state has no chance of satisfying these external demands without risking the democratic stability. On another level, we also find the emergence of the post-industrial society in Latin America.

Two important scenarios have emerged from a comparative study which was carried out in 20 Latin American countries. The first, a pessimistic scenario which is unfortunately the most likely, is an increase in social exclusion and a persistence of social fragmentation, and a deepening of the economic crisis which would pose serious difficulties, even to the extent of reverting to the level of development of the 1960s. This trend would imply a weak democracy, where Latin American governments would emphasise the governability of the economy and procedural legality more than their own legitimacy. Schmitter [*1985*] has called this '*democradura*'.

The second scenario indicates several alternative trends in social and cultural action which imply that the best way to consolidate democracy is to increase a society's capacity for action; in other words to strengthen social movements and the political system along the lines of the democratic regime which would allow better communication between social and political actors. Theoretically, the question is how to increase a society's resilient capability, and how a society can consciously develop its capacity for social creation. Globally, five kinds of change are needed:

(1) The revitalisation of the will to change the political game in a complex, pluralistic and substantial sense. By pluralistic, we mean a political system which recognises the diversity of social identities, and by substantial we mean social integration and ethical values. In short, progressive modernity.
(2) The strengthening of autonomy of social movements which are able to transform their needs and demands into political action. A society's autonomy must promote interaction between different types of social action, being the best way to arrest the process of social fragmentation. The recent experience of workers in Sao Paulo (the CUT organisation) is a good example.
(3) The build up of an entrepreneurial ethos, not only in relation to entrepreneurial behaviour, but in the reconstruction of a collective will of solidarity against political demoralisation and in the construction of a process of efficiency in social action. Entrepreneurs should act like entrepreneurs, not like Las Vegas gamblers.

(4) The reinforcement of the state's capacity to regulate social and political relations with the help of a renewed democratic regime. The state must strengthen the country's relations with the external sector in regard to its own domain, the state area and public and private areas.

(5) The innovation of the political regime. This final point could lead to the most important political change in the continent, a change which could end the elitist pattern that was inherited from the colonial period. However, would it be possible to think of a renewed political regime, and would such a regime be able to boost the plurality of social and cultural actors in the decision-making process?

Every study to date has shown high inconsistencies between society and political representation. Parliaments do not represent the multiple forces of a society, and in any case are subordinated to the executive branch of the government. Social forces tend to ask for institutional changes such as decentralisation or plebiscitary mechanisms.

The principal question is how social actors can be both represented and representable in the political arena, and how participation can be achieved in the political system. Social actors are not able to express their actions without an adequate institutional frame. In short, the main challenge in Latin America today is how to create some capacity of response from the state and the political system in order to meet society's needs and demands, and to achieve this in an adverse international system. The answer can only be found within a world-wide system of historical action, which implies the reformation of democratic regimes as well as modifications in the behaviour of political and social actors serving in this renewed political regime.

However, it is evident that in the sociopolitical process in Latin America today, there has not been any tendency towards the institutionalisation of new arenas of collective decision-making through the participation of social actors. Majority parties become the main actors in the political system and create long lists of demands and expectations. There is a greater exchange between parties and social movements prior to the transition to democracy, but after the transition the exchange loses intensity, eventually establishing distance between social and political dynamics.

Thus the potential of redefinition of social behaviour and identity has not been explored, but in the process of democratisation, the issue of recomposition of both the social network and the political system has to do with the ability to articulate political and social action. For this reason, a 'new social pact' that would - in the words of Norberto Bobbio - 'attempt simultaneously to solve a problem of both power and justice in the region,' is still a long way off.

One sure thing is that the different actors demanding democratisation do not necessarily share a model of democracy that is able to redesign institutions. While the construction of state sovereignty and the stability of recovered, new or debilitated democratic governments seem to be inconceivable without reform and political or institutional creation, the exploration of this field is still in its early stages. Nevertheless, the potential for renovating democracy in the region is closely tied to this, and is an indicator of the degree of political creativity and a recourse for the improvement of decision-making systems.

The lack of constitutional technology capable of institutionalising the management of conflict has been pointed out as characteristic of the region. To this must be added the necessity of overcoming the favouritism of certain clients and corporations and of broadening social representation in the process of decision-making. All this is not possible without the creation of an institution capable of amplifying the public arena; the only space in which political and social identities can be redefined in accordance with progressive governability.

Whilst this does not endorse a strict institutional understanding of democracy, transition or the improvement of democracy, it does support the thesis that a model of enclosing development (or a situation of progressive governability) requires an institutional modification that redefines the rules of distribution and exercise of power, framing the behaviour of political and social actors with regard to the model of enclosing development.

In fact, democratic routines and their discipline can only be attained by institutionalising the conflict which guarantees the different actors that their contribution to democratic stability and development will be compensated almost immediately, both formally and substantially.

The symbolic integration acquired through the revaluation of democracy by the majority will be continuous and profound as long as the political order furnishes the institutional means for non-exclusive development. Of course one must see where and how the political regimes advance, and without using abstract formulae for improvement, as these regimes are not abstract but rather incarnate in certain political parties, pressure groups, executive orientations, etc., beyond procedural order.

Moreover, constructing the state's democratic sovereignty means that politics regain control of its own sphere, and this is a principal task of transition or revitalisation of the democratic order. This construction requires much more than a democratic institutional order, rather an accumulation of democratic power beginning with a respect for democratic procedures (conspiratorial ways of undertaking politics), dating from agreements on the perfection of institutional frameworks and on the substantial contents (ethical and material) of the regime. Social representation in political decisions and their technical/political compatibility are indispensable.

The context of political relations has been modified profoundly by the closure of the state cycle described above. A revision of the new conditions manifests the difficulties that political and social systems have in order to comply with their role. The growing complexity of the social universe fragments and diversifies demands without remission to the global models of development which validate them and make them compatible.

Partisan organisations, in turn, do not manage to rechannel participation exclusively through themselves: The obstruction they face in monopolising representation is evident. Likewise, there are hindrances to a fluid interchange between partisan and sectoral representation, and in fact social movements in general, which impede, especially after a democratic system has been put in place, an adequate representation in this new complex society. In general an instrumental retreat is taking place in the political parties, perhaps due to the penury of governability.

Concomitantly, there is a crisis in present constitutional designs, as shown by the institutional reforms presented by a majority of countries in the region. However these are ambiguous in content and while the modifications to the institutional frame seem to prohibit improvement in the system's problems of governability, changes in human or social rights must give priority to the construction of the political system's democratic sovereignty and the amplification of the spaces and topics subject to public regulation.

In fact there exists an inverse relation between democratisation and governability, and in the identity crisis of socioeconomic actors, one can neither redefine an exchange with reciprocal limitations nor expand partisan capacity to undertake social conflict. The dismantling of this system has been a cost that governments do not tend to calculate if it is found to be immediately governable. Institutional innovations which amplify political citizenship (modifying institutionalised participation in decision-making) can, nevertheless, settle political designs, even if additional factors are required.

The deterioration of organisational and social integration, violence and a regime's loss of legitimacy could be ascribed to the strategy of fixing politics by executive powers and shielded partisan systems which tend to reject the introduction of substantial progressive compromises in the political system's functioning.

In action - even in politics - strictly economic criteria prevail. The characteristics of political reform and modernisation prompted by these actors clearly reveal the displacement of the nucleus of decisions towards the political system due to the recession of the state and its autonomy, and also to the democratisation of the regime, which does not actually imply a greater capacity for public regulation, but a major input from the private sector and a brutal concentration of power.

In contrast, a series of incidences in collective action which point towards political reform in different institutional and sociocultural contexts can be seen. In the institutional context, innovation has occurred - and is being promoted - in the furthering of political and social representation and its influence in decision-making, and in the sociocultural context the shaping of consensual values of integration in development is being promoted.

This aggregate of practices, orientations and values of collective action is not present in any degree of great consistency or clarity except in specific and barely intercommunicated ways. However, potentially this indicates that a society is capable of acting for itself.

In fact, it is possible to recognise new social movements among actors related to this orientation, such as the new Brazilian unionism, new Indian movements in various countries, new movements based on gender consciousness, incipient ecology movements, new socio-cultural movements (for example the Rastafaris; the youth movement of rock and salsa), urban community and religious movements. In addition, there are changes in traditional social actors like the union movement, be it rural or urban labour.

Likewise, the emergence of new political parties and fronts (for example the PT in Brazil and Cardenism in Mexico) show similar intentions. Processes of innovation and internal democratisation have even begun to demand this type of perspective in political parties with long traditions, such as populist parties.

Joining this amalgam of practices and orientations are new layers of intellectuals and technicians who are fully conscious of the challenges of the so-called post-industrial culture. The development of an internationalised civilian society with important political and cultural exchanges is not indifferent to this either, and contributions from peripheral business groups, the armed forces, the Catholic Church etc., can also be traced.

These practices generate complex processes of identification, with traces of social autonomy in many cases, which to a great extent are constructed in opposition to prevailing political orientation and which put their efforts into articulated representation of social and political actors. They are particularly concerned with shortening the distance between the elite and the masses and with attaining material and symbolic results appropriate to the whole society. This version of the political system could create space for public expression and reduce conflicts between different forces in society, a process in the framework of improved procedures of representation and public control of decisions.

In short, they would try to make politics into representation and deliberation, so as to change the modern orientation of the state and the determination of policies of reactivation and economic reconversion. The margins of viability of other types of modernisation, and economic policies which include a social content capable of attaining the objective of reactivation and reconversion will be seen in future development, as well as the existence of specific socioeconomic actors to support a project of this nature.

Until now, there has not really been a true field of conflict around the described orientations, and even less so regarding any type of conflict with the capacity of historical determination. However, the demands set by the weakest actors are not static, as they have been able to gain technical consistency due to their greater political consistency in the immediate time frame.

In reality, a democratic state in the long run would be marked by these mixed orientations towards political reform. It is thus possible to express hypothetically that as they establish themselves - within the framework of democratic stability - they will be able to interchange their orientations, recognise each other and admit modifications. Perhaps it is this which will fully mark the beginning of a new cycle of historical democracy.

BIBLIOGRAPHY

The interpretation brought forward in this essay are refering to a number of processes of contemporary Latin American history: hence bibliographic backing would be too extended to be included here. Nevertheless the empirical base of our elaborations comes to a great extent from the UNDP-UNESCO-CLACSO Project RLA 86/001: *Crisis and the need of new paradigms in the relationship state/economy/society*. This study has been achieved by national research teams in 18 countries of the region and published by CLACSO's Library of social sciences in 8 volumes (in Spanish).

Volúmenes 1 y 2: *Democratización/modernización y actores socio-politicos.*
Volúmenes 3 y 4: *Los actores socio-económicos del ajuste estructural.*
Volúmenes 5 y 6: *Centralización/decentralización del Estado y actores territoriales.*
Volúmenes 7 y 8: *Innovación cultural y actores socio-culturales.*
Bobbio, Norberto, 1982, 'Perché torna di moda il contrattualismo', *Mondoperaio*, No 11, pp.84-92
Bobbio, Norberto, 1984, *Il future della democrasia*, Einaudi, Torino, pp.126-47
Bovero, Michelangelo, 1985, 'Societá di contratto sociale, democrazia reale. Sui significato del neocontrattualismo', in *Teoría política*, I, No 3
Schmitter, Philippe C., 1985, 'La transición del gobierno autoritario a la democracia en sociedades en proceso de modernisación: ¿puede invertirse la proposición (y el pesimismo) de Gino Germani?', in *Los límites de la democracia*, CLACSO, Buenos Aires, Vol 2, pp.146-147
Vallejo, Cesar, 1965, *Obra Poética Completa*, Colección Literatura Latinoamericana, Casa de Las Américas, La Habana, p.155. 'Todos han partido de la casa, en realidad, pero todos se han quedado en verdad.', en el texto *No vive ya nadie...* de los poemas en prosa.

6

Participatiom and Development: Emerging State-Civil Society Relation in India

R.B. JAIN[1]

The very nature of 'development' calls for community involvement in the process of development. Although many developing countries adopted a centrist theory of development during the 1950s and 1960s, the failure of these centrist policies, especially in the implementation of development plans and the delivery of benefits to a large section of the poorer community, started a re-evaluation of the practicability of the centralist strategies of development.

During the 1970s, various politico-administrative decentralisation programmes, coupled with the evolution of a number of institutional devices to affect people's participation in development, were instituted in many developing countries.

After independence, the constitution makers in India devised a political strategy that was essentially federal in character but heavily weighted in favour of centralisation. This was considered important to curb the secessionist tendencies at that time and to have a uniform economic development pattern. However, in recognition of the fact that uniform policies were not the answer for complete development of the country, the constitution makers, through the provisions of the Directive Principles of State Policy, established a system of Village Panchayats (village councils) to involve the people at grass-root levels in the decision-making process.

Thus, decentralisation and people's participation, both in economic as well as in political and social development, became important policy issues in the development strategies of India. These policies were encouraged by the United Nations Economic and Social Council which recommended that the government adopt popular participation as a basic policy measure in national development strategies. It also suggested that non-governmental organisations, such as trade unions and youth and women's organisations, be involved in setting goals, formulating policies and implementing plans in the process of development.[2]

A brief survey of the principles and characteristics of people's participation in development will now be undertaken, along with the institutional innovations which have been adopted in India for this purpose. In addition, we will analyse the new demands, actors and processes which are emerging, with a view to examining the relationship between the social actors and the state following the changes in the socio-political practices.

I. DEVELOPMENT PHILOSOPHY IN INDIA

The philosophy of development which evolved under the stimulus of India's struggle for freedom from colonial rule attached great importance to the participatory approach. In fact, this approach was upheld for its intrinsic value and for its instrumental rule by the most important leaders in the national struggle.[3] The basic premise of the participatory philosophy is spelled out in Mahatma Gandhi's statements: 'Man is the most wonderful machine in creation', and 'technology must serve man and not lord over him'. His greatest statement supporting a participatory approach stated that people are the roots and the state is the fruit; that the 'classes' at the top which are crushing the 'masses' at the bottom must get off their backs, and that true democracy cannot work through 20 men sitting at the centre. 'It has to be worked from below by the people of every village'.[4]

After independence in 1947, Jawaharlal Nehru became the first Prime Minister of India. Although his vision was not identical to Gandhi's, his firm commitment to 'the democratic approach' and to the concept of a 'just society' aimed at extending and enlarging the scope of popular participation. Nehru showed full awareness of the fact that there cannot be full mass participation in an unequal society and that the conventional framework of the right to vote according to the principle of universal adult franchise allowed for extremely restricted mass participation. Participation helps man to be himself, to make decisions himself and to grow to his full status as a man. As Nehru put it, 'development is but the means to an end - the building up through effort and sacrifice, widely shared, of a society without caste, class or privilege, which offers, to every section of the community and to all parts of the country, the fullest opportunity to grow and contribute to national well-being'. This concept of opportunity to grow and be human is the essence of participation.

Some major developments during the post-Nehru era released contradictory forces both in favour of and against mass-oriented and participatory development. A centralised planning system for industrial and agricultural development came into existence along with programmes for social development at the grass roots level. During the Indira Gandhi era, major policy initiatives were witnessed, such as the nationalisation of large commercial banks, the formulation of a new land reform package, legislative enactment against debts, minimum wages for agricultural labour, homestead lands for the landless, the introduction of a crop loan scheme, the launching of the Twenty Point Programme under Garibi Hatao (to remove poverty), and the introduction of several anti-poverty programmes for backward classes and regions. All these were meant to create pre-conditions for mass-oriented and participatory development.

In the centralisation-decentralisation continuum, the system of government that India inherited from the colonial period was in many respects more decentralised than centralised. With the arrival of a democratically-elected government at the centre and in the states, the balance was heavily tilted towards centralisation. However, decades of experience has yielded the lesson that centralised planning does not work well. In the meantime, mass politicisation has begun to generate a demand for participation, and it has become necessary to turn more towards a decentralised system of government and planning.[5] Before examining the specific programmes and strategies adopted in India to turn decentralisation and people's participation into a reality, it would be pertinent to consider the meaning of the term 'participation'.

People's participation has no doubt emerged as the most difficult and controversial issue of our time. As it is conceptually integrated with the redistribution of economic and political power in the process of development, it is therefore subject to value judgements. Moreover, it is controversial because its content is operationally the function of the ideology and moral philosophy of each country.

However, in practical terms it is assumed that participation in development means:

(1) sharing in economic power through increased access to productive assets;
(2) sharing in socio-political power by taking part in decision-making through organisations of one's own choice;
(3) having incentives to contribute to increasing production through institutional organisational arrangements; and
(4) sharing in opportunities for rewards and benefits of growth to improve nutrition, productive skills and abilities, and to enable an exchange of labour and production for essential needs.[6]

71

Such an interpretation of participation implies that the socio-economic order, which excluded people in the past from sharing in development, has to gradually give way to a newly-ordered system, based not only on opportunities for increasing productivity and income but also on social power and freedom from a high degree of dependency for survival. It is recognised that redistribution of economic power opportunities in agriculture alone cannot resolve the crisis of rural poverty: The structural change in urban power relations is therefore complimentary.

In addition, the extent to which the rural poor participate is dictated by the operational ideology of the state, and this can be derived from either extensive experience in its people or by importation from oth. cultures, or a combination of both.

II. INDIA'S STRATEGY FOR PARTICIPATIVE DEVELOPMENT: THE INSTITUTIONAL INNOVATIONS

People's participation in development and nation building in India has posed a number of crucial issues, such as the adoption of new institutions at different levels between the citizens and the administration. Citizen involvement in development calls for improved mass-communication facilities so that the governmental agency responsible for development can reach the masses and learn their views on different areas of urban/rural development.

Effective management of civic affairs and rural services calls for an effective participation and a sense of responsibility on the part of the citizens to bridge the gap, not only between the well-to-do and the rest of the population, but also between urban and rural dwellers.

In the urban areas, inter-group or inter-person dialogue can take place during group discussions, organised through the mass media such as radio, television and newspapers. Structural arrangements like the 'People's Forum for Integrated Development', based on territorial and functional representation, can be created to solve community issues as well as group interests.

In 1959, the Government of India launched the Urban Community Development Programme which was designed to transform, socio-economically, the lives of villagers and urban slum dwellers. It was called the 'People's Programme', and included the participation of the people together with the local authorities.[7] Some of the studies relating to urban development in India have shown that people's involvement can occur, even in a government programme, if those involved as animators are committed to the people and can develop their capacity to organise themselves for social and political actions.

Such studies have recognised 'poor' people as the most important social and economic resource in urban development. Urban community development has great potential for building systematic linkages between physical improvements, social services and people's participation.[8]

However, as India was predominantly an agricultural society at independence, development basically meant the development of rural India and rural society, although there was concomitant improvement in urban and industrial infrastructure for further growth plus work on the problem of linkages between urban and rural development.

The discussion of people's participation in development in India is thus related more to rural than to urban areas. In fact, since independence, various experiments in participatory development in India have taken place through community development programmes which have established the institutional framework of Panchayati Raj institutions. This is an infrastructure of cooperative bodies and government-sponsored development agencies and an encouragement of voluntary organisations to help and assist in development programmes.

Gandhi's Movement

Even before independence, Mahatma Gandhi had already launched his constructive programme of rural development through the voluntary efforts of the people. He experimented with a self-sufficient and self-supporting village economy. The society envisaged by him was to be self-initiated and non-violent, and the individual would have maximum freedom for himself, whilst still being part of his immediate community. The smaller community would be linked to a larger community until, ultimately, all became part of the larger world community.[9]

In his concept of rural development, he believed in decentralisation of social and political power, and was sure that the imbalance of power between urban and rural India would be removed through the mechanism of Panchayati Raj working as the basic and effective unit of the government, as it would enable rural India to have its share of political power. Gandhi planned to give shape to his ideal of the total reconstruction of rural society with the help of voluntary workers.

However, when Gandhi plunged into the political movement for independence, the village reconstruction plan lost its momentum. After his death in 1948, Vinoba Bhave developed a variant of the

Gandhi Plan in the form of the Sarvodaya and Bhoomi Dan movement (land donation movement). Nevertheless, this did not succeed as the people were more attached to the family and the land than their community and they only accepted the movement for the benefits conferred by it. In addition, government aid robbed the movement of its specificity and uniqueness.[10]

Despite its failures, it was Gandhi's philosophy of the village as being the nerve centre of the peoples' universe which became the basis for India's development programmes. It also shaped a new programme that came to be known as the 'Community Development Programme' (CD) with the village as the focal point for development. The Gandhian model of decentralisation of political power was later taken up in the Panchayati Raj institution which was introduced during the Second Five Year Plan.

The Community Development Programme

As part of the strategy to bring about socio-economic and cultural transformation in the rural areas, a massive community development programme was launched throughout the country in 1952. This programme drew its inspiration from the experiments in Albert Mayer's Etawah Project in the Uttar Pradesh State in 1948, and S.K. Day's Nilokheri Project in Punjab (now in Haryana) in 1950.

The Community Development Programme was launched throughout the country in 1952. Initially it covered 55 projects comprising 27,388 villages and 16.4 million people. However, within a very short period of time it was felt that the programme needed to be extended to cover the whole country. Hence, a less intensive programme, called the National Extension Service, was formulated and put into effect on 2 October 1953. The CD programmes were described as 'the all round rural development programmes', aimed as material development by encouraging rural people to create better living conditions through infrastructural facilities provided by the state.

In fact, it was assumed that as the programme caught on and became acceptable to the rural people it would move from officially motivated self-help to self-motivated self-help. The goals of the Community Development Programme were:

(1) to increase employment and increase production by the application of scientific methods in agriculture, including horticulture, animal husbandry, fisheries, etc, and the establishment of subsidiary and cottage industries;

(2) self-help and self reliance and the largest possible extension of the principle of cooperation;

(3 the need to develop a portion of the vast unutilised time and energy in the countryside for the benefit of the community.

It was assumed that the desired changes could be introduced into the villages through an administrative machinery capable of providing infrastructural facilities and technical know-how. This would increase the rural society's growth potential, creating economic prosperity, which would in turn begin to minimise, if not completely eliminate, poverty and social and economic inequalities. However, these expectations were not met as there had been no recognition of the fact that a new social order based on the values of democracy, secularism and socialism could not be easily implanted on a caste-bound feudal and hierarchical society without shaking off the age-old values and beliefs of the people, and reorganising the socio-economic structure.

In fact, the blending of centralised planning with the parliamentary form of government had created opposing pulls within the Indian polity.[11] The logic of centralised planning was antithetical to people's participation. If the goals of development were already determined by centralised planning, the role of the bureaucracy, in the absence of a cadre-based political party, was to mobilise the people, and participation in its real sense was all but a total farce.

The main drawback of the CD Programme was that it had been conceived in purely administrative terms, and remained primarily a bureaucratic activity where officials were 'target-oriented' and showed little sensitivity to the social process generated by economic programmes. People's participation was substituted by bureaucratic mobilisation which was directed towards achieving set development goals. The programme was not conceived in response to the 'felt needs' of the people. In addition, the human and material resources were inadequate considering the scale and magnitude of the task that was to be accomplished. In community development, there was greater dependence on the government for material resources and these were not supplemented by popular contributions, as had been expected.

Despite these shortcomings, however, the CD Programme did succeed in shaking up the rural society from its extreme passivity and inertia, and gave it a momentous start. For the first time, it brought the people closer to the government through its bureaucratic apparatus and accrued political consciousness. It also familiarised people with many new concepts and techniques of agricultural development.

Moreover, an awareness was generated that facilities which were being made available by the state could be used for general good, if access to them was not restricted by people of influence or the government.[12]

The Panchayati Raj Institutions

During the period of the second Five Year Plan (1956-61), the National Development Council appointed a Committee on Plan Projects (Balwant Rai Mehta Committee) to examine the work of the Community Development and National Extension Service. The committee's recommendations mark the beginning of a new experimental phase in people's participation in Development through what has come to be known as the process of democratic decentralisation.

The committee realised that development without popular participation would have a weak foundation, and clearly saw that in order to be self-sustaining and self-generating, development had to go hand in hand with participation. It advocated that rural development and welfare are only possible with local initiatives and direction, and must be an instrument of expression of the local people's will. Therefore, the committee recommended a devolution of power and a decentralisation of machinery, which should be controlled and directed by popular representatives of the local areas, thus laying the foundations of the Panchayati Raj institutions.

The establishment of a three-tier system of rural local self-government with full powers to assume responsibility for local development was the core of the Balwant Rai Mehta Committee recommendations. Rajasthan was the first state in India to introduce the Panchayati Raj system on October 2, 1959, which was followed by a number of other states, including Andhra Pradesh, Uttar Pradesh, Maharashtra, Gujarat and Madhya Pradesh. There were two main variants in the adopted Panchayati Raj model which depended on whether greater authority was delegated to Samitis (groups of villages) or Zila Parishads (the districts). By the 1970s, the Panchayati Raj system had been introduced in practically all parts of the country. The new institutional set up was intended to be an experiment involving the poorest of the poor in rural areas in the process of self-consciousness for national reconstruction and to channel energies towards the refashioning of community life.

The Panchayati Raj institutions have been in operation in almost all states in India for nearly three decades, but with a number of variations in their structure concerning their decision-making, implementation and resource-allocation, staffing pattern, training and recruitment of staff and the degree of autonomy allowed to different units. A number of research studies have been conducted by various scholars in the functioning of the system on an empirical basis, and these have generally pointed to the limited extent of the involvement of people in decision-making at grass-roots level, the interactional resistances between the official and the non-official functionaries, the paradoxical resistances and tensions of the system in operation, the problems of caste-elite domination and political influences, and more significantly the non-achievement of developmental goals.

While the Panchayati Raj institutions have acquired stronger roots in some states such as Gujarat and Maharashtra, these have not made any impact in other states due to a number of reasons, including the postponement of elections, declining and inadequate material and human resources, tensions between the officials and political leaders, and the lack of the very premise of popular participation in development programmes, which has been the raison d'etre of the entire concept.

The Ashoka Mehta Committee was set up in 1977 by the Janata Government which came into power after the short aberration of 19 months of emergency regime imposed by the then Prime Minister Mrs. Indira Gandhi. It reviewed the Panchayati Raj institutions at various levels and noted that the system had passed through three distinct phases: the phase of ascendency (1959-64); the phase of stagnation (1965-69); and the phase of decline (1969-77). The Committee proposed some structural and organisational changes to revitalise the PR system, but with the fall of the Janata Government in 1980, the recommendations were put into cold storage. However, it is doubtful whether the proposed changes by the Ashoka Mehta Committee would have made any impact on the relationship between state and Civil Society in the absence of the realisation that the decentralisation of power had more deeper cultural problems rather than merely the organisational and managerial efficiency of the PR institutions. From 1980 until 1989, when a new proposal to revitalise the PR institutions by giving them a constitutional status was initiated by the Rajiv Gandhi Government, the PR institutions virtually remained in suspended animation.

The Participation Crisis: Growth of Development Bureaucracy

Since the early 1970s, a number of special rural development programmes were initiated by the government in order to cater to the demands of various target groups in the rural areas through the Integrated Rural Development and the Poverty Alleviation Strategies. These could be classified as

(a) Sectorial programmes;
(b) Employment oriented programmes;
(c) Area programmes
(d) Target-group oriented programmes.

Sectorial programmes were farmer oriented, and aimed at intensive agriculture development through improved technology. Employment oriented programmes fell into two broad categories: Target group oriented schemes, such as SFDA, MFAL, DPAP, TADP, HADP, DDP and WDP;[13] and continuous employment/income providing schemes, for example, Rural Work Programme, Crash Schemes, Pilot Intensive Rural Employment Programme, Employment Guarantee Scheme, Food for Work Programme and National Rural Employment Programme. Recently the Rural Landless Employment Guarantee Programme (RLEGP) and the Self Employment to Educated Unemployed Youth (SLEEUY) have been launched to provide gainful employment for at least one person in every family in rural areas and opportunities for self-employment in urban areas.

Training of Rural Youth for Self-employment (TRYSEM) has also been expected to prepare 200,000 youths for self-employment each year. However, most rural employment programmes are operated as short-term measures rather than as permanent solutions to either employment or poverty problems, and offer low wages. The schemes, being grant based, are thus of only an ad hoc nature.

Programmes such as the Backward Area Development Programme, Command Area Development Programme, Hill Area Development Programme, Desert Development Programme and Tribal Area Development Programme are included in the Area Programmes. The Target group oriented programmes have included SFDA, MFAL and ERRP (Economic Rehabilitation of the Rural Poor). While under SFDA and MFAL, target groups have received loans in cash, whilst the Minimum Needs Programme and ERRP were designed to serve the poor by quantifying their basic needs such as food, clothing, shelter, health, education, water and sanitation. Resource problems have reduced the effectiveness of the Minimum Needs Programmes. Antyodaya/ERRP identifies the poorest of the poor families in every block, assists them under the usual banking schemes with concessionary rates of interest. However, all the programmes are beset with the problem of improper identification of beneficiaries.

A very penetrating and critical study on the functioning of rural development programmes has indicated that none of these programmes have made any significant impact on either poverty or on rural inequality. This failure has been inherent in the approach and methods adopted for these goals, and representative bodies have been replaced by a colonial pattern of administration. The people have been substituted by the state bureaucracy with serious short and long-term consequences for development and democracy.[14]

The study further states that confidence in the bureaucracy, as a better agent of social change than elected Panchayats, has turned out to be misplaced. The people themselves have no place in rural development, as every available inch is occupied by the bureaucracy. The community which was once central to the rural development strategy is now peripheral to it. A vast development bureaucracy has replaced elected Panchayats, with no elections being held in village Panchayats in most states during the last 12-14 years. Even where they have been held, the Panchayats have not been endowed with any worthwhile development functions and resources.

The precondition for any development scheme being undertaken in a village today is not community contribution as in the past, but government subsidies. Unless government subsidy is forthcoming, the bureaucracy has little incentive to push a development scheme. There are no longer any village sponsored schemes which are fundamental to the concept of community development, as there are now only centrally sponsored village development schemes which have necessitated an elaborate system of central guidelines and approval. To further its control, the central government has fostered a District Rural Development Agency (DRDA) in each district, which is a registered society headed by the Collector. Central grants for rural development are channelled directly to DRDA, bypassing not only the Zila Panchayats, but also the State Government.[15]

One of the arguments for the replacement of elected Panchayats by the bureaucracy has been the belief that Panchayats could not be expected to emancipate the poor, dominated as they have been by powerful elements. However, it has been noted that despite total direction and control being in the hands of the bureaucracy, poverty groups have only peripheral access to IRDP resources, child development services or nutrition. The idea of the Antyodaya approach was to meet the poor in person, but the poor are still eluding the bureaucracy. It is the rural rich who are more aligned with development administration, and the nexus between the rural rich and the bureaucracy is also being backed up by the MLAs and the MPs. The institutional arrangements for development thus continue to be top-heavy without the pillars of public support, and today democratic decentralisation is practically non- existent.[16]

Cooperatives: The Institutional Innovation for Economic Participations

Although the cooperative movement in India started at the beginning of the 20th century, the first Five Year Plan (1951-56) envisaged that all agricultural families would become members of multi-purpose village cooperatives. After the third Five Year Plan (1961-66), the cooperatives spread throughout India. To give support to the cooperatives, the National Cooperative Development Corporation and the Agricultural Refinance Corporations were established in 1962 and 1963 respectively, and by 1965, the cooperatives accounted for one third of short- and medium-term loans and long-term credits for land development, irrigation wells and pump sets. In 1972, a number of multi-purpose farmer's service societies came into existence to help the weaker sections of the rural areas and were backed up by the National Bank for Agricultural and Rural Development. In practice, however, these societies did not benefit either weaker sections or small and marginal farmers or agricultural labourers. Only in some areas of Maharashtra and Gujarat did the cooperative movement actually succeed in involving people in the development process. While Panchayats were envisaged as representing political participation, cooperatives were to provide a companion institution for economic participation by the people. However, cooperatives are now being supplanted by corporations (another administrative body) in almost all spheres e.g. handlooms, milk, credit marketing, scheduled caste development and even women's development.

Field evidence from various studies has confirmed that the share of the weaker sections in cooperative credit continues to be low. India has a large number of cooperatives (300,000, with over 110 million members), but there is a stagnation in their numbers.[17] Panchayats and cooperatives apart, the local population is not considered fit to be associated with development in an advisory capacity. While there are a number of advisory committees in the towns and the cities, and in various ministries/departments of the Government of India as well as state governments, there are no advisory committees in the programmes for rural development - be it the nutrition centre, fair price shops or anything else. In short, while there has been a sporadic showering of development assistance from above, in the absence of community involvement this has failed to generate a process of development where people would take matters into their own hands after initial assistance from the state. In the words of a critical observer, 'All that has been generated is dependency. The resulting development is grass without roots'.[18]

III. NEW DEMANDS, ACTORS AND PROCESSES

New Areas and Actors in Participative Development

Realising the importance of participatory development, the sixth Five Year Plan (1980-85), emphasised the importance of non-governmental organisations, both formal and informal in nature, as new actors, which could motivate and mobilise people in specific or general developmental tasks and meet the new demands of the growing sphere of developmental activities. The new areas where awareness and conscious participation of the people is critical for success were identified as:

(1) Optimal utilisation and development of renewable sources of energy, including forestry through the formation of renewable energy associations at the block level;
(2) Family welfare, health and nutrition education and relevant community programmes in this field;
(3) 'Health for all' programmes;
(4) Water management and soil conservation;
(5) Social welfare programmes for weaker sections;
(6) Implementation of minimum needs programme:
(7) Disaster preparedness and management (floods, cyclones etc.);
(8) Promotion of ecology and tribal development;
(9) Environment protection and education.

The new actors who sought to be associated with these tasks were: (i) youth and women's organisations at different spatial levels, particularly for promoting eco-development and environmental protection; (ii) voluntary organisations of specific beneficiary or interest groups such as self-employed women, or farmers or people who have common economic interest such as marketing; (iii) voluntary organisations engaged in general developmental work in an area or a specific activity; (iv) farmers' organisations for the improvement of land and water management through irrigation projects, catchment areas in the hills, and watershed areas in unirrigated regions; (v) religious, social or cultural organisations or clubs (Rotary, Jaycees, Lions etc.) which often undertake developmental activities in selected areas; (vi) professional organisations or educational institutions which take up study, research and social action programmes as part of their professional or social commitments.

In the field of rural development in India, a number of voluntary organisations have come into existence at the national level during the past two decades. These fall into three categories: (a) The Techno-Managerial Voluntary Agencies, which work on the premises that the process of rural development can be accelerated through modern management techniques and technology, (b) Reformist Voluntary Agencies, which try to bring about changes in the social and economic relationships within the existing political framework, and (c) Radical Voluntary Agencies, which seek to challenge the existing production relations. They attempt to organise the exploited against the exploiters through economic, health or educational programmes as an 'entry point' to mobilise masses for political action.[19] Included in this category are also the voluntary organisations and movements begun for the purpose of environment protection, such as the 'Chipko Andolan' led by Sunderlal Bahuguna, the Narmada Valley Protection Movement or the Sulabh Sauchalya movement.

Such non-governmental organisations (NGOs) get a much more practical, people-based view of environmental issues than the state with its unimaginative, inflexible structure. Therefore, the viewpoint of the NGOs as the eyes of the state in terms of grass-root monitoring of environmental quality needs to be properly recognised. Prominent among the national level voluntary agencies in India are:

(1) Agriculture and Allied Fields: The Bharat Krishak Samaj, New Delhi; the Young Farmers' Association, New Delhi; the Action for Food Production (AFPRO), New Delhi; the Appropriate Technology Development Association, Lucknow; and the Council for the Advancement of People's Action and Rural Technology (CAPART), New Delhi, which is a voluntary organisation for promoting people's awareness towards innovations in rural technological development.

(2) Food and Nutrition: Catholic Relief Services, New Delhi; CARITAS India, and Peoples Action for Development, India (PADI) New Delhi.

(3) Child Welfare: The India Council of Child Welfare, New Delhi; the Balkanji Bari, Bombay; and the Federation of Organisation Working for Children in India (FOWCI), New Delhi.

(4) Harijan Welfare: The Harijan Sewak Sangh, New Delhi.

(5) Tribal Welfare: The Bhartiya Adimjati Sewak Sangh, New Delhi, and the National Institute of Social Work and Social Service (NISWASS), Bhubneswar.

(6) General Rural Development and Coordination Functions: The Bharat Sewak Samaj, Church Auxiliary for Social Action (CASA), New Delhi; the Asian Institute of Rural Development, Bangalore; the Centre for Agrarian Research Training and Eduction (CARTE), Ghaziabad; the National Christian Council of India, Nagpur; the Association of Voluntary Agencies for Rural Development (AVARD), New Delhi; the Remarkrishna Mission, Belurmath, Calcutta; the Gandhi Peace Foundation, New Delhi; the India Council for Social Welfare, Bombay; and CARITAS, New Delhi.[20]

The seventh Plan (1985-90) envisaged a more active role for the voluntary organisations in order to make communities as self-reliant as possible. These were expected to show how village and indigenous resources, as well as human resources, rural skills and local knowledge, could be used for their own development. Furthermore, these were to be utilised to demystify technology and to introduce it in a simpler form to the rural poor, to train grass-roots workers, to mobilise financial resources from within the community and to mobilise and organise the poor and generate a demand for quality services and impose a community system of accountability on the performance of village level government functionaries.

Recently India has seen a considerable shift in the attitude of the government towards the NGO/Voluntary sector. Earlier the relationship tended to be one of patron and supplicant, with the state as the grant-giver drawing the parameters not only for performance requirements, but also for the structural and spending patterns to achieve these ends. This is now acknowledged often to have imposed conditions that were unrealistic and to have deterred many people or groups from seeking government support. However, these changes have failed to percolate down the line, particularly to the field level where day to day cooperation between the governmental and non-governmental sectors must become a reality if the development objectives are to be realised.

The nature and character of voluntary agencies have also undergone a noticeable change. In the past such agencies adopted a religion-oriented mass approach in an informal atmosphere, stressing programmes of education, medicine and social reforms in their plans of action. The services provided by its members were free. At present, the agencies are adopting a nationalist-oriented group approach in a formal atmosphere, the objective being socio-economic development of the specified target group through paid, fulltime and formally trained workers. They raise funds from the masses, take interest in government/international aid and collect token fees for services rendered.[21]

Many of the voluntary agencies today are sponsored by industry for publicity and image building, or for sentimental and emotional reasons for the welfare of one's own place, caste, or community, for tax benefits granted by the state or for economic benefits accruing to the industry on a long term basis. However, to be more effective these need to have proper coordination at the town/district/state level.

People's Participation in Planning

Although planning was mentioned as one of the functions of Panchayati Raj institutions in the legislation of many states, in actual practice the PRIs have had very little or no involvement in the planning process. Some experiments in the State of Karnataka and West Bengal made the PR institutions responsible for planning at the district level and below, but by and large the role of Panchayats in the planning process has been negligible or at the most peripheral. It is argued that the involvement of Panchayats in the planning process would provide, at the local level, an opportunity for advancement on the basis of self-help and mutual cooperation. It would be especially useful in laying down priorities for the needs and problems of the people. This involvement would also be useful in identification, formulation, selection and location of schemes of local importance, in monitoring and evaluation of projects/programmes, as well as in the collection of reliable data and information. However, these functions cannot be performed by Panchayats alone without the help of local level bureaucracy as well as Experts. Before deciding on specific projects or schemes, it would be better if the socio-economic and financial viability of the Panchayats were determined by some expert planning team. This would ensure that 'public involvement did not result in the plan becoming merely a list of demands from a narrow local perspective'.[22]

In 1978 The Dantwala Committee, which was appointed to draw up 'Detailed Guidelines for Block Level Planning', stressed the need to strengthen the planning capability at district level. The Committee recommended that the planning team at the district level - who had the responsibility of preparing block plans - consist of a core group comprising a Chief Planner, Economist/Statistician/Cartographer/

Geographer, Agronomist, Engineers, Industry Officer and Credit Planning Officer. However, the Committee did not visualise block-level planning as a purely bureaucratic or Expert dominated exercise and emphasised the importance of public participation at the stages of plan preparation and implementation. It also suggested that the planning team at district level seek the assistance of the voluntary agencies in their area while preparing the plan, and selectively entrust to them the implementation of some Sectorial plans in which they may have requisite expertise and experience. It would also be necessary to make special endeavours to ensure the participation of the weaker sections in the planning process.[23]

However, not much progress has been made in putting local level planning on a sound footing. Similarly, again in 1984, the Hanumantha Rao Working Group on District Planning noted that 'if decentralised planning has to make headway, institutional mechanisms have to be made more broad-based with the active involvement of local representatives and endowed with a greater degree of autonomy in local decision-making. Ultimately, district planning has to be taken over by the Panchayati Raj institutions, which would have to be strengthened'. People's participation, to be really meaningful, should take place at every state of planning, including pre-planning, strategy setting, scheme formulation, monitoring and review, and not merely at the time of plan-finalisation. Similarly, full benefit of the experience and special merits of voluntary agencies should be availed of wherever possible and desirable.[24]

In order to ensure a more participatory role of Panchayati Raj institutions and decentralised decision-making in development, the former government, led by Prime Minister Rajiv Gandhi, sponsored the 64th and 65th Constitutional Amendment Bills in 1989 to give the Panchayati Raj institutions and urban local bodies a constitutional status and making it obligatory for all the states to establish a three tier system of Panchayats at village, intermediate and district levels. The state legislatures were expected to enact laws to devolve powers to the Panchayats to enable them to plan and implement schemes of econ-omic development and social justice. The Bills included provision for the reservation of seats for Scheduled Castes, Scheduled Tribes and women in the elected bodies and ensured Panchayats a fixed term of five years. The control of elections was vested in the Election Commission and provision was also made for the audit of accounts under the auspices of the Controller and the Auditor General. It also made a provision for the constitution of Finance Commission every five years to review the finances of Panchayats and to recommend the principles for apportioning an assignment of taxes to the Panchayats.

Although there was a general appreciation of the need to decentralise powers at grass-root levels, the two bills, which the Congress-I Government had recommended for the restructuration of Panchayati Raj Institutions and urban local bodies, could not be accepted by Parliament during its tenure. The opposition had voted against the bills, mainly because of their anti-federal provisions. However, the most important reason of their non-acceptance was the wrong approach and wrong timing of the introduction of the bills. The impression among the people was that both bills were intended by the Government as election gimmicks to serve the electoral ends of the party in power, hence they did not attract the kind of serious attention they deserved.

With the election of the National Front Government led by Prime Minister V.P. Singh in November, 1989 the move to reform the PR institutions and to give them a constitutional status was again considered, and the question was taken up at a Conference of the Chief Ministers held at New Delhi on 9-10 June, 1990. The broad agreements on the reform measures which emerged at the Conference were the granting of constitutional status to the Panchayati Raj Institutions, reservation of seats for women and weaker sections and provision of safeguards to make supersession of local bodies difficult. The thrust of the reform, however, is expected to make the Gram Sabha (The village council body of the elected representatives in a village) the base of the rural set-up. In short, the aim is to make democracy more effective at the grass-roots level and to pave the way for greater people's participation.[25]

The eighth Five Year Plan (1991-95), entitled 'Towards Social Transformation' also envisages a major shift in the approach to rural development from the departmental schemes to the completion of the process of democratic decentralisation within the first year of this plan.[26]

IV. CONCLUDING OBSERVATIONS SOCIAL ACTORS VERSUS THE STATE

The foregoing analysis of India's experiments with participatory democracy highlights the importance of a number of social actors and institutions which can effectively perform the role of mobilising people for development. Such actors and institutions often come into conflict with the state, although the goals of both seem to be identical. The gradual changes occurring in the socio-political culture and processes also precipitate such a conflict. In India, people's participation in development has been an integral process of socio-economic and political change since Independence. The institutional, managerial technological, infrastructural, participative and human development service oriented changes have also affected its rural and urban social structure in terms of occupational diversification, social mobility, reduction in income disparities and changes in values and social relationships for integrated social living. Other factors, such as leadership, social consciousness, organisation and political awareness have also affected the process of participation necessitating a new relationship between the state and the Civil Society. Experiences in India have demonstrated that the state by itself can neither initiate technological or societal development nor mobilise people to accept its processes of change.

Recent events in the east European countries have further strengthened the role of new social actors in mobilising the people to accept the concomitant socio-political change brought out by a state through its bureaucratic apparatus and technological and material resources. Even if the state does succeed in physically delivering the minimum or the basic needs through centralised planning and bureau-cratic implementation, people are unlikely to acquire the necessary capabilities and quality. Technology is an aid but not a substitute for the people's conscious activity as individuals, as groups, or as large collectives.[27] A reorganisation of state power structure from village level onwards which institutionalises the political participation of the masses, their role in policy-formulation, decision-making, economic bargaining, political and economic management, and which brings the dominant elite under the framework of community discipline is essential if the basic goals of development - transformation of the outlook of the people, inculcation of the spirit of self-reliance, generation of habit of cooperative action through popular bodies leading to enlightenment, strength and hope - are to be realised. In the most comprehensive sense of the term, participation implies the restoration of interaction, communication and dialogue between the forward-looking sections of the elite at the top or the people in authority and the people below impatient for a new socioeconomic order. The conflict between the state and the emerging social actors and institutions must give way to cooperative endeavour towards development and 'to a long term equilibrium between state and society - an equilibrium fundamental to the survival of democracy and human dignity and also for equality within society'.[28]

NOTES

1. The author is grateful to Shri T.N. Chaturvedi, former Comptroller and Auditor General Government of India, for his valuable comments and suggestions on an earlier draft of the paper.
2. United Nations Commission for Social Development, *Report of 24th Session* (January 1975). Official Records of the Economic and Social Council, 58th Session, Suppl. No. 3 U.N. Document No. E/CN. 5/526, Para 4.
3. See Joshi, P.C., 'Participatory Approach to Growth and Social Change', John Barnabas Memorial Lecture delivered at the national Institute of Public Cooperation and Child Development, New Delhi, February 5, 1988.
4. *Ibid.*
5. Mukarji, Nirmal, 'Decentralisation below the State Level', *The Hindustan Times* New Delhi, Magazine Section, May 7, 1989, p.2.
6. See El Ghonemy, M.R., 1984, 'The Crisis of Rural Poverty: Can Participation Resolve it?, in M.R. El Ghonemy, R.P. Sinha, N. Uphoff and P. Wignaraja, *Studies on agrarian reform and rural poverty*, Rome: UN Food and Agriculture Organisation, p.2.
7. For a critical evaluation of such programme see Gangrade, K.D., 1985, 'Development and People - A Participatory Approach', in S.C. Bhatia (ed.), *The Rural-Urban Continuum*, Delhi: University of Delhi, pp.31-53.
8. See for instance Cousins, William J. and Catherine Goyder, 1979, *Changing Slum Communities*, Delhi: Manohar Publications. Also see R.K. Wishwakarma and Gangadher Jha (eds.), 1983, *Integrated Development of Small and Medium Towns: Problems and Strategic Policy Issues*, New Delhi: Centre for Urban Studies, Indian Institute of Public Administration. See also Government of India, Ministry of Works and Housing, 1983, *Report of the Study Group on the Strategy of Urban Development*, New Delhi: Ministry of Works and Housing, p.23..
9. See Gangrade, K.D., 'Plan: People's Involvement', *The Hindustan Times* June 11, 1990, p.11.
10. For details see Padhy, Kishore Chandra, 1986, *Rural Development in Modern India*, New Delhi: B.R. Publishing Corporation.
11. See Chaturvedi, H.R. and Mitra, Subrata K., 1982, *Citizen participation in Rural Development*, New Delhi: Oxford & IBH, p.9.
12. *Ibid.*, pp.9-12.
13. SFDA: Small Farmers Development Agency; DPAP: Drought Prone Area Programme; MFAL: Marginal Farmers and Agricultural Labourer; TADP: Tribal Area Development Programme; HADP: Hill Area Development Programme; DDP: Desert Development Programme; WDP: Women Development Programme.
14. Jain, L.C., B. Krishnamurthy and P.M. Tripathi, 1985, *Grass Without Roots*, New Delhi: Sage Publications, p.196..
15. *Ibid.*, pp.197-98..
16. *Ibid.*, p.205.
17. *Ibid.*, p.207.
18. *Ibid.*, p.210.
19. Shah, Ghanshyam and H.R. Chaturvedi, 1983, *Gandhian Approach to Rural Development*, New Delhi: Ajanta Publications, pp.7-8.
20. I. Udaya Bhaskara Reddy, 1884, 'Role of Voluntary Agencies in Rural Development' in *Indian Journal of Public Administration*, New Delhi: Vol. 30 (1984),

p.551. See also Alliband, Terry, 1989, *Catalysts of Development: Voluntary Agencies in India*, West Hartford, Connecticut: Kumarian Press.

21. See Pady, n.9, p.389.
22. See Prasad, Kamta, 1989, 'Decentralisation of Planning through Panchayati Raj', in *Centre for Area Development and Action Research Studies*, National Symposium on Panchyati Raj - Decentralised Planning. Role of Communication, New Delhi: CADARS, p.33.
23. See Government of India, Planning Commission, 1978, *Report of the Working Group on Block Level Planning*, (Known as Dantwala Committee Report), New Delhi: Planning Commission, pp.139-142.
24. See Government of India, Planning Commission, 1984, *Report of the Working Group on District Planning*, headed by C.H. Hanumantha Rao; New Delhi: Planning Commission, pp.12-13.
25. For Comments, see the Editorial, 'Raj for Panchayats', *The Hindustan Times* June 14, 1990, p.11.
26. See '8th Plan's Accent on Growth and Justice', *The Hindustan Times* May 25, 1990, pp.1 and 20.
27. Joshi, n.2.
28. Jain *et al.*, n.12, p.220.

PART III

ECONOMIC REFORMS AND CHANGES IN THE ROLE OF THE STATE

7

Economic Reforms and Transformation of the Role of the State

MICHEL BEAUD

Is the state going through a crisis? Is its role called into question? A whole body of facts point to that direction.

In the West, the welfare state which ensured security, solidarity and a certain equity and was set up in some countries by social democratic and left-wing parties with the support of the trade-union movement and the workers, is now facing some difficulties and is even losing ground. This has gradually been the case in Germany, France and Sweden, and more abruptly so in the United Kingdom.

In the East, countries where the construction of socialism led to strengthening an 'all-state' system, with control over the economy, society and the ideology, are now changing course and fostering the development of a market economy and a business mentality. This process, together with the combined effect of democratic aspirations and long suppressed discontent, has led to student and mass demonstrations followed by repression in China, while in the USSR and in eastern Europe it has led to challenging the established order and has revealed innumerable difficulties including nationalistic claims and ethnic or religious clashes.

In the South, the failure of most development policies and the greed of some leaders and governing circles, combined with the consequences of the economic crisis, the debt burden and the strategies of multinational banks and firms, have driven many states into serious difficulties - even to bankruptcy or utter helplessness - compelling many of them to appeal to the International Monetary Fund and to accept their stringent lending conditions.

Thus the state appears to be facing crises everywhere in the world except for a few rare cases, notably in Asia (e.g. Japan and South Korea). The aim of this chapter is to suggest some explanations.

The main explanatory elements to the crisis are as follows:

(1) Although some important progress has been made in the name of socialism, nowhere has a global socialist logic (in particular a logic

of production) succeeded in imposing itself upon a whole country;

(2) The generalised state control system, for a long time presented as 'real socialism', has reached a dead-end and led to situations made unbearable by examples of capitalist dynamism from elsewhere in the world;

(3) The on-going phenomena of internationalisation, multinationalisation or worldwide *modi operandi* have deeply affected the concept of national economy or nation-state and called national economic and social policies into question.

1917-1949. the period of the socialist revolutions.

The opponent was clearly identified: beyond the former established order, it was capitalism and imperialist domination. The goal was clear: the construction of socialism. However, changing a society implies some engineering as mysterious as changing life. No one masters it except for the worse, as dictators and masters of totalitarian regimes have shown. So no-one had a recipe for the successful transition to socialism: the simple recipes of the 19th century idealists were not good, the social-democratic recipe allowed the amendment of capitalism by strengthening the role of the State, and the Soviet recipe tried to generalise government control. However, the social formation process is the same as life: whatever the obstacles, the difficulties or the hostile environment, survival instincts are stronger, forms of adaptation are sought and tried so that, one way or another, social reproduction soon gets organised.

After the Bolshevik revolution, the leaders surrounding Lenin had hold of the state. Overnight the hated symbol became the irreplaceable tool. The state machinery proved essential for the war (either external or internal), for compulsion and repression against counter-revolutionaries, for transportation and the food supply of cities, and for controlling and organising production.

For Lenin, the state was supposed to be useful during a short period only, i.e. during the transitory period of 'state capitalism'. With Stalin, the state could not and must not be called into question, so it received the label of 'socialist'. Socialism was going to be built with the help of the state. In the past catch phrases had been 'I am the state', or 'You are the state', from then on one would be able to say 'the state is socialism'.

In fact, the system which spread was *state control* but neither capitalism nor socialism. The contribution of the state control system has been important: it helped to build a heavy industry, some infrastructures, to define an arms policy or conduct a war economy, and it also helped systematic urbanisation, to mechanise agriculture or the promotion of major research programmes. But as soon as the whole system becomes more complex, its limits are revealed by administrative bottlenecks, malfunctions, waste, shortages, etc.

However, what the state could not provide, social reproduction forces were able to substitute for through household or market activities, either open or clandestine, and even real firms more or less linked to the sectors of the state economy - i.e. through grey or black markets and an underground economy. Therefore, going through successes as well as difficult periods, social forces managed to set up around the core state system the conditions for social reproduction where the features of the past were at times able to find a new efficiency.

Thus, in the name of socialism and because the logic of socialist production could not be applied on the scale of an entire country, a state control system developed in Eastern Europe.

Simultaneously in the West, and specifically in western Europe, the trade-union, cooperative and political struggles against capitalism had led, between the end of the 19th century and up to the beginning of the second half of this century, to the development of 'social-democratic compromises' which enabled important social and democratic progress to be made and contributed to a renewed capitalist dynamism through mass consumption and new markets for leisure, health, education and culture. In this context, a strengthening of the state occurred, particularly in the social sphere, for example the size of the state sector grew through nationalisations.

Though this path was at times given the label of 'socialism' (Swedish, British, West German or even French style), it still remained a long way from the socialist dream of the 19th century.

The main characteristic of a state control system is of course the central and essential role played by the state:

Institutional base for the leaders (statocracy) and the upper-middle classes (techno-bureaucracy);
- It gives the main orientations to and organises the processes of production, accumulation and negotiation;
- It decides on the priorities: industrialisation, war economy, reconstruction, modernisation, consumption, production levels, etc;
- It ensures the overall cohesion, resorting to the ideology (e.g. construction of socialism), to compulsion through police control and repression, to the quest for a social compromise between the various classes and social strata, or to a combination of all three.

Regimes where accumulation was organised by the state were first set up in the USSR, and subsequently in eastern Europe and China. The main objective was the concentration and reinforcement of the power held by the leaders. This 'state control regime' is referred to as *Etatisme* by Beaud [*1982; 1985*]. In contrast to the caricature of capitalism, 'a logic of profit for profit's sake', the characteristic of the state control regime would be 'a logic of power for power's sake'.

However, describing a particular country as a 'state control regime' does not mean that government control is the only logic at work. Any social formation is structured by the articulation of many different economic and social logic. For instance, in capitalist countries the capitalist logic predominates but the logics of the market, of the household as well as the logics of dependency an .... state intervention also exist, albeit secondary and subordinated. Equally, in socialist countries the state control logic predominates, but other logics - those of the household, the market and also of dependency and ... capitalism - are at work in the formal sector as in the grey or black economy. For a long time prohibited and confined to secrecy, capitalist realities seem to be assigned a new position within the framework of the current mutations: here tolerated, there accepted, even encouraged in places.

It remains that in view of the weight and influence of the planned sectors on other sectors, and the check kept over free markets, the Soviet-style economy is essentially an economy managed and directed from one and only centre. This type of economy is efficient in such situations as a war or 'social mobilisation' (to fight a calamity and for a national or social project). But it can also be cumbersome to handle with its bureaucratic rigidities and its lack of emulation. It has proved unsuited to periods of fast mutation, innovation, mobility and diversification. Such a period has, in fact, started with the recent evolution of capitalism.

According to the official Soviet line of the past few decades, capitalism was considered as dying - it was considered to be in the final phase of collapse. In reality, capitalism was able to generate successive waves of revival and forceful dynamics. Though the American prosperity of the 1920s, based on mass production and consumption, stumbled over its own limitations, i.e. European protectionism, over-indebtedness and over-consumption, it found a new lease of life in the Second World War, the reconstruction of the damaged countries, the Cold War, and finally the powerful wave of new consumer demand in the 1950s and 1960s. The wave reached the reconstructed western Europe, hit Japan and East Asia and finally, through various channels, reached the elite classes and the new rising generations in the Third World and also in socialist countries.

In fact, this is a key explanatory element in what appears today as the failure of state socialism. If capitalism had reached final collapse, as communist analysts had so often predicted, socialist countries would now appear as havens of security if not of prosperity. But, within the spirale of the worldwide social reproduction and from its American, European and now Far East poles, capitalism has developed and created new needs, new products, new technologies, new ways of life, new dressing habits, new transportation means, new types of recreation and culture acquisition, new ways of working, producing, administrating, informing, controlling, etc. New references valid for almost every country, every generation, every class, every social stratum, etc. have been created on a world scale.

First Lenin and then Stalin had indeed talked about the ground which had to be made up, but it had seemed within arm's reach since capitalism was dying and socialism had an aura of promises for a bright future. And yet Krutchev, Breznev and Gorbatchev had still a lot of ground to make up and the distance had been growing bigger and bigger despite all the efforts to reduce it. The challenger had been able to find a second wind, to open new fields, to create new needs and new expectations, and introduce new products to satisfy those demands, thereby creating new production lines and profit opportunities.

Such has been the unflagging capitalist 'destructive creativity' in the face of which bureaucratic apathy has shown its ineffectiveness. In a static world, the socialist regimes would have been able to provide their state leaders with appropriate tools to uphold power and satisfy the basic needs of the people. But in a world unremittingly revolutionised by the national/worldwide capitalist dynamics and its new needs, new references and new aspirations, the socialist system has appeared crippled, lame, short of steam and unable to follow. Once the political or material incentives and sanctions had worn away, the only possibility left to the power holders was either to make the state sector more efficient through reforms or to create and develop a private and capitalist sector and thereby call the whole socialist system into question.

To sum up:
- The socialist countries have cut themselves off from the world capitalist system, and been indubitably marked out.
- Their state sector, with its whole range of fringe activities (official or underground) has created the economic conditions for the social reproduction.

- Those countries have proved unable to adapt to the capitalist dynamics, and unable to respond to the needs and aspirations which, among their own people, have sprung from the influence of western capitalist societies.

The limitations and the incapacities of an all-embracing state system are at the origins of the difficulties experienced by socialist countries which, for decades, have represented 'real socialism'. But socialist countries are not the only ones going through a crisis of the state.

During the past few centuries, the nation-state has been the favoured context for various major accomplishments and the framework for the emergence of the modern state.

Unlike some earlier forms of statehood, the state has not been only a site for power and armed forces - i.e. a conqueror, an empire builder, an undertaker of major works programmes building pyramids and temples, ports, canals, irrigation systems and road networks. It has been much more: the creator of a national entity, with accepted borders and sometimes encompassing various peoples, and the catalyst of social compromises, consensual agreements and feeling of community belonging - despite class, religious or language differences. It has also created a national market, a national currency, national laws and regulations, a tax system, a public administration, public services, a national diplomacy, national forces, a national police, an educational system;...it has defined national policies for agriculture, industry and technology and, at a later stage, set up systems of national health care and social protection, national radios, national television, national accounting.

Nation-states were first established in western Europe, where and when the logics underlying the capitalist and socialist systems were formalised. They gradually spread all over Europe as national consciousness grew - here grouping together small kingdoms and princedoms, and there ripping apart old empires. They spread to the other continents with independence movements and decolonisation. Hence, likewise 19th century Europe, the world of the last third of the 20th century appears essentially made of nation-states.

In fact, the nation-state is the main organised form under which a society does exist in the contemporary world. The peoples without state (the Palestinians, Armenians, Kurds, Basques etc.) claim and fight for the right to have a territory with boundaries, and be acknowledged as nation-states by other countries. The peoples whose sovereignty is limited demand full sovereignty. From the League of Nations to the United Nations system, nation-states have equipped themselves with ways to listen and talk to each other as well as discuss and cooperate. Thus, the nation-state is not only the main basis of social reproduction but also the prime mode of collective living in relation to the 'others' of the contemporary world at large.

For two centuries, the nation-state has been the main frame of reference of social reproduction. This does not mean that other frames had disappeared: the family (nuclear and extended), the village community, the ethny, the tribe and the clan (traditional or new one) existed, but they had become secondary and dependent parts. Let us just remember the policies for agriculture, industry, foreign trade, education and also the infrastructures (especially transport)....; we may refer to Colbert, Fichte, List, Carey, Mélines, Lenin and Stalin, but also to Hobbes, Locke, Rousseau, Montesquieu and De Toqueville. Social reproduction is global and concerns all facets of life, including production, power, ideas, values, culture, institutions, defence, desequilibria and conflict resolution. In each of these fields, the control of the nation-state now predomines.

In capitalist countries the control of the nation-state has been strengthened by the search for solutions to the economic and social desequilibria of the past sixty years - hence the economic nationalism, the New Deal, the social-democratic compromise, the national-socialism and national-corporatism supported by doctor Schacht, Hitler, Roosevelt, Keynes, Blum, Pétain, Mussolini, Franco, Scandinavian social-democratic parties, the British Labour Party, the parties of the French left, de Gaulle, the German SPD, etc. Despite following different and even diverging paths all have contributed to increasing the role of the state, and not solely within the economic and social fields.

State control was also reinforced in countries where revolutionary minorities came to power with the objective of implementing socialism (with the assumption that the state will wither away), and tried to catch up with capitalist advances. Stalin imposed total state control i.e. a totalitarian regime which structured the economy, the society, the mentalities and behaviours though, deep down within each individual and society, something continued escaping its hold. Others followed the same path: Mao Tse Tung, Enver Hodja, Fidel Castro, Nicholae Ceausescu, the Khmers and Kim Il Sung.

State control has also been strong in countries which gained their independence during the post-war process of decolonisation, especially among new nations.

Growth, inflation, distribution, income, savings, investment, credit, working conditions, town and country planning, population, youth, old age, employment, unemployment, information (radio and television), and of course through taxes various situations involving the individual, the family, the firm, the municipality i.e. industrialisation, development, security, prosperity and welfare, all, at one time, appeared to be the responsibility of the state - even happiness. Some economists have tried to build an indicator of 'gross national happiness' in order to work at increasing it.

Keynesian thinking and social-democratic ideas have carried powerful messages. In every country, political debates and trade-union debates have been rich, particularly at election time. The national experiences (miracles or models) have been varied: the United States, Germany or Japan among countries from the West, Albania, China or Cuba from the East, and Nasser's Egypt, Algeria or India at the time of the green revolution among countries from the South. But all this is history now and even seems to belong to the distant past.

Today, as national borders disappear, the pre-eminence of the state is eroded. A national economy is not what it used to be. It is no longer confined to a domestic product (derived from mining, agriculture, manufacturing and services), a labour force, unemployed workers, consumers, territorial activities and straight-forward contacts with the outside world (imports/exports, incoming/outgoing capital, emigration/ immigration and dumping/protection) - all those items adding up to make the national accounting matrix. Conceived in the 1930s and 1940s, it bloomed in the 1940s and 1950s, flourished in the 1960s and 1970s but became superseded in the 1980s - though very few people readily admit it.

Nowadays, things are more complex. The proportion of what is produced on the national territory but by firms controlled by foreign capital reaches 25 per cent in Mexico and France, 33 per cent in Belgium, 55 per cent in Ivory Coast, 58 per cent in Canada and 70 per cent in Nigeria. In contrast, the equivalent of 15 per cent of the domestic production of Sweden, 16 per cent of the United States's, 21 per cent of the Netherlands's, 27 per cent of the United Kingdom's and 64 per cent of Switzerland's is produced by national companies abroad.

There are European components on the new Boeing aeroplanes, and American components on the new Airbus models. The spare parts and components necessary to produce the European model of the Ford Escort are manufactured in 12 different European countries, as well as Japan, Canada and the United States, whilst the assembly plants are located in the United Kingdom and Germany.

Two hundred firms - all multinationals - have a turnover equivalent to one quarter of world production. François Perroux has evaluated the share of multinationals as being 70-80 per cent of international direct investment flows, and their share in world trade as being 90 per cent. However, an important part of that trade is intra-trade within the circuit of the multinationals, which makes it a peculiar type of international trade.

Is there a world currency? The American dollar - i.e. a national currency - still plays the part of a world currency. But it is now, to some extent, beyond the control of the monetary authorities of its country of origin. Loans in dollars granted by banks outside the United States allow payments in dollars and thereby create eurodollars, petrodollars and other xenodollars. In many countries where the national currency is weak, the dollar is considered - officially or not - by banks, companies and the rich minority as a substitute currency.

The exchange rate, the interest rate, economic and monetary conditions, financial analyses and anticipation, speculation and behaviours and, of course, the information and interpretation related to all these domains are deeply interconnected and interdependent to a degree hard to perceive. Following the October 1987 crash, the *Wall Street Journal* wrote: 'We have learned that, in the world, only one thing spreads faster than information: panic'.

Similarly, under the triple pressure of internationalisation, multi-nationalisation and worldwide *modi operandi*, 'nation-state control' is being eroded in the fields of defence, culture, information, leisure and health. Nations are increasingly interpenetrated and interdependent.

External constraints are increasingly numerous and stringent and the room for manoeuvre of any government is shrinking. Hence, the growing difficulties encountered by 'welfare states' over the last few decades. Hence, the new obstacles that the three interventionist currents - nationalist, Keynesian and social-democratic - have had to face and the actual strong return of liberalism through deregulation and privatisation.

The weakening of the state is often compensated in two ways:

(1) by plurinational grouping: where an isolated state is powerless, cooperation may help a group of countries to restore a capacity for action;

(2) by means of regionalisation and decentralisation: when a central government proves inefficient, regional and local bodies can take or relay the initiative for action.

These two solutions contribute to cutting back the responsibility and commitments of the state, in other words they lead to less state-control. For some the choice will be ideological, for others it will result from short term interests, for others again it will be the result of helplessness or confusion, like those sailors who let the helm free when steering becomes too difficult. The destabilisation of socialist countries has made the confusion worse.

In some ways the current trend in 'less state-control' is only a surface wave which will soon ebb. In fact, liberal capitalism has never worked well without an efficient and interventionist state administration. In present-day capitalism, the role of the state remains essential: one only has to look at the United States, Federal Germany, other west European countries, Japan and South Korea.

Nonetheless, the fact remains that the weakening of the state, linked to the new expansion in markets and products, to the triple pressure of internationalisation, multi-nationalisation and worldwide *modi operandi*, as well as to the definition of policies at the plurinational, regional or local levels, will have some lasting effect.

CONCLUSION

The above diagnosis can be summarised in a few phrases: in a period of strong capitalist and trade expansion and when national logics are weakened by the dynamics of international, multinational and world-wide *modi operandi*, we are witnessing not only the failure of the 'all-state' system in state-managed countries but also the limitations of the welfare-state and, in the South, of the state as development entrepreneur.

If one accepts the main lines of this assessment, many analyses and ways of thinking should be re-examined. Three examples can be presented here:

(1) Regarding political practice, notably in France and in some other west European countries, political thinking, speech and debates remain deeply 'nation-state oriented', and all the more so since the most prestigious elections are still the national ones (both legislative and presidential). The candidates continue acting as if things were settled at the national level, even though they do not believe this themselves and that their electors have understood or perceived that such pretence does not hold together anymore.

It would be much clearer to search for and identify what should be done at each level (local, regional, national, plurinational and worldwide), and then build up a new type of speech explicitly saying: 'we are confronted with this problem (e.g. unemployment, pollution, violence or information retrieval), here is the policy we will follow at the national level, but here are the actions we are also proposing to favour and support at the local and regional levels, and finally, here are the decisions we will press for at the plurinational (European) and international levels'.

Of course the explanation would be lengthier, but it would certainly be better received and better understood. Democracy would gain by it, and perhaps it could initiate a process with the view of improving the articulation between the various levels of democratic life (i.e. municipal, regional, national and European elections).

(2) The loss of substance in the 'national state control' is accompanied by two closely linked phenomena which are: firstly, the reinforcement of the power and capacity for action of multinational firms and banks, as well as of all types of transnational organisation such as churches, sects, mafias, etc.; and secondly, the fact that an increasing number of problems extend beyond national boundaries (e.g. pollution, the international monetary system, drugs, ecology, poverty, the spread of the deserts, malnutrition and famines, etc.) but are either ignored or badly taken care of.

Therefore, we must become more aware of the urgent necessity to develop some structures of state control capable of matching these new forces and challenges, at both the continental and the world levels. Then it would become possible to arrange for 'stateless nations' to be represented in various pluri- or international organisations if they so wished. In a world where societies are less and less confined to their borders, it would be a way of giving inter-national recognition and a voice not only to nation-states but also to nations that historical vicissitudes and power relations have prevented setting-up a nation-state.

(3) Finally, there are the Third World countries which suffer the most from the reduction in the room for manoeuvre at the national level and from the new limits imposed on the actions of the state. They are caught in the world system through trading, monetary relations, investment and credit, migration, etc, but also through knowledge, as well as the norms for consumption, social organisation, the functioning of the state and the production process etc.

In this context, how is it possible to build a 'national economy', and how can a 'modern national economy' be created, when, nowadays, no national economy, even the strongest, has the benefit of both a complete system of production and a strong position in sectors and technological fields with good future prospects (which was still possible at the end of the nineteenth century, and even until the 1950s)? Therefore, the room for manoeuvre is particularly narrow for nation-states from the Third World. Autarky is an illusion and deconnection [see *Amin 1986*] deceptive. In fact, a national strategy can only aim at widening the room for manoeuvre by:

(a) trying to make external dependence less stringent;
(b) strengthening the coherence of the domestic economy;
(c) developing products able to capture a share of the world market;
(d) building or reinforcing plurinational, regional and other solidarities.

To reach those objectives it is necessary to implement the following mix:

(i) to safeguard, promote or consolidate national products (from all sectors - traditional, informal, state or capitalist) apt to satisfy the vital and important needs of social formation under good conditions (i.e. at a reasonable cost);
(ii) the creation and development of new activities (either private or public) capable of securing some outlets on the world market, in conjunction with traditional productive units (for instance in agriculture), the goods and service sector (formal and informal) and, if need be, foreign firms;
(iii) the development of plurinational agreements and cooperation. In each of these spheres, protectionism could be advisedly used as well as international competition.

Obviously the content and the significance of these strategies could not be the same for: continent-sized countries from the Third World; important regional countries; small and medium Third World countries; the 'annexes' of capitalist poles.

Neither would the chances of success be the same: in countries where state efficiency is based on a social and national cohesion which has progressively developed through history; in countries where the state is controlled by a few families or oligarchies; and in countries where the state is a structure not yet well rooted into the society.

However, in all cases, the capacity to define a national strategy, to help it to be accepted and to implement it is a decisive factor. But success has rarely been lasting and quite often hardship has followed euphoria. Causal factors have been varied: the pressure of foreign interests, the selfishness of local oligarchies (in South America, for example), the difficulties linked to too rapid economic and social mutations (in Africa south of the Sahara), the worsening of internal contradictions (Egypt after Nasser, the Shah's Iran, the Philippines and perhaps tomorrow's South Korea), and the inordinate convulsions of the world economy during the period 1978-88.

Beyond the specific situations mentioned above, various questions for the 1990s, which are not only pertinent to Third World countries, remain unanswered:

(i) Which place and which role should the nation-state assume?
(ii) Which forms of plurinational organisation should be developed at the regional level?
(iii) How to change the world system so that the constraints of dependence become weaker and the uncontrolled effects of erratic development less damaging?

BIBLIOGRAPHY

Amin, Samir, 1986, *La déconnexion: pour sortir du système mondial*, Paris: La Découverte.
Arnoult, Erik, 1977, *Espace national et déséquilibre monétaire*, Paris: PUF.
Balibar, Etienne and Immanuel Wallerstein, 1988, *Race, nation, classe: les identités ambigües*, Paris: La Découverte.
Barry Jones, R.J., 1986, *Conflict and Control in the World Economy*, Brighton: Wheatsheaf.
Beaud, Michel, 1982, *Le socialisme à l'épreuve de l'histoire*, 2nd Edition, Paris: Le Seuil.
Beaud, Michel, 1985, 'L'avènement du système étatiste', *Le Monde diplomatique*.
Beaud, Michel, 1987, *Le système national/mondial hiérarchisé (une nouvelle lecture du capitalisme mondial)*, Paris: La Découverte.
Beaud, Michel, 1989, L'économie mondiale dans les années 80, Paris: La Découverte.
Beaud, Michel, 1990, *Histoire du capitalisme (de 1500 à nos jours)*, 3rd Edition, Paris: Seuil.
Bellon, Bertrand and Jorge Niosi, 1987, *L'industrie américaine fin de siècle*, Paris: Le Seuil.
Bernis, Gérard de (ed.), 1988, *Théories économiques et fonctionnement de l'économie mondiale*, Paris et Presses universitaires de Grenoble: UNESCO.
Bernstein, Henry and Bonnie K. Campbell, 1985, *Contradictions of Accumulation in Africa*, Beverly Hills: Sage.
Bertin, Gilles, 1981, *Les objectifs extérieurs des Etats*, Paris: Economica.
Bonin, Bernard, 1984, *L'entreprise multinationale et l'Etat,* Saint-Laurent: Editions Etudes vivantes.
Bourguinant, Henri, 1985, *L'économie mondiale à découvert*, Paris: Calmann-Lévy.
Bourguinat, Henri, 1987, *Les vertiges de la finance internationale*, Paris: Economica.
Bowles, Samuel, David M. Gordon and Thomas E. Weisskopf, 1983, *L'économie du*

gaspillage. *La crise américaine et les politiques réaganiennes*, New York: Anchor Press, translated from English, Paris: La Découverte, 1986.

Boyer, Robert, 1986, *La théorie de la régulation: une analyse critique*, Paris: La Découverte.

Brown, Lester R., 1989, *State of the World*, London and New York: Norton.

Campbell, Bonnie K., 1983, *Les enjeux de la bauxite*, Montreal: Montreal University Press.

CEPII - Centre d'études prospectives et d'informations internationales, 1983, *Economie mondiale: la montée des tensions*, Paris: Economica.

CEPII, 1984, *Economie mondiale 1980-1990: la fracture?*, Paris: Economica.

CEPII, 1986, *L'après-dollar*, Paris: Economica.

Chavance, Bernard (ed.), 1987, *Régulation, cycles et crises dans les économies socialistes*, Paris: Editions de l'EHESS.

Chavance, Bernard, 1988, *Le système soviétique: de Brejnev à Gorbatchev*, Paris: Nathan.

Chevalier, Jean-Maris, Philippe Barbet and Laurent Benzoni, 1986, *Economie de l'énergie*, Paris: PFNSP and Dalloz.

Chonchol, Jacques, 1987, *Le défi alimentaire, la faim dans le monde*, Paris: Larousse.

Coquery-Vidrovitch, Catherine and Alain Forest (eds.), 1986, *Décolonisations et nouvelles dépendances*, Lille: Presses universitaires de Lille.

De Bandt, Jacques and Philippe Hugon, 1988, *Les tiers nations en mal d'industrie*, Paris: Economica.

Dehove, Mario and Jean Mathis, *Le système monétaire international*, Paris: Dunod.

Delapierre, Michel and Jean-Benoit Zimmermann, 1986, *L'informatique du Nord au Sud: un complexe industriel internationalisé*, Paris: La documentation française.

Drach, Marcel, 1984, *La crise dans les pays de l'Est*, Paris: La Découverte.

Duchene, Gérard, 1987, *L'économie de l'URSS*, Paris: La Découverte.

Dumont, René, 1988, *Un monde intolérable (le libéralisme en question)*, Paris: Le Seuil.

Dunning, John H., 1981, *International Production and the Multinational Enterprise*, London: George Allen & Unwin.

Dunning, John H. and Robert D. Pearce, 1981, *The World's Largest Enterprises*, Farnborough: Gower.

Dufourt, Daniel, 1979, *L'économie mondiale comme système*, Lyon: Presses universitaires de Lyon.

Fouquin, Michel (ed.), 1986, *Industrie mondiale: la compétitivité à tout prix*, Paris: Economica.

Frobel, Folker, Jurgen Heinrichs and Otto Kreye, 1986, *Umbruch in der Weltwirtschaft*, Hamburg: Rowolt.

GEMDEV, 1985, *Economie mondiale, économies nationales et multinationales*, Paris: Cahier No. 5 (Nov.), multigraphié.

Gilpin, Robert, 1987, *The Political Economy of International Relations*, Princeton: Princeton University Press.

Girling, Robert H., 1985, *Multinational Institutions and the Third World*, New York: Praeger.

Goldfinger, Charles, 1986, *La géofinance*, Paris: Le Seuil.

Graziani, Giovanni, 1982, *Comecon, domination et dépendance*, Paris: Maspero.

Grjebine, André, 1982, *La nouvelle économie internationale*, 2nd Edition, Paris: PUF.

Grjebine, André (ed.), 1986, Théories de la crise et politiques économiques, Paris: Le Seuil.

Economic Reforms and Transformation of the Role of the State

Grou, Pierre, 1983, *La structure financière du capitalisme multinational*, Paris: PFNSP.

Guillaumont, Patrick and Sylvaine (eds.) 1988, *Stratégies de développement comparées*, Paris: Economica.

IPSHU - Institute for Peace Science Hiroshima University, 1988, *Le Japon face à l'internationalisation*, Hiroshima: Research Report No. 4.

Judet, Pierre, 1981, *Les nouveaux pays industriels*, Paris: Ed. ouvrières.

Kolko, Joyce, 1988, *Restructuring the World Economy*, New York: Pantheon Books.

Kornai, Janos, 1980, *Economics of Shortage*, Amsterdam: North-Holland.

Krassner, S.D., 1985, *Structural Conflict: The Third World against Global Liberalism*, Berkeley: University of California Press.

Lacoste, Yves, 1980, *Unité et diversité du Tiers-Monde*, 3 volumes, Paris: La Découverte.

Lacoste, Yves, 1986, *Contre les anti-tiers mondistes et contre certains tiers mondistes*, Paris: La Découverte.

Lavigne, Marie, 1979, *Les relations économiques Est-Ouest*, Paris: PUF.

Lavigne, Marie, 1985, *Economie internationale des pays socialistes*, Paris: A. Colin.

Lavigne, Marie et al., 1986, *Les relations Est-Sud dans l'économie mondiale*, Paris: Economica.

Lavigne, Marie (ed.), 1980, *Stratégie des pays socialistes dans l'échange international*, Paris: Economica.

Lavigne, Marie and Wladimir Andreff (eds.), 1985, *La réalité socialiste*, Paris: Economica.

Lessard, Donald R. and John Williamson, 1987, *Capital Flight and Third World Debt*, Washington: Institute for International Economics.

Levy-Garboua, Vivian and Gérard Maarek, 1985, *La dette, le boom, la crise*, Paris: Atlas-Economica.

Lewin, Moshé, 1985, *La formation du système soviétique*, New York: Panthéon Books, translated from English, Paris: Gallimard, 1987.

L'Hériteau, Marie-France, 1986, *Le Fonds monétaire international et les pays du Tiers-Monde*, Paris: PUF.

Lipietz, Alain, 1985, *Mirages et miracles*, Paris: La Découverte.

Maddison, Angus, 1964, *Economic Growth in the West*, New York: The Twentieth Century Fund.

Maddison, Angus, 1987, 'Growth and Slowdown in Advance Capitalist Economies', *Journal of Economic Literature*, pp.649-698.

Marchand, Jacques, 1987, *Nationalisme économique et multinationales minières dans le système national/mondial hiérarchisé*, Thèse de doctorat, Université de Paris VIII, 3 vol.

Marris, Stephen, 1985, *Deficits and the Dollar: The World Economy at Risk*, Washington: Institute for International Economics.

Michalet, Charles-Albert, 1985, *Le capitalisme mondial*, 2nd Ed., Paris: PUF.

Michalet, Charles-Albert, 1983, *Le défi du développement indépendant*, Paris: Ed. Rochevignes.

Ngo Manh-Lan (ed.), 1984, *Unreal Growth: Critical Studies in Asian Development*, 2 vol., Delhi: Hindustan Publishing Corp.

Niosi, Jorge (ed.), 1985, 'Les multinationales et l'Etat', special number of *Etudes Internationales*, Quebec: Laval University.

OCDE, 1981, *Investissement international et entreprises multinationales*, Paris.

OCDE, 1988, *The Newly Industrialising Countries*, Paris.

Ohmae, Kenichi, 1985, *La triade, émergence d'une stratégie mondiale de l'entreprise*, Paris: Flammarion.

Ominami, Carlos, 1986, *Le Tiers-Monde dans la crise*, Paris: La Découverte.

Parboni, Riccardo and Immanuel Wallerstein (eds.), 1987, *L'Europa e l'economia politica des sistema-mondo*, Milan: Franco Angelli.

Perroux, François, 1982, *Dialogue des monopoles et des nations*, Presses universitaires de Grenoble.

Rivière, Jean, 1986, *Les Etats-Unis à l'horizon de la troisième révolution industrielle*, Nancy: Presses universitaires de Nancy.

Robinson, John, 1983, *Multinationals and Political Control*, Aldershot: Gower.

Rouillé d'Orfeuil, Henri, 1987, *Le Tiers-Monde*, Paris: La Découverte.

Rudloff, Marcel, 1982, *Economie internationale*, Itinéraires et enjeux, Paris: Cujas.

Salama, Pierre and Patrick Tissier, 1982, *L'industrialisation dans le sous-développement*, Paris: La Découverte.

Sautter, Christian, 1987, *Les dents du géant: le Japon à la conquète du monde*, Paris: Olivier Orban.

Szentes, Tamas, 1986, *Economie politique du sous-développement*, Paris: L'Harmattan.

Strange, Susan, 1988, *States and Markets*, London: Pinter Publishers.

Taylor, Robert, 1986, *L'axe Chine-Japon: une nouvelle force mondiale?*, Paris: Economica.

UNCTAD, *Trade and Development Report*, New York: United Nations (annual report).

Vidal, Jean-François, 1989, *Les fluctuations internationales de 1890 a nos jours*, Paris: Economica.

Vincze, Imre, 1984, *The International Payments and Monetary System in the Integration of the Socialist Countries*, The Hague: Martinus Nijhoff Publisher.

Wallerstein, Immanuel, 1985, *Le capitalisme historique*, Paris: La Découverte.

Williamson, John (ed.), 1983, *IMF Conditionality*, Cambridge Mass.: MIT Press.

World Commission on Environment and Development, 1987, *Our Common Future*, Oxford: Oxford University Press.

Zachir, Fayçal, 1987, *Enjeux miniers en Afrique*, Paris: Karthala.

8

Adjusters or Followers? A Different Approach to the Role of the State in Arab Economic Life

ALI AL-NASSAR

It is not very objective to discuss the role of the state in economic life in purely economic terms in any country. However, some people are perplexed by the enthusiasm shown by many economists and consultants who claim to have a recipe for adjustment in Third World countries.

This adjustment recipe mainly presents packages of economic policies for capital ownership and pricing systems. This chapter considers the possibility of developing the concept of 'adjustment' to the 'feasible area of objectivity' in the case of the Arab world.

A variety of meetings and publications on adjustment and privatisation have taken place in the Arab World, but the Arab Planning Institute (API) hesitated in joining such fora. However, it did take part in a seminar in 1989[1] which took Arab specifications into account. Whilst Arab specifications can be historic, the API has tried to read them in the light of future challenges in order to be able to supply decision-makers with applicable ideas.[2]

The results of this seminar have been worrying. The state can end up interfering economically, but without greatly expanding its dominance over economic projects, giving little hope of creating a successful private or public sector, as the handicaps preventing success in this area are enormous. Out of the Arab-Islamic heritage, the 'social contract' between the state and civil society includes many of the state's economic responsibilities. The question of adjustment in Arab economic thought has grown in importance following pressure by international institutions and the reshuffling that is taking place in Eastern Europe politics. But this adjustment cannot simply mean privatisation or integration in a new interdependent world. In fact, it is most unlikely that Arab countries will be able to achieve much without a minimum of economic integration or cooperation between each other.

I. THE SOCIOLOGIST'S CONTRIBUTION:
THE ARAB STATE REVISITED

The emergence of the modern state has been correlated with society's role in economic life.[3] Its perceived role has changed depending on the different economic theories being applied by western culture, whether mercantilist, classical, neoclassical, Marxist or Keynesian. Even the present monetarist thoughts need state interference to accomplish the conditions of their promised stable economic achievement.

The Independence Movement

The independence of many Third World countries has been associated with the growth of a new 'national state' to secure economic development, stability and independence. Most of the Arab states have emerged following this independence movement and were initially unable to create economic stability. Modern Arab states differ in their degree of interference in economic life, but it can generally be proved that these states have developed since their independence.

There have been many criteria used to estimate state growth, not only government expenditure and public ownership, but also the presence of the state in individual and community life and the degree of power it holds (as it appears in political science research).[4]

With the declining socioeconomic performance of Arab countries and the continuing world market crisis, the heavy heritage of errors in development are becoming much more noticeable. Weak government reactions and mismanaged responses from the International Monetary Fund have led to uprisings, including street riots, and subsequently to contradictory government policies. The Arab governments, whether they are interfering in the economics of their countries or not, are being held responsible for the dispersion of Arab surpluses abroad as well as the general lack of any benefits from inter-Arab dimensions reaching the common society. They are also being blamed for the lack of any efficient long-term export policy.

The State in Social Science

Is the role of the state in economic life a subject for economists? During the last two decades, no other subject has had so much attention from sociologists as 'the state'. Studies began with the state-phenomena in Europe and other capitalist societies as a field of social research, later expanding to cover the Third World. Other disciplines, such as political science, psycho-politics and general development research, have also become interested in the question of the state.[5]

However, sociologists in the Arab world do not accept the idea of fitting the 'modern' state of many Arab countries into one of the prototypes of classical social research. What are the characteristics of an Arab state? Why is it difficult to see a solution for any Arab state problem through a government change or change from public enterprise to private, or vice-versa?

Sociologists seem to have a very comprehensive approach. For them, it is unwise to discuss the limits and inadequacy of the tools for state intervention without going back to an historical perspective. The most important elements are the specific concepts of the 'legitimacy' of the Islamic ruler, and cultural identity and the relations between the state and civil society. For sociologists, the Arab experiments in centralisation and socialism have different explanations to those which economists generally refer.

Recalling History

The environmental endowments that some Arab countries have, and their geopolitical situation, have always played an important role in the state's growth rate and the heaviness in its interference in economic life. This is easy to understand in the cases of Egypt and Iraq, and to a lesser extent in Syria.[6] Historically, this centralism has been a beneficial and positive factor in development at certain times, but a curse at others. These countries formed the very ancient states, but later, as Islamic states, they exercised certain forms of decentralisation and economic freedom, leading in some instances to fragmentation and collapse.

A look at the periods of famine in the past shows a greater correlation with the way the state was run than with weather irregularity. Even under the most arduous climatic conditions, famines were essentially due to the bigotry of the ruler and the continuous deprivation of the peasant of a large share of his produce. Nevertheless, the central role of governments - the state and its ruler - in economic life was the responsibility of securing basic needs, food storage, and controlling natural resources and equity amongst the people. This was a common popular request during the ancient civilisations of today's Arab region, and also in the different Islamic nations until the beginning of the nineteenth century.

State intervention in the nation's economy is usually through taxes, ownership policy, creation of demand, etc. It could additionally involve tax relief and liberalisation. No historian has ever said that a state is weaker in moments of low economic intervention. Taking the example of Egypt, with more liberalisation Ibn Toulon built his mighty state out of the ruined economy of the Abbassides. Ismail Pasha was able to achieve the same success.

Arab agriculture is now mainly privatised, and represents - besides trade - the major economic activity. The strength, or dominance, of the state in agricultural activities has never been simply correlated with private ownership.[7] Stronger state interference has been achieved in many Arab countries through 'national agricultural guidance', both directly and indirectly affecting the price system and the expansion of urban projects and infrastructure. Community development missionaries have also been involved in this process.

How deep is the issue of the role of the state and its ruler in Islamic economic life? The answer lies in Islam's flexibility towards wealth ownership. However, it is obvious in Islamic traditions that man is the trustee of God's gifts and that he has been called upon to preserve them. Three features characterise the attitude of Islam to the environment,[8] and consequently to the nation's economy. First, there is the clear commitment of Islam to social justice and the collective responsibility for the well-being of all believers. Excessive consumption has been considered as an encroachment on others' needs. Secondly, Islam recognises holistic and integrated views, with moderate choices between the present life and the 'life to come', between material and immaterial and between rationalism and irrationality. Finally, there is the responsibility of the ruler for the satisfaction of the basic needs of the Islamic community, which are differentiated between 'complementary' and 'luxury' goods in Islamic terms. In fact, these were considered pre-requisites for a lawful government. Arabic-Islamic culture has not managed to accomplish any deep and lasting transformations towards 'secularism' or 'Calvinism'.

Change and Reorientation

Before departing from the past to the present, it is important to note that the reorientation towards western values has occurred twice in the Arab region's history. The first occurrence coincided with the arrival of Alexander the Great, and lasted until the arrival of Islam. The second relates to the arrival of Napoleon and the fall of the Osmani Dynasty.

In comparison to the first western cultural invasion, the second was more violent in terms of domestic values and the institutional framework.[9] As a result of this violence, Arab politics has tended to adopt a policy of rejection rather than a more positive form of dialogue comprising diversity and compromise. The form of rejection has been extended not only towards the negative consequences of western values, but also any positive impact they may have had.

The deep-rooted Islamic values, and their reflections in the concepts of the state and ruler have been neither permanently positive nor permanently negative during the past 14 centuries. Some writers relate the collapse of development projects over part of this period to the co-existence of political reactionary forces in politics and in religion. Throughout history, these periods of failure have been associated with narrow-mindedness concerning the needs of adjustment, and have led to other states assuming the responsibility of consolidating previous development efforts. In fact, as the role of the priests and sheikhs increased during these periods of decline, the teaching of science and art was curtailed. Moreover, failure to abide by the 'dictates' meant ex-communication. Many of these symptoms of decline are still seen today in some Arab countries. Meanwhile, the world is changing rapidly and 'adjustment' is becoming a must.

II. THE FUTURE AT STAKE: WHAT ADJUSTMENT?

During discussions, the Arab seminar seriously considered all schools of thought, but it was more difficult to differentiate between the political 'left' and 'right' than expected, particularly when one considers the transformations and overlapping which occur in the social strata of the Arab world. Towards the end of the conference, the dialogue acquired more of an Arab flavour with all of its complications. Most of the contributors developed ideas proving that a genuine theoretical contribution is necessary, as the future is at stake.

A Need for Theorisation

A contribution towards theorisation is needed not only from an historical perspective, but also from the possible future challenges. Extrapolating the past and interpolating the future, maintaining the indigenous and harvesting the new, extracting the objective causalities and practicing normative choice; all must be coupled to the dialectics of theory. One could not expect a unique theory, nor even a standard orientation, for all countries and stages of development. But when beginning with Arab state characteristics and performance, the future determinants must be integrated. This is a type of effort which could be beneficial to all social science disciplines, even psycho-politics.

113

Revision and Interpretation

World developments are occurring so rapidly, and the changes are leaving behind all those who are neither generators nor contributors. These helpless observers will either become part of the 'fringe' of the labour division, or part of the 'modernisation curse'[10] and be alienated. Alternatively, they could simply remove themselves from the newly emerging economic order.[11]

Both groups of countries - those which want to join and those which refuse to comply with the negative sides of the global trends - must adapt and adjust. In this case, adjustment is more nation-wide and revolutionary, and goes beyond ownership and the price system, including values, patterns of decision-making, the education system and the organisation of knowledge. All of these conditions raise the question of the maturity of the civil society and the dynamics of correcting bad political choices.

Any project for a modern state, now and in the future, will be challenged by prerequisites of adapting to specific features of the three technological revolutions (biology and biological engineering, material substitution, and restructuring, computing and telematics) and post-industrialisation (division of labour).

Adjustment in the Whole Structure

These prerequisites cannot mean anything less than an institutional restructuring, or an Arab 'Perestroika', to cope with the changes:

- Industrialisation needs, which are more than simply building up industrial projects. Industrialisation raises many issues, including adequate values, media, roles of behaviour and the culture in general.
- Disengagement between technocrats and bureaucrats within the institutional frame of decision-making. The concept of 'govern-ance' should accept that people who are 'leaders we can trust' are not necessarily those who will be able to help in the long-run.
- The concept of 'governance' must be settled in the light of the current 'independent world' concept and the new ways of life which have been generated following the third communication revolution ('telecommunication', after the first and second communication revolutions, respectively 'language' and 'printing').
- The Arab world must create a clear distinction between the 'government' and the 'state' in order to be able to appraise philosophical and political issues of representativeness of govern-ment.[12] This is really the question of maturity of the civil society and

114

the degree of crystallisation of political strata and centres of power in the society.

In other words, people's participation must have a continuing solid objective, and political plurality can only be considered as a first approximation of this objective.

This restructuring must be put at the top of the list of priorities of a country so that a suitable environment for the 'Big Science' era can be created, thereby opening up possibilities for domestically-oriented research and development and vertical integration between basic knowledge and production.

Strengthening or Weakening

This quest for the re-evaluation of the role of the state in Arab economic life to cope with the international market developments and increasing interdependence does not necessarily mean an inevitable weakening in its role. The question is more how to modify and strengthen this role in a vertical fashion. The domain is totally open for work and organisation to achieve a development-oriented infra-structure, educational and training systems, research and development, etc, to initiate new economic sectors and activities and to rebuild values based on development.

In addition, the three contemporary revolutions mentioned above will have positive contributions to make by aiding vertical integrations of production and institutions and creating shorter paths between basic sciences and their application. These revolutions will also affect indigenous capabilities, independence of choice, etc. The question is, how will each state consciously interpret this and plan its own action? This raises the issue of centralisation versus decentralisation.

Politics

It is important to review some of the elements of the newly emerging world political order in order to better understand the consequences of a sustained national state. In fact, the world would be more interrelated and human beings would have greater mobilisation than at any other period of history, including even the Islamic nations between the seventh and nineteenth centuries. The traditional example of a 'closed economic model' appears to be impossible to repeat. Furthermore, according to the interpretation of most of the available studies of the future, there will be no place for small national identities. Anyone who is unwilling to respond to dramatic changes in the basic sciences, and consequently the education system, will be unable to utilise the type of capital - machines, equipment, services - currently available in the international market.

Governments, and centres of power within any nation, use many concepts which should reflect the institutional framework and government structure. Therefore each nation must 'adjust' to the basic transformations in these concepts. What will the following terms mean: national security, national cause, colonialism and imperialism, national resources, sovereignty in culture and life patterns, direct productive labour, workers and bourgeois classes, leisure time, armed forces and logistics, etc? What could be the role of people's participation in theory and in practice?

We have the prerequisites to cope with the international phenomena of standardisation in agreements, codes of conduct and in products. Remote-controlled production, the appearance of 'new crimes and criminology', the cross-national parallel institutions and the non-governmental organisations already exist and must be dealt with.

Economics

On the international level, economic fiscal developments have, in some circumstances, led to economic physical developments. The huge growth in money and financial markets have created more internationalisation of money and circulation. For the first time in history, the currency system has become separated from the national domain: currency used to be a main economic manifestation in the emergence of state phenomena.

In contrast, the state must now play a greater role in preventing capital flight, in reducing vulnerability in financial market crises and in defending its wealth abroad. Nowadays, the Arab world economy may be the most vulnerable, as its inter-trade is less than 10 per cent of its total trade and two-thirds of its exports to industrial countries are raw materials whilst two-thirds of its imports are finished goods.

Politics and Economics

The new peaceful world conditions and the calming of regional tensions will alter the interest and priorities between productive activities and military needs and also the links between these. This change in advocated interest will affect not only state interference in economic life, but also the legality of such interference in most Arab countries.

In addition, one could also argue that the possibilities of a more positive and active role of the state towards regional economic integration could be realistic whilst the foreign resistance to Arab unity could become weaker and a more solid base to resist the downfall of real oil prices could be created.

Participation

How could the link between people's participation and the state be enforced? The workers of today and of the future are intelligent and highly qualified. They have the ability to store, analyse and retrieve information, and are part of a new management order. It is a generation of workers which must be built up so as to be able to cope with the age of 'micros' - where micro-analysis allows treatment of information without directly visualising what is going on. This is the age of information and soft tools which are comparable to manual effort, materials and hardware in preceding stages of man's economic activities.

This appears to be the type of working class which is emerging. The concept and practice of governments and participation, which could cope with these trends in people's capabilities and in the structure of society in general, are very far from the actual situation in most Arab countries. Instead of the patrimonial systems in the Arab states, any new political system must adapt to the new 'production relations' which are continuously changing. The classic Marxist analysis, where the 'production factors' are able to progress, despite fixed 'production relations', is no longer valid. The technological progress of today has combined the development of both groups - factors and relations - in significant positive correlations, and examples can be seen throughout the Arab world. Children are 'playing electronics' and consumers and housewives are 'storing and retrieving'. Very small units of production are highly developed in technology, whilst still classified as informal industries!

The concept of governance must cope with these new elements and working conditions of society, as well as new forms of specialisation, trade unions and a different hierarchy between leaders and citizens. The state must consciously contribute to the development of culture as well. In fact, the Arab-Islamic culture must develop more as a culture of 'plurality and diversification' within a 'politico-cultural developmental project for Arab renaissance'. The very basic elements behind the reform must be the protection of identity and individual freedom of creativity as a part of a new 'social contract' between the civil society and the state.

Participants at the API seminar agreed on the need for a theory on a 'normative scenario',[13] because the current, 'exploratory', scenario is unsatisfactory. The exploratory forecasts state that privatisation - free prices and debt versus equity swaps - will not help overcome the critical financial problems of the majority of the Arab countries. Instead, the emphasis should be directed to rationalising and increasing the efficiency of the public sector, but not through merely using simple cost-benefit or direct short-run economics.

The Arab state interference in economic activities is expected to be more permissive and less restrictive, meaning more competitive prices, relatively free interest rates, fewer constraints on private investment, greater correlation between wages and productivity increases and fewer state-owned projects. Furthermore, the international institutions are expected to stop pushing privatisation, to concentrate on the rationalisation of the public sector and draw Third World attention to the technological and training needs necessary to cope with the emerging world market.

These steps are only economic and are considered naive and of a short-term duration. They are not far removed from creating 'followers' rather than 'adjusters', because they have not taken into account Arab politico-cultural ideas.

The socioeconomic part of the 'politico-cultural project for Arab renaissance' is crystalised by many participants as the theoretical frame of an 'autonomous development'.[14] The question has been, how can any country's development be independent in an interdependent world? The ad hoc answer, which needs more investigation, is that the autonomy of the country is a state decision as far as possible. The suggestion is to build on this autonomous development, or rather autonomy in economic decision-making, in the following areas:

- dominance on natural resources, which will need indigenous technological capabilities as well as regional Arab cooperation;
- structural reorientation of all resources, meaning the adoption of a clear strategy of people's participation and institutional restructuring;
- building-up the appropriate infrastructure in education, research and development and allowing freedom in the cultural scientific media and in community development;
- coping with the new concepts of 'national resilience', which will emphasise the road to technological self-reliance, people's participation and regional Arab integration;
- structural development towards basic domestic needs;
- concentration on human development as a concept totally different to human-resource or manpower approaches. In the long-run, the human being is the main resource, and the highly qualified human being is the 'determining factor' in development.

Other areas to work on, in order to complete comprehensiveness of the politico-cultural project, are those of participation, governance, the 'modern' state and the value system.

III. THE COMPROMISE BETWEEN 'FOLLOWING' AND 'ADJUSTING' DEVELOPMENTS IN ECONOMIC THOUGHT

Economists, after examining the results and ideas demonstrated, may ask if they have done anything wrong. Supporters of the public sector, or those responsible for rationalising its performance and developing the role of the state in economic life, may ask how things went wrong. The answer to both questions can be seen as a lack of theorisation, violating abstraction and the failure of the system of relations between the state and public enterprise.

Economists have not helped the administrative science much with the problem of restoration of relations between the state and public enterprise. To enable identification of the quality of Arab state intervention and to differentiate between failures or successes in performance, the stability of growth, self-reliance in food production and the mastery of technological change should be the indicators used. The Arab picture is not encouraging in the light of these indicators. The apparent relations between the state and public enterprise in most of the Arab countries which have a significant public sector reveal some general features leading to failure in achieving development goals set out by the state. These features are:

- the adoption of 'ideal' economic theories in cases where tribal, elite and patrimonial scales dominate over accomplishment scales and efficiency;
- lack of integrated types of control and coherent actions in favour of partiality of financial control and short-term decisions;
- the bureaucratic burden, or the absence of accountability: the neglect of economics and trade-offs within the bureaucracy.

Avoiding any of these features demands much input from economists. It is hoped that the future trends in developing economic theory will utilise simulation which could deal with such details as man-machine interactions, thus enabling a comparatively more realistic theory.

Work Agenda

After having undertaken the necessary theorisation, it is important to:
- establish a theory for the dynamics of modification of the price system;
- set up procedures for identification, evaluation and establishment of public enterprise. A most crucial question is that if shortcomings, such as environmental hazards and uneven income distribution, can be avoided now instead of having to treat their consequences later on, what could be a typical state's proposal for long-term development?
- adopt a concept of scientific management which will be adequate for the changes taking place in the world.

IV. CONCLUSION

There is now common agreement between the majority of economists that economic cooperation and Arab integration on a regional level can help. However, it is also important to believe that cooperation and integration between disciplines of social science can play their role.

The final question is, can our institutes and institutions provide an adequate base for the coordination between planning activities in different Arab countries and between research activities in different social disciplines?

NOTES

1. Seminar on 'The Role of the State in Economic Activities in the Arab World', API, Kuwait, May 27-29, 1989.
2. This request was the main issue made in the opening speech by the Planning Minister for Kuwait, Dr. Abdel Rahman Al Awady, who is deeply involved in planning and the environment in the Arab world.
3. The classical works dealing with the emergence of the 'modern state' of the nineteenth and twentieth centuries (M. Weber, K. Marx, Bodin, E. Durkheim, V. Pareto) have helped here. One can also find a good review in: King, A., 1986, *The State in Modern Society*, London: Macmillan Press
4. A summary of such developments can be found in Ibrahim, S., *et al.*, (1988, 'The Future of the State and Society in the Arab Homeland' (in Arabic), in the series *Istishraf Mostakbal Al-Watan Al-Arabi* (Prospective Analysis of the Future of the Arab Homeland), Beirut: Centre of Arab Unity Studies.
5. This was very clear in all the sociologists' contributions made in the API seminar. See the contributions by Dr. A. Zaid, Dr. M. Al-Rumehy, Dr. Kh. Al-Nakeeb and Dr. B. Serhan. See also Halpern, M., 1963, *The Politics of Social Change in the Middle East and North Africa*, Princeton University Press, and Geertze, G. (ed.),

1967, *Old Societies and New States*, New York: The Free Press.
6. See Ibrahim, S., *et al.* (*op. cit*) and El-Kholy, O., *et al.*, 1981, 'Scientific Technological Potential of the Tradition and Heritage of Egyptian Rural Communities and their Possible Utilisation in the Satisfaction of Basic Needs', Project (SCA), *Socio-Cultural Development Alternatives in a Changing World*, The United Nations University.
7. *Ibid.*
8. To be seen in the Holy Koran, in the heritage after Omar Ibn El-Khattab ad Ali Ibn Taleb, and in works of Abu Hamed Al Ghazali and Ibn Khaldoon.
9. See A. Toynbee, G. Sartan and Anouar Abdel-Malak.
10. See Tahranian, M., 1981, 'The Modernisation Curse', *The International Magazine for Social Sciences*, UNESCO.
11. Al-Biblawi, Hazem, 'Perspectives for the Role of the State in the Arab World in light of Recent and Expected Techno-Economic Changes', paper presented at the seminar in Kuwait, 1989.
12 Thapar, R., 1982, 'The Changing Concepts of Governance', Stockholm: *World Future Studies*.
13. For different future scenarios, see the results of the scientific Arab work: The final document of the 'Prospective Analysis of the Future of the Arab Homeland', (in Arabic) entitled: The Future of the Arab Nation: Challenges and Choices, Centre of Arab Unity Studies, Beirut, 1989.
14. Abdulla, Ibrahim S., 'The Role of the Arab State in Economic Activities: General Issues and Perspectives', paper presented at the Seminar in Kuwait, 1989.

REFERENCES

Allen, Chris, 1989, 'State, Society and the African Crisis', *Third World Quarterly*, pp.189-193.
Alexander, R.J., 1989, 'A Keynesian Defence of the Reagan Deficit: the Real Issues. How Big Should the Federal Budget be and How Should it be Met', *The American Journal of Economics and Sociology*, Vol. 48, No. 1, pp.47-54.
Allende, Juan A., 1988, 'Towards a Theory of State Enterprises in Less Developing Countries', *Public Enterprise,* Vol. 8, No. 2, pp.147-164.
Amin, Samir, 1988,'Matha ya Hadouthe fi al-itiHade as-soufiati' (What is Happening in the USSR?), *Al-moustaqbel al-' arabi*, Vol. 11, No. 114, pp.49-60.
Antosenkov, Evgenni, 1989, 'The Impact of Economic Restructuring on Employment in the USSR', *Labour and Society*, Vol. 14, No. 1, pp.23-38.
Bennett, A.H.M., 1988, 'Theoretical and practical problems in determining criteria for performance evaluation of public enterprises', *Public Enterprise*, Vol. 8, No. 1, pp.18-27.
Bergsten, C. Fred, 1988, 'The U.S. Economy at a Turning Point', *Challenge*, Vol. 31, No. 6, pp.17-25.
Bowring, Joseph, 1987, 'Competition in a Dual Economy', *Review of Radical Political Economics*, Vol. 19, No. 3, pp.93-96.
Burnett, D. *et al.*, 1979, *The Organisation, the State and the Community,* London: Sweet & Maxwell.
Butenko, A.P., 1988, 'On the Nature of Property Under the Conditions of Real Socialism', *Problems of Economics*, Vol. 31, No. 8, pp.25-42.
Chakravarty, Sukhamoy, 1988, 'Market Mechanisms Versus Balanced Growth', *Development*, No. 2/3, pp.34-36.

Chamley, Christophe, 1988, *The Effects of Financial Liberalisation on Thailand, Indonesia, and the Philippines: a Quantitative Evaluation*, Washington: World Bank.

Cotton, James, 1988, 'Reforming the Chinese Political System; Reflections on Talks with Political Scientists in China, 1987', *Korea and World Affairs*, Vol. 12, No. 3, pp.548-562.

Edwards, Michael, 1989, 'The Irrelevance of Development Studies', *Third World Quarterly*, pp.116-136.

Elmandjra, Mahdi, 1989, 'China in the Twenty-First Century', *IFDA Dossier 70*, pp.18-20.

Finger, J. Michael, 1988, *Economists, Institutions and Trade Restrictions: a Review Article*, Washington: World Bank.

Gelb, Alan, 1988, *Lewis Through a Looking Glass: Public Sector Employment, Rent-Seeking and Economic Growth*, Washington: World Bank.

Ghaussy, Ghanie, 1988, 'Attempts at Defining an Islamic Economic Order', *Economics*, Vol. 37, pp.9-30.

Hariq, Ilya, 1979, 'Ad-dawla(t) ar-ra'awiya(t) wa moustaqbel at-tenmia(t) al-'arabia(t)' (The National State and the Future of Arabic Development), *Al-moustaqbel al-'arabi*, Vol. 11, No. 121, pp.4-28.

Hemming, Richard, and Ali Mansour, 1988, 'Hal at-taHouil ila al-qiTa' al-khaS houa al-ijaba(t)?' (Is the Transfer to the Private Sector the Answer?), *At-tamouil wa at-tanmia(t)*, Vol. 25, No. 2, pp.31-33.

Hettne, Bjorn, 1988, 'Three Worlds of Crises for the Nation-State', *Development*, No.2/3, pp.14-25.

Jankowsk, Richard, 1987, 'The Profit-Squeeze and Tax Policy: Can the State Actively Intervene?', *Review of Radical Political Economics*, Vol. 19, No. 3, pp.18-33.

King, Robert E., 1988, *International Macroeconomic Adjustment 1987-1992; a World Model Approach*, Washington: World Bank.

Krauss, Melvyn B., 1978, *The new Protectionism: the Welfare State and International Trade*, New York: New York University Press.

Lindauer, David L., 1988, *Government Pay and Employment Policies and Government Policies and Government Performance in Developing Economies*, Washington: World Bank.

Marsh, Robert M., 1988, 'Sociological Explanations of Economic Growth', *Studies in Comparative International Development*, Vol. 23, No. 4, pp.41-76.

Mas'oud, Madjid, 1988, 'Haoul al-itijahat at-taHdithia(t) al-mou'aSira(t) fi al-iqtiSad as-soufieti' (On the Contemporary Orientations in the Soviet Economy), *Al-iqtiSad (Syria)*, Vol. 21, No. 293, pp.20-32.

Mathur, V.B.L., 1988, 'The Role of the Public Sector in India', *Development*, No. 2/3, pp.37-38.

Mdaghri, Driss Alaoui, 1981, 'The Limits of State Control over Public Enterprises in Morocco', *Public Enterprise*, Vol. 2, No. 1, pp.41-52.

Meed, 1988, 'Economic Briefing; Libya - a More Liberal Economy', Vol. 32, No. 27, pp.29-30.

Meed, 1989, 'Feature Story: Arab Economies until 1993', Vol. 33, No. 11, p.14.

Mohtadi, Hamid, 1988, 'Growth-Distribution Trade-offs: The Role of Capacity Utilisation', *Cambridge Journal of Economics*, Vol. 12, No. 4, pp.419-433.

Nair, Govindan, 1988, *How Much do State-Owned Enterprises Contribute to Public Sector Deficits in Developing Countries, and Why?*, Washington: World Bank.

Nerfin, Marc, 1989, 'Another Liberation', *IFDA Dossier 70*, p.2

122

Nicholaides, Phedon, 1988, 'Limits to the Expansion of Neoclassical Economies', *Cambridge Journal of Economics*, Vol. 12, No. 3, pp.313-328.

Quijano, Anibal, 1988, 'A Different Concept of the Private sector, a Different Concept of the Public Sector', *CEPAL Review* No. 35, pp.105-120.

Al-Saadi, Abdullah Juma'an Saeed, 1986, *Fiscal Policy in the Islamic State: its Origins and Contemporary Relevance*, Newcastle-under-Lyme: Lyme.

Sayegh Yousouf, 1988, 'Fi al-iqtiSad as-siassi wa al-ijtima'i li idara(t) at-tenmia(t)' (Managing Development Through the Politico-Social Economy), *Al-moustaqbel al-'arabi*, Vol. 11, No. 114, pp.4-21.

Shirley, Mary, 1988, 'Khibra(t) at'taHouil ila al-qiTa' al-khaS' (The Experience of Transferring to the Private Sector), *At-tamouil wa at-tanmia(t)*, Vol. 25, No. 2, pp.34-35.

Stanford Research Institute, 1974, *Social and economic impacts of the Kuwait Government Compensation increase of 1971-72 and recommended national compensation policies*, final report/Stanford Research Institute; prepared for the Planning Board, State of Kuwait, California.

Stern, Robert M. (ed.), 1987, *U.S. Trade Policies in a Changing World Economy*, Cambridge, Massachusetts, and London: MIT Press.

'The State and the Crisis in Africa; in Search of a Second Liberation (Seminar), Uppsala 15-19 September 1986', 1987, *Development Dialogue*, No. 2, pp.5-29.

Tarasov, L.A., 1988, 'The Economy of the Socialist Community; Emergence, Development, Problems', *Problems of Economics*, Vol. 31, No. 7, pp.82-99.

Thapar, Romesh, 1982, 'The Changing Concepts of Governance', Stockholm: World Future Studies Federation. Paper presented to the VII World Conference on Future Studies, 'The Future of Politics', June 6-8, 1982.

United Nations Commission of the European Communities, 1987, *World Comparisons of Purchasing Power and Real Product for 1980*, New York: United Nations.

Wisman, Jon D., John Willoughby and Larry Sawers, 1986, 'The Search for Grand Theory in Economic History: North's Challenge to Marx', *Social Research*, Vol.55, No. 4, pp.747-773.

Wolfe, Marshall, 1988, 'The Social Actors and Development Options', *CEPAL Review*, No. 3, pp.143-147.

World Economic Survey, 1988, *Current Trends and Policies in the World Economy*, New York: United Nations.

9

Economic Reform in Latin America: Groping for Ways out of the Crisis

JORGE SCHVARZER

Latin America is facing one of its greatest challenges ever: that of reforming its economic structure whilst being caught in the middle of a deep and lasting crisis. Such a challenge leaves no options, since the crisis giving rise to the problem is, at the same time, the main reason for reform, and is defining its rhythm and course.

Pressed by short-term urgency, the chief decisions on change are being made amid intense pressure and with insufficient leeway to analyse any prospective effects in the long run. The old debate on the ways and conditions of development has left the spotlight, and its place has been taken by a number of questions put forward in a pragmatic and defensive way: How is the crisis to be resolved? How are foreign creditors' demands to be met? How will the productive system be restarted after its progress broke down some years ago? Most of the reform measures currently under way promise to solve these problems in the future but their immediate results do not always appear to provide reassurance that progress is being made in the right direction.

It may be said that the new economic policy strategy being applied throughout the continent tends to adapt itself to the demands posed by those sectors capable of imposing their views. Any rejection of such views entails the risk of deepening the crisis, as the reaction of major economic agents can bring about negative effects almost immediately (capital flight, drop in investment, higher external imbalances, and so on). Instead, adoption of the proposals would mean a chance to alleviate some of the perverse short-term phenomena and to nourish a hope of future improvement. With all other alternatives blocked, the only remaining possibility is a *fuite en avant*.

In fact, this appears to be the crucial point. The reforms are being envisaged as part of the process of developing a new economic and social model to operate throughout the continent; a process which is certainly in progress. But for the time being, the course appears to be determined by the will to leave the crisis behind rather than by the attractions the future may hold. The pressing urge of circumstances is therefore more powerful than a discussion of ideas and is prodding the nations in the area along an unexplored road towards a different destination.

Some elements on the dimension and significance of the crisis are to be outlined here, in order to present its main cause and galvanising factor: foreign debt. Only some parts of the problems which stem from foreign debt and its impact on proposed solutions are to be discussed, along with some reflections on future prospects.

The unusual extent of the crisis is the first outstanding factor accounting for the present evolution of the continent. This point should be stressed as many phenomena are apt to be disguised by the way global statistics are presented. The most widespread and well-known indicator of the crisis is the drop in the population's income since the outbreak of the debt crisis. The Economic Commission for Latin America (ECLA) estimates that per capita income in Latin America dropped 8 per cent during the 1980s - a figure which allows for an appreciation of the scale of the reversal in the continental productive system but which does not really explain the actual deterioration in income. The parallel between income and Gross National Product cannot be assumed when the transfer of wealth abroad, arising from the payment of foreign debt interest, reduces the former to a greater extent than the GNP. With only this correction, per capita income at the end of the decade is 11 per cent below the level corresponding to 1980.

Of course, this figure expresses a mathematical average for the region and its society as a whole, thus concealing - as every average does - the actual evolution of different social groups. In order to overcome this problem, we must consider some hypotheses based upon an elementary stratification of the population according to income brackets. Let us assume that the 20 per cent highest income earners were able to maintain their income in absolute figures throughout the last decade - and in fact, indicators on income evolution in different Latin American societies suggest that this estimation could even turn out to be somewhat conservative. In any case, even if actual indicators showing a worse distribution are left aside, this means that the relative participation of such a group, representing about 50 per cent of the total wealth available, has actually increased during this period.

The wealth available for the rest of society has been accordingly reduced: A simple mathematical calculation allows an estimation that the remaining 80 per cent of the population has lost an average of 22 per cent of its income in 10 years. Any stratification within this large group would show sharper than average falls for the large social masses at the bottom of the scale and would thus provide an explanation of the intensity and diffusion of the phenomenon of extreme poverty throughout Latin America.

The crisis can likewise be verified using other indicators. The drop in productive investment is a widespread feature of Latin America and has reduced both the possibilities of economic growth and the capacity to meet social demands in the foreseeable future. The inflationary explosion has revealed the difficulties encountered in reshaping the economy under the pressure of external and internal demands and has shown the degree of disarticulation of the whole system. The strangling of public finance has prevented the operation of social security schemes and has substantially limited chances of investment in infrastructure - a task traditionally undertaken by the state.

Strong variations in both exchange and interest rates resulting from sharp swings in external financial flows have hindered the construction of a stable and predictable economy, and have accentuated adverse effects on the distribution of income. The deterioration of the state regulatory capacity is another phenomenon derived both from the consequences of existing economic restrictions and the new operating conditions of the market system. If the present appears difficult, the future looks unpromising unless expectations in social progress are reduced to levels far lower than those contemplated during the early 1980s.

All these situations pose formal contradictions, because they all call for urgent solutions in spite of the fact that corrective measures are of a structural nature, and are therefore slow in their effects. Latin American governments are compelled to act as quickly as possible in the middle of a crisis, in spite of all kinds of pressure and with minimal margins in reaching solutions. At this point economic difficulties are intertwined with socio-political problems. Paradoxically, the massive return to a democratic system in a number of countries within the region was partly propelled by the crisis, but the expected impacts of democracy have been checked by the growing effects of the crisis itself.

Democracy, a system implying social debate and interest conciliation, has had its growth somewhat curbed by current pressing needs and has also been distorted by the necessity of responding to compulsive and immediate demands. Parliaments end up yielding their places to executives who, in turn, give in to those who are accumulating power and leading the way of the economy and society at large.

Foreign creditors, associated with the ruling classes within each country, have achieved an unprecedented capacity to promote economic reforms in whatever direction they wish, and to the point where reforms become social goals. The crisis, which was brought about by the foreign debt of the early 1980s, has now turned out to be the decisive factor in the short term, and its analysis is imperative if the changes in progress are to be understood.

The foreign debt cannot be reduced to mere financial, monetary or payment flows, nor to mere analysis of the relationships between Latin American nations and foreign creditors. From the time its scale reached critical levels, and negotiations about it acquired a political character, the debt became a structural factor closely linked to the present and the future of the whole region.

In fact it has affected the behaviour of every economic - and consequently political - decision within the countries of the continent. Its presence cannot be limited to its specific impact on one area as the network of macroeconomic relationships built around it makes its presence felt in the whole system. Thus, only some of its decisive aspects are being examined here, and we will look at its relations with the economic reforms currently under way before drawing some conclusions in this regard.

Until the outbreak of the crisis in 1982, very high amounts of foreign credit were available for Latin America. Although part of the resources provided served to cancel the interest on previous loans (and in this sense it was only an accounting device which cloaked the actual flow received) some funds remained available to offset deficits in the balance of trade as well as to supply foreign currency for the privileged groups within each national society.

The positive effect of these loans in the late 1970s should not be exaggerated. In fact, taking them as a whole and forgetting important national differences in distribution, only a portion of them was used to import capital goods required by those economies, whilst a significant proportion served, instead, to facilitate capital flight from the continent towards international financial centres.

From 1982 onwards there has been a flow reversal. Big private international banks began to refuse loan renewals and the commitments they have made since then are actually lower than the interest due on previous loans. Latin America has since been forced to generate a positive trade balance to cover this gap. The results have been striking: During the past decade, the continent started with a trade deficit of US$ 2 billion and ended up with a surfeit of US$ 30 billion. This change stems from a drop in imports during the first five-year period and, since 1988, an increase in the exportable supply of the region. This first significant structural transformation has led to an extensive alteration in the composition of the domestic supply of goods and services as well as to a number of seldom-mentioned consequences on macroeconomic equilibrium.

As the supply of imported goods is curtailed (consisting, to a considerable extent, of capital goods, because of the impossibility of stopping the inflow of strategic inputs required by those economies) and the activity is reorientated towards exportable products, there is a modification of relative prices in the economic system at large. Such a transformation implies massive transfers of income - through price changes - from sectors linked to the domestic market towards exporters, and from wage-earners to capital owners.

It is fairly well known that this process can only take place by means of a certain inflationary effect whose drive is reinforced by other factors which will be examined below. In other words, the first structural response of the continent to the challenges posed by foreign debt is a balance of trade in the black together with recession, a modification in relative prices, income transfers and a first inflationary drive.

At the same time the positive result in the balance of trade implies an imbalance in the domestic market of goods and services, and the monetary income corresponding to the exported surplus (that, by definition, does not have an equivalent local supply) must be sterilised lest it results in an inflationary effect, and even more so when the positive balance is at the level mentioned. The commercial surplus of the continent has only been exceeded in absolute terms (but not as a proportion of the GNP) by Japan, a country which applies careful economic strategy to neutralise the negative effects of such a balance by means of investment abroad and through the encouragement of domestic savings. This task is not easy in the case of the weak Latin American economies and the effects of the surfeit balance tend to accelerate the inflationary process. This phenomenon is less pronounced when the state exports goods directly through its enterprises, and in this case the trade surplus in foreign currency is not converted into local currency but directly services the debt. It is highly likely that the experience of lower inflation rates enjoyed by Mexico, Venezuela and Chile has much to owe to the fact that the states in these countries - in contrast to what is generally the case in the region - are the main exporters of goods.

Brazilian economists, in particular, have developed the concept of transfer to explain this issue. Indeed, the profit from balance of trade belongs to private sector exporters and must be purchased by the public sector in order to service the debt. The government must, therefore, generate a *superavit* in revenues and domestic currency equal to the balance of trade. If this is successful, private agents end up having an amount of money without a counterpart in local goods that, if not saved, causes inflation. If the government cannot levy taxes to the extent required it must then resort to other methods affecting the macroeconomic equilibrium: It must either secure loans in the local market, thus quickly raising the domestic rate of interest, or issue new currency which automatically increases the inflationary process.

Some global figures may give an idea of the scale of the problem. In terms of the Gross Domestic Product of each country, the interest payment on debts amounts to 6 per cent of the GDP, and must be serviced by the public sector whose budget represents about 25 per cent of that variable. Consequently, from the start of the debt crisis, governments have been compelled either to collect six extra points in taxes or to cut down expenditure by one quarter, just to be able to meet the yearly interest payments.

It should not be surprising, therefore, that all the countries affected are facing enormous budget cuts without, as yet, being able to find any satisfactory combination of those two alternatives. The reduction of public spending is not easy since it involves sharp cuts in social investment, public employment and salaries, while an increase in taxes is likely to meet a strong adverse reaction of those potentially affected who are generally able to neutralise any measure of this sort. In addition, inflation appears to perform a functional role, and issuing new money to cover the deficit allows the state to collect a tax on the society at large (thus limiting the burden on privileged sectors), to feed the monetary demand already in force on account of other factors of inflation and to contribute to the process of reconstruction of the system of relative prices.

In the long run, the process is self-defeating because inflation itself decreases public revenue (through the so-called Tanzi effect), thus neutralising the expected effects of new issues of money. This compulsory strategy tends to raise inflation rates to levels incompatible with the normal functioning of the economy and encourages the demand for 'reduction of the state' based upon the widespread idea that the latter is accountable for the prevailing chaos.

It would seem appropriate at this stage to consider some figures on the inflationary phenomenon. In the period 1977-81, prior to the debt shock, the average rate of inflation for the continent as a whole was, according to ECLAC, 49 per cent but by 1983-84 it was 158 per cent and in 1989 it exceeded 1,000 per cent yearly with several dramatic cases beyond the 3,000 per cent level. Even if the particular evolution of each country in this regard could be explained in specific terms, the generalisation of the phenomenon is a good example of the debt shock effects through mechanisms such as those already briefly outlined.

The pressure arising from the crisis and the soaring inflation has been addressed by cutting down public expenditure and reducing the role of the state. This conjunction of demands, concurring with the aims set down by creditors and ruling groups within the continent, has lead to the sale of public assets. In order to solve their cash problems, the different states have been divesting themselves of their more valuable property, usually their enterprises and other real estate and mining assets. Thus, these assets have become one of the targets of the so-called privatisation of the economy and, when put in a more bombastic way, of the reform of the public sector. No doubt in the long run these privatisation measures will deeply affect the operation of the economies within the region, the relationship between the market and the state, income distribution, productive dynamism, etc.

However, doubts are being entertained as to whether these impacts will be positive since there are many reasons to make opposite forecasts in this respect. But long-term problems are not the immediate topic here, nor are the main causes underlying the decisions taken. Such decisions are only concerned with responding to the immediate needs that condition and define them, and moreover there is every indication that these decisions can be applied, thereby overcoming enormous social and political resistance due to the pressing urgency posed by the debt problem.

Unable to resolve short-term demands, the role of the state in each country must be reduced in order to give place to other social and economic actors. Debt has forced the state to contract the public sector (through cuts in spending and personnel and the closing of offices) while inflation has curbed the autonomy of its monetary policy. At the same time, external financial flows have forced the opening up of the economy, until then half-closed to the impact of other countries' supplies, and have imposed the conditions of the world market to the local system.

None of the aspects involved in the current strategy can be separated from the restrictions and requirements imposed by the presence of the foreign debt. Any speech on the subject is apt to outline a bolder future on account of the reforms presently being undertaken, but the dire facts show that every decision is driven by short-term needs rather than by the expected resulting model.

The Weimar hypothesis

Of course these cause-and-effect phenomena are the object of intense controversy, basically a re-enactment of the 1920s dispute concerning German hyperinflation. The Weimar government placed war reparations (equivalent to the present Latin American debt) as the origin of the inflationary spiral, while the Allied Powers accused the German government of excesses in public expenditure and its monetary policy. The issue was not only theoretical but different stands clearly mirrored the interests at stake. Discussion on the German experience has been renewed in recent years and new arguments have been put forth. These arguments, both in their substance and in their nature, appear to be closely entwined with the positions and interests present in the dispute on the Latin American debt and soaring inflation. It is not possible to state that the issue has been settled, either theoretically or historically. It is a fact that German stabilisation in 1923 was able to put an end to the inflationary problem thanks to internal adjustment together with a de facto moratorium on reparations payments. Each side, therefore, feels free to emphasise one of those two aspects in order to defend its views.

Even though the current controversy follows a course similar to that of the 1920s, the resemblance is closer with regard to the views than with the actors, since the latter do not correspond precisely to present creditors and debtors. A stand reflecting the prevailing position presents the Latin American crisis as a consequence of mistaken local strategies (which is partly true) and tends to deny the harmful effects of the debt. This view is held by the creditors but also by the ruling classes who are willing to pay for different reasons. The other view, presenting the debt as the cause of the crisis, has been losing ground and is increasingly reflecting a theoretical diagnosis whose validity seems to have an inverse relation to its diffusion.

The last stand, placing the debt as the cause underlying the crisis and the reforms, logically deduces a political corollary: the so-called foreign debt generating a radical reshuffle of domestic power relationships within Latin American societies. To accept this means to adopt certain strategies and to turn down others, thus eliminating the possibility of different alternatives which have been attempted in the past; such as in a take-it-or-leave-it game where one puts everything at stake. To reject it implies, in turn, breaking with the system as a whole, something that conditions all decisions in this respect. It is not the first time in history that a similar situation has provided the creditors with a negotiating capacity unthinkable under other circumstances. Due to the debt predicament, creditors have mostly allied themselves with different power sectors (both in creditor and debtor countries) so as to be able to impose their views and interests in theory and practice. It is not only a matter of collecting their dues but also of the consolidation of a political and economic system in accordance with their perspectives and those of their allies.

An historian dealing with the relationship between the world of finance and the United States government at the end of the 18th century has vividly described the way bankers and their associates managed to gain control of national decisions based upon their credits against the state. The study in question culminates with these - in our view - decisive words: 'the creation of the debt was the economic counterpart of the Constitution'.[1] Likewise, it may be said that in Latin America the debt turned out to be the economic counterpart of democracy; the renewed presence of national popular majorities within the political system found their possibilities of economic and social reform neutralised in part by the domestic restriction imposed by foreign commitments. Unfortunately, the analogy cannot be extended further. The United States were able to combine such a restricted democracy with an economic system favouring development, but nothing at present indicates a similar occurrence in Latin America.

It is possible, and hopefully desirable, that economic reforms end up helping development of the continent. Until now, however, all the measures have had to go through the filter of urgency and their need has not been consistent with the goal of reaching macroeconomic balances which will raise investments and allow social progress.

Latin America will still have to undergo a long process of change before a way out may be visualised, and in the meantime the problem will, for the most part, be not a matter of argument on the prospective contours of such a future, but rather a question of immediate and pressing demands coming from large human masses who have been plunged into misery. These masses may remain subject to restrictions and pay a tremendous price in doing so, whilst waiting for long-term prospects of a more consolidated democracy with an economic boom and social welfare. They could also reject these restrictions in a number of ways, from passive resistance to revolt against the system.

In this regard, it would be better not to make predictions but to turn back to examples supplied by historical experience. If debt pressure had a happy ending in the United States, it was not the case in the Weimar Republic, where it led to Nazism and bloodstained racist and military consequences before Germany was finally able to recompose its social organisation. The possible scenarios for the Latin American future cover a similar range when they are envisaged without prejudice among the creaks and crackles of crisis and change. But of course lack of prejudice does not imply no worries: Some of the alternatives contemplated may be highly dangerous for the survival of a continent that is a decisive element of the planet.

NOTES

1. Ferguson, James, 1961, *The Power of the Purse: a History of the American Public Finance (1776-1796),* University of North Carolina, quoted by James O'Connor, 1973, in *The Fiscal Crisis of the State,* New York: St. Martin Press.

10

Economic Reforms and Changes in the Role of the State: The Taiwan Experience

FOH TSRANG TANG

I. INTRODUCTION

In some ways, the process of economic development is similar to that of a child's growth. The mother takes care of her child when he is young, but leaves him alone and encourages him to participate in all kinds of social activities once he grows up. The Government of the Republic of China in Taiwan has approached the economic development of Taiwan in a similar way.

In the early stages of economic development, Taiwan had an agricultural predominated economy with limited natural endowment, a weak industrial base and a shortage of capital, but with an abundance of labour. The government laid down foundations for industrial development through increasing agricultural productivity, something made possible through policies of agricultural reform.

The government then started playing an active role in the planning and encouragement of industrial development. Many effective measures, mostly restrictive or protective in nature, were taken at different stages, the major one being subsidies in the form of tax reductions, tax exemptions, low interest rates, etc., which have been used to encourage the investment or manufacture of specific industries and products. Another means adopted by the government to promote the development of import substitution and export-oriented industries has been the establishment of protective measures such as high tariff and non-tariff barriers to support the growth of infant industries. There have also been limitations on factory establishment to maintain development order, and control of foreign exchange to make effective use of the very limited foreign exchange available for the importation of machinery, equipment and raw materials necessary for industrial production.

Since the late 1970s, both the domestic and the world economy have experienced dramatic changes. The Government of Taiwan has changed its policy from protecting the baby to encouraging him to live alone and independently. In other words, economic liberalisation and internationalisation have been the new strategies adopted by the government. More recently, political liberalisation, interaction across the Taiwan Strait, and other environmental factors have changed, meaning that a further adjustment in the role of the government has become necessary for the 1990s, but it is not yet clear how.

II. THE IDEOLOGY AND NATURE OF ECONOMIC PLANNING AND POLICY-MAKING

Taiwan's economic development is basically guided by the principle of creation and equal distribution of wealth. Accordingly, Taiwan's economic development is both planned and market-oriented in nature.

Back in the early 1950s, Taiwan faced high inflation and huge unemployment rates, a lack of capital or foreign exchange, a weak infrastructure, and an absence of farsighted entrepreneurs. The private sector was characterised by small, traditional, and even backward, enterprises that had neither investment knowledge, nor any money to carry out any large-scale industry. As measures had to be adopted to overcome these difficulties, the government tried giving direction to national economic development, while at the same time encouraging and supporting the development of the private sector.

It should be noted that the nature of economic planning in Taiwan is different to the rigid system that exists in centrally-planned economies. Even in the public sector, planning is usually formulated with a bottom-up and not a top-down approach, while planning for the private sector has been done in a different way. The government did not invoke its authority in order to force private enterprise to adhere to government policies or regulations, but rather implemented policy measures such as tax reductions or exemptions to encourage the development of private enterprise.

Protective policy was preferred by the policy-makers in Taiwan. They claimed this was necessary and justifiable on the grounds that the newly set-up infant industries were as weak as babies, and that protection and care were necessary for their survival into maturity.

In fact, parenthood has been the major role the government has played in Taiwan and many protective policy measures have been adopted during the past four decades. Another major characteristic of economic planning in Taiwan is that much emphasis has been placed on public enterprise, because private enterprise has been weak and few in number due to lack of capital, entrepreneurship, and other necessary requirements for industrial development.

Another important factor has been Dr. Sun Yat-Sen's doctrine - the supreme policy guideline and also the major source of the national constitution of the Republic of China. According to Dr. Sun, industries or businesses such as electricity, railroads, banks, etc., which are either monopolistic in nature or inappropriate for private operation due to their large scale, public service, or for other reasons, should be owned and run by the government. Therefore, public enterprise has held a significant proportion of the economic system, and most of the large scale and capital-intensive industries are still public. However, this has gradually been changing during the process of economic development, with private enterprise growing at a relatively high rate and dominating the economy since the late 1970s.

III. ECONOMIC REFORMS AND CHANGES IN THE ROLE OF THE STATE: HISTORICAL REVIEW OF THE PAST FOUR DECADES

The Launch and Scope of the Reforms

The process of Taiwan's economic development can be roughly classified into five phases, with different goals in each phase.

The first phase (prior to 1952) was a restoration period, during which the damage caused by the war was cleaned up, and the foundations for economic development were laid. The second phase (1952-60) emphasised import substitution while increases in agricultural productivity was the central issue of the government's efforts.

The third phase (1961-70) was one of export expansion in which the labour-intensive, light-industrial sector began to dominate the economy. The fourth phase (1971-80) was the structural adjustment period in which the economic structure changed from labour-intensive to capital- and technological-intensive industries, and finally the fifth phase (1982-89) is one of economic liberalisation and internalisation in which the economic structure continued to adjust itself to the drastic and rapid changes in the internal and external environment.

The first phase (prior to 1952): restoration period

During World War II, Taiwan was occupied by Japan and was seriously damaged by allied bombing. When the Chinese government

137

resumed its sovereignty over the island in 1945, restoration of the infrastructure and plants was naturally the government's top priority. After the civil war and economic collapse on the mainland, the Central Government was forced to move to Taiwan in 1949.

Hyperinflation was experienced during the late 1940s and the beginning of the 1950s. The index of prices escalated from 1.00 in 1948 to 36.73 in 1949, continuing to rise to 103.85 in 1950, 154.37 in 1951, and 189.60 in 1952. Price stabilisation was therefore the most urgent job that the government faced.

Monetary reform was implemented in June 1949 to counter hyperinflation. Measures included transforming the Taiwan Dollar to the New Taiwan Dollar (40,000 to 1), devaluing the currency to 40 New Taiwan Dollars to one US Dollar, restricting the amount of currency in circulation, and prohibiting speculation on the price of gold. Inflation was brought down to an annual average of 8.8 per cent between 1952 and 1960. The government also introduced preferential interest savings in March 1950, which helped accumulate the capital necessary for economic development, and also helped keep inflation in check.

More than two million soldiers and civilians moved with the Central Government from the mainland to Taiwan in December 1949, creating many new economic and social problems, such as food supply, huge unemployment rates and social conflict and disorder. Countermeasures for all these problems also became top priorities.

The land reform programme was implemented in 1949 to increase agricultural production and social stability. The first step of the land reform programme, the 37.5 per cent reduction programme, was announced in February 1949, under which farm rent paid to landowners was forbidden to exceed 37.5 per cent of the total yield of the main crop. At the same time, extra burdens, such as advance rent payments and security deposits, were abandoned; farm lease contracts were to be for a minimum of six years, and landlords could not terminate the contract except for certain legal reasons.

The second step of the programme was the sale of public land to farmers. A total of 139,688 farming families purchased 171,763 acres of land in six land sales held between 1948 and 1958. The land reform programme affected 43 per cent of Taiwan's 660,000 farming families, and greatly strengthened the overall incentive to invest in and cultivate the land. With higher yields and lower rents, the average income of tenant farmers rose by 81 per cent between 1949 and 1952.

Although this was a disturbingly abnormal transition period, the government still tried to develop some basic industries. Lack of foreign exchange was a major constraint on the importation of the necessary

138

raw materials for production, and measures to increase the supply of food and clothing for domestic demand had to be adopted. The electrical and fertiliser industries were developed and the government implemented a protection policy to encourage the development of the textile industry.

Other programmes implemented during this period included construction of facilities for water conservation, advances in agricultural technology, and reformation of farmers' organisations. These policies helped agricultural production attain an average annual growth rate of 13 per cent between 1949 and 1952, which was far in excess of the rate of population growth.

All these policies and programmes resulted in rural stability, and helped lay foundations for agricultural development and the consequent industrial development, and also made a significant contribution to the overall post war social stability and economic reconstruction.

The second phase (1952-1960): agriculture, industry and import substitution period

Beginning in 1953, the government implemented a series of four-year economic development plans in which the key agricultural policy was to develop agricultural resources and to increase food production. The principle aim was to achieve self-sufficiency in food production and to improve the nutritional intake of the people. Furthermore, the plans tried 'Using Agriculture to Cultivate Industry', which was the major strategy adopted during the 1950s. Such measures as the 'land tillage' programme, the fertiliser paddy system, the land tax-in-kind system, and the compulsory rice purchase plan were implemented, thereby increasing and controlling food production and supply, and stimulating the transfer of surplus capital from the agricultural to the industrial sector.[1]

Increased agricultural productivity also brought about the transfer of labour from farms to the non-agricultural sector, which made a cheap labour force available for industrial development. The increase in food production not only supplied the raw materials necessary to stimulate industrial development but also promoted the export of agricultural products to earn foreign exchange which was necessary for the importation of the equipment and raw materials needed for industrial development.[2] At the same time, the increase in income for farming families also created a domestic market for the weak infant industrial sector which had no competitive ability in the international market.

In fact, development of import-substitution industries was a top priority for the government during this period. Any industry that could increase exports or reduce imports and make a significant contribution to the improvement of the balance of payments was encouraged, together with industries appropriate to the development of private enterprise. Measures taken by the government included:[3]

(1) The privatisation of four public enterprises in 1953;
(2) The adoption of a protective policy which focused on various tariff and non-tariff measures (the former comprised raising tariff rates in 1955, and the latter included restrictions on imports, import licensing and restrictions on the setting-up of new factories);
(3) Strict controls on the allocation of foreign exchange due to its shortage.

By the end of the 1950s, Taiwan's economic situation showed significant improvement. To encourage the expansion of foreign trade, several major policies were changed:

(1) Tax rebates on industrial exports were liberalised in 1956;
(2) A foreign exchange reform was adopted in 1958, and the multiple exchange rate system was gradually replaced by an effectively devalued uniform rate in 1958;
(3) A large multifaceted package of fiscal incentives for both domestic and foreign investors was implemented. Perhaps the most important incentives were the '19-point Financial and Economic Reform Programme' and the 'Statute for the Encouragement of Investment' in 1960.

The third phase (1961-70): export expansion period.

This phase was a time of economic transformation where industry and commerce developed rapidly, and the rate of migration of workers from the countryside to the cities increased. Although farm wages rose steadily, agricultural profits and growth dropped, and the rate of self-sufficiency in food began to decline. The role of agriculture changed from that of supporting economic development to requiring assistance from other sectors.

In fact, agricultural policy focused on integrating agriculture into the overall economy, adjusting the structure of agricultural production, protecting the environment, strengthening rural development, and raising farm incomes. In addition, since 1969 'the Outline of Agricultural Policy Review', 'Guidelines for Strengthening the Current Stage of Agricultural Reconstruction', and 'the Agricultural Development Act' have been implemented to better address the needs of agriculture.

Because of limited natural resources, a high population growth and a relatively small domestic market, Taiwan's economic development has had to be heavily dependent on the expansion of foreign trade. Thus, export-oriented industries continued to be under the protection of import controls and high tariffs during this period.

In order to accelerate industrial development, two important and effective measures were adopted during the 1960s. The first one was 'the Statute for the Encouragement of Investment', promulgated in 1960, whose main intention was to reduce production costs through tax reductions and exemptions, thus facilitating the acquisition of land for industrial use and increasing competitiveness. The other was the establishment of 'Export Processing Zones' in 1966.

The fourth phase (1971-1980): structural adjustment period

During this phase, Taiwan not only suffered from the oil shocks of 1973-74 and 1978-80 and the general world recession, but also experienced major diplomatic crises, including internal problems.

Since the early 1970s, Taiwan's economic structure has changed from being primarily agricultural, supporting the development of the rest of the economy by providing an abundant and steady supply of food, labour and surplus capital, as well as maintaining economic stability, to a situation where the agricultural sector must seek support from other sectors to ensure its own survival and continued development. With greater stress on the environment, its role in protecting soil and scenic resources has become more important. Other roles such as the enhancement of the welfare of farmers and the continued rise in farm incomes to help maintain a balanced development between agricultural and non-agricultural sectors are equally important, and to this end, since 1973, the government has successively launched plans of reconstruction.

In the long-run, high economic growth has been experienced, but this has caused some other important problems to emerge, such as the lack of physical infrastructure, the shortage of technicians and skilled labour, insufficient diffusion of technology, and the inefficiency and disadvantages of too many small and medium-sized industries. To conquer these problems the government undertook ten major development projects in 1973 and 12 others in 1978 to increase the supply of physical infrastructure. It has also encouraged capital-intensive and technological or heavy industries to replace the light, labour-intensive industries in the economy, set up the Hsinchu Science-based Industrial Park in 1980 as a strong base for the introduction of key technologies, and established an administration and a Business Bank of Taiwan to specifically help small and medium-sized industries.

The fifth phase (1981-89): economic liberalisation period

The 1980s have been an period of challenges characterised by increasing protectionism and keen competition in the world market. However, many social movements, such as the labour movement, the environmental protectionists and the so-called self-rescue movement, have not only changed traditional relationships between employers and employees but have also changed the relationship between the government and the people. Several measures have been implemented by the government, such as speeding up the process of economic liberalisation and internationalisation, and improving the investment climate.

In August 1984, the government announced its intention to promote a policy of economic liberalisation and internationalisation, but it was not effectively implemented until 1987. After a rapid growth of foreign exchange reserves and a huge trade surplus, The New Taiwan Dollar appreciated against the US dollar from NT$ 40.47 in September 1985 to NT$ 28.17 by the end of 1988, (43.7 per cent increase) thus inflicting heavy pressure on local enterprise. In order to reduce the pressure of any further revaluation, the government lifted the controls on foreign exchange on 15 July 1987, and reduced the tariffs on a further 3,574 items by an average of 50 per cent beginning on 1 February 1988. Furthermore, the government embarked on 14 major development projects, most of which focused on developing transportation to enlarge domestic demand.

The 1980s have also been a period of world and national economic uncertainty. Domestic financial operations are still thought of as backward by private enterprise - the tax system needs to be improved and government agencies lack efficiency - and the willingness to invest in domestic enterprise had been sluggish for years. This all indicated that the overall investment climate had deteriorated and that there would be unfavourable effects on economic development. In response to this, the government set up a Consulting Committee on

Industrial Development in 1984 to look at upgrading the industrial structure, and in 1985 organised an Economic Renovation committee which made 56 policy recommendations towards the improvement of the investment climate. In 1987 the Taxation Reform Committee was established to improve the Tax administration and tax structure.

In order to tackle the problems caused by the social movements, the government set up the Labour Commission on 1 August 1987 to formulate labour and dispute settlement policies. The Environmental Protection Administration was also established in 1987 to strengthen the effectiveness of protection and conservation of the natural environment.

Private enterprise upgraded its technological level to raise productivity, and increased the level of automation in the production process to reduce labour costs and disputes with workers. It also started investing overseas, mainly in Mainland China and in Southeast Asia, to procure an adequate supply of materials and low-wage workers.

In addition, the agricultural sector developed along the same lines as in the past. The government adopted 'the Program to Improve the Structure of Agriculture and Boost Farm Income, 1986-91', to further rural reconstruction and increase farm income. In addition, the rice field diversion plan was implemented to solve the problem of over production of rice.

Significant Achievements in Development

Although many problems and difficulties have emerged during the different stages of economic development, the quick and accurate response of the government with its appropriate policies and measures, the cooperation of private and public enterprise, and the hard-working Taiwanese people, have resulted in the distinguished 'Taiwan Economic Miracle'.

The economy has evolved from an agricultural to an industrial economy, and its society has changed from being poor and underdeveloped to being affluent and progressive, and can be illustrated by six items:

(1) the maintenance of a high level of economic growth without the emergence of a huge gap between poor and rich;
(2) thriving exports, which has helped amass large amounts of foreign exchange reserves, and successive years of surplus, revealing a durable competitiveness;

(3) sound financial administration, generally free of the burden of annual budget deficits or public bonds, and without foreign loan restraints;
(4) the maintenance of stable commodity prices for many years with little inflation;
(5) an exceptionally low unemployment rate;
(6) a rate of saving which is the highest in the world.[4]

High and Stable Economic Growth

From 1952 to 1988, the real Gross National Product grew at an average annual rate of 8.94 per cent, or, if the factor of population growth is taken into account, 6.40 per cent per capita GNP (See Table 1). This high economic growth was mainly due to a policy of export-orientation. As Taiwan lacked natural resources and foreign exchange reserves during the early development stages, raw materials and machine equipment for industrial production had to rely on imports, which themselves depended on the foreign exchange earned from exports.

TABLE 1

ECONOMIC GROWTH   Unit: %

	1952-60	1961-70	1971-80	1981-88	1952-88
GNP	8.07	9.63	9.75	7.95	8.94
Per Capita	4.51	6.75	7.66	13.01	6.40
Commodity Exports	9.37	22.43	17.20	15.61	19.41

Source: 'National Income in the Taiwan Area, Republic of China'. Taipei: Directorate General of Budget, Accounting and Statistics (DGBAS), Executive Yuan, Dec. 1987
'Statistical Abstract of National Income, Taiwan Area, Republic of China', 1951-1988. Taipei: DGBAS, 1988

Foreign trade has grown exceptionally rapidly during the past four decades. Exports accounted for 9.7 per cent of the GNP in 1952, but increased to 50.7 per cent by 1987, with an average growth rate of

19.41 per annum. The main force supporting the expansion in foreign trade was domestic fixed capital formation: During this period, the average growth rate of fixed capital was 12.29 per cent, the greatest portion of which went to industrial development.

The economic structure has also experienced rapid change. See Table 2. Agricultural production accounted for 36 per cent in 1952, but dropped to five per cent by 1988. Correspondingly, industrial production increased from 18 per cent to 46 per cent during the same period. The service industry has grown significantly in the past few years, reaching 49.3 per cent in 1988, for the first time becoming the largest sector in the economy, and this percentage increased to 51.5 per cent, compared to 43.6 per cent for the industrial sector by 1989.

TABLE 2

ECONOMIC STRUCTURAL CHANGE   Unit: %

	1952-60	1961-70	1971-80	1981-88	1952-88
Agriculture					
Distribution	29.06	21.84	11.11	6.38	-
Average Growth Rate	6.19	4.52	1.79	0.99	3.40
Industry					
Distribution	29.90	35.34	48.68	48.31	-
Average Growth Rate	10.14	13.74	12.70	7.89	11.26
Service Industry					
Distribution	44.04	42.82	40.22	45.31	-
Average Growth Rate	8.61	9.28	9.04	8.14	8.77

Sources: See Table 1

Even Income Distribution

The economic institutions of Taiwan are based on Dr. Sun Yat-Sen's Principle of Social Well-Being. It stresses equitable distribution of wealth, and a steady elevation of the people's standard of living and quality of life through economic development. In fact, with effective economic planning and policies, Taiwan has made considerable achievements in this area over the past four decades.

TABLE 3

DISTRIBUTION OF INCOME

Year	Gini Coefficient	Ratio of earnings of highest income group to lowest
1953	0.588	20.5
1961	0.461	11.6
1964	0.360	5.3
1970	0.321	4.6
1975	0.312	4.3
1980	0.303	4.2
1981	0.306	4.2
1982	0.308	4.3
1986	0.322	4.6
1987	0.323	4.7

Source: Wu Hui-lin, 'A Comparison of Wages and Productivity of Taiwan and its Competing Trading countries', Economic Papers, nº60. Chung Hua Institute for Economic Research, 1985.
National Economic Trends, Taiwan Area, the Republic of China. DGBAS, Executive Yuan, 1988.

Generally there are two ways of measuring the distribution of wealth, the Gini Coefficient and the ratio of earnings of the highest group to the lowest. The Gini Coefficient (Table 3) shows a decrease from 0.558 in 1953 to 0.461 in 1961 and 0.321 in 1970, and with a continued fall to 0.303 by 1980, before resuming an annual increase. It shows that disparities in the distribution of wealth in Taiwan narrowed steadily, during 1953-80, giving a more even income distribution during the process of economic development. However, the disparity in the distribution of wealth began to widen during the 1980s, and the ratio of earnings from the highest income group to the lowest has confirmed this finding, with only a slight difference in 1981.

Low Inflation

Taiwan suffered from severe inflation both during and in the five years which followed the end of World War II. Inflation was slowly brought under control in the 1950s. Expressed in terms of changes in the consumer price index, the inflation rate in the 1950s averaged 9.84 per cent. It dropped to 3.4 per cent in the 1960s, climbing back to 11.08 per cent in the 1970s due to the energy crises. A period of minimum inflation was entered in the 1980s, averaging 2.80 per cent per year. However, there was an upward trend from 0.5 per cent in 1987 to 1.3 per cent in 1988, followed by 4.5 per cent in 1989.

If expressed in terms of the wholesale price index, the degree of inflation is shown in a better light: 8.87 per cent in the 1950s, two per cent in the 1960s, 10.73 per cent in the 1970s, and -0.46 per cent in the 1980s.

Compared to both developed and developing countries, Taiwan has maintained a low level of inflation. This is attributable on the one hand to government efforts in controlling the money supply; and on the other hand, to the fact that rises in labour productivity have consistently outpaced wage increases, although this is now beginning to change. At the same time, the government has exercised strict budgetary controls, and there has only rarely been a fiscal deficit. But this is also beginning to change. In addition, drops in import prices and tariffs have made a positive contribution to keeping inflation in check.

Low Unemployment Rate

Employment opportunities were scarce during the 1950s when refugees from Mainland China continued to pour into Taiwan, and private enterprise had not yet developed. However, a sizable pro-portion of the surplus labour was absorbed when the government developed export-oriented labour-intensive industries. In the 1960s, export processing zones were established, industrial zones were delimited, and foreign and domestic investments were encouraged, again absorbing a large amount of labour, and thus enabling Taiwan to maintain a relatively low level of unemployment over a prolonged period of time.

IV. RADICAL CHANGES AND REFORMS IN THE 1990S

The Launching of Economic Reforms

Although Taiwan has enjoyed successful economic development during the 1980s, there have been many external and internal major environmental changes which require radical reforms if Taiwan wants to maintain its economic development. The major changes include the following:

Political Liberalisation

- the lifting of the 38-year-old Emergency Decree on 15 July 1987;
- the Law on Assembly and Parades;
- guaranteeing the right of peaceful demonstration;
- allowing Taiwan's residents to visit relatives on the mainland;
- dropping the restrictions on new newspaper registrations and the limitations on the number of pages permitted;
- revising the Law of Civic Organisations to legitimise new political parties

These political liberalisation measures will undoubtedly affect social stability and economic development.

Trade Imbalances

The trade surplus grew steadily between 1985 and 1987, but fell in 1988. In 1985, a trade surplus of US$ 10.61 billion was registered. In 1986 the figure rose to US$ 15.61 billion, and in 1987 to US$ 19.03 billion, but in 1988 a surplus of only US$ 10.94 billion was recorded. The bulk of the trade surplus comes from trade with the United States. In 1985, for example, the trade surplus with the United States was US$ 10.03 billion. In 1986 it was US$ 13.58 billion, in 1987 US$ 16.1 billion, and in 1988, it was down to US$ 10.43 billion, which accounted for about 95 per cent of the total trade surplus.

Such large trade surpluses have evoked protectionist feelings in the United States, and the US government has instituted various protectionist measures to limit imports of Taiwan-manufactured goods, and used political pressure to force the continued appreciation of the New Taiwan dollar. As of January 1989, Taiwan-manufactured goods have no longer received preferential treatment from the United States.

Adjustments in the Domestic Economy and Society

Labour problems: Over the past 40 years, labour and management have enjoyed relatively harmonious relations, although on a rather different level to those in industrialised countries. Strikes were illegal before the Emergency Decree was lifted in July 1987, and labour problems were not conspicuous.

Since the lifting of the Emergency Decree, however, numerous labour disturbances and disputes have erupted. Part of the source of the problem has been the five-year-old Labour Standards Law, which failed to the needs of either the workers or the management. A work strike by railroad engineers on 1 May 1988, called a 'leave of absence' by the striking workers, was followed by a go slow by drivers of private bus companies. Labour-management disputes over year-end bonuses have also occurred, sometimes leading to go slows or strikes.

Another problem has been a labour shortage and a failure to keep the increase in productivity in line with rises in wages. As a result, many labour-intensive industries have relocated to Southeast Asia and the Chinese mainland.

Environmental protection: Lack of concern for the environment has helped industry to achieve phenomenal growth. Taiwan now suffers a pollution problem that has reached health-endangering levels, and public opinion has recently changed to concern about the environment. Petitions and demonstrations in opposition to the construction of new chemical or electrical power plants have been held. People demonstrated against Du Pont's proposal to open a titanium plant in Kukang in early 1986, and against the construction of the fifth and sixth naphtha cracking plants. Public opposition is one of the factors that has caused 14 major construction projects to fall behind schedule.

Petition actions: In recent years people have increasingly taken unsolved problems involving individual rights and interests to the streets in order to reach a solution. Some unscrupulous politicians have taken advantage of this opportunity to instigate mass demonstrations to enhance their political prestige. War veterans have

149

demanded compensation for government-issued land deeds from the mainland (these were issued to soldiers accompanying the central government to Taiwan, to be redeemed after recovery of the Chinese mainland) and farmers have opposed the importation of US turkey meat. The government has been blamed for drops in stock prices, and demands have been made for new parliamentary elections.

These problems must be effectively resolved in order to maintain social order and national confidence, a sound investment climate, and continued economic growth.

Business environment: With vigorous industrial development, rapid changes in the economic structure, and the increasingly complicated face of international trade, a number of unethical practices have interfered with the normal functioning of the market mechanism. For example, artificially high prices have been fixed by monopolies, unfair business practices have been used to boycott competitors and illegal businesses have even been set up. How national corporations, large-scale enterprise, and underground economic activities can be satisfactorily regulated is without doubt one of the greatest problems in industry today, and one that urgently awaits an effective solution.

Insufficient Domestic Demand and Reinvestment

Lack of sufficient domestic demand and investment induces large surplus saving to buy stock and real estate, and an escalation of stock and real estate prices will widen the disparity of income distribution, reduce the willingness to work, and cause many other unfavourable social effects.[5]

Insufficient Investment in Services

With too much industrial development, insufficient investment in transportation, recreational, medical care and environmental protection facilities is inevitable.

The Scope of the Reforms

Facing this new environment, the government, as in the past, is presently considering various policies and measures to conquer these problems. Social and cultural development will be adhered to, in addition to the economic structural adjustment which has been the major role played by the government over the past 40 years.

ECONOMIC STRUCTURAL READJUSTMENT

Reducing the trade surplus

The government has adopted, or is considering a number of measures to correct the trade imbalance:

(1) The lowering of tariffs, increase of imports, reduction of other import barriers, relaxation of restrictions on purchasing zones, and simplification visa procedures;

(2) Market diversification to balance trade between each region, while at the same time consolidating existing markets by raising product equality, and opening new markets through loan financing, insurance, and competence training;

(3) The relaxation of restrictions on inland transportation, and the internationalisation of the service industry;

(4) Expansion of domestic demand and public investment, amelioration of the quality of life, enhancement of the investment environment.

Under the new regulations drafted by the Board of Foreign Trade (BOFT) of the Ministry of Economic Affairs, the government is actively developing trade with East European nations such as Poland, Hungary, Czechoslovakia, Yugoslavia, Bulgaria, and Romania.

In October 1988, the private Taiwan Imports and Exports Association organised Taiwan's first trade delegation to the Soviet Union to explore trade opportunities. Only indirect trade is allowed with the Soviet Union under current regulations.

A trade delegation visited Canada in 1990, and Canadian visas are now issued in Taiwan. 'Buy American' missions have been sent to the United States in an attempt to boost US imports and reduce the US trade deficit with Taiwan. Furthermore, the BOFT and the China External Trade and Development Council (CETRA) have set aside US$ 1.5 billion to establish a 'Taiwan Trade Center' in Tokyo to help reduce Taiwan's trade deficit with Japan.

Further readjustment of the economic structure includes:
- Increasing investment in public works to promote investment from the private sector in transportation, environmental protection, and other infrastructures;
- Privatisation of public enterprises;
- Renewal of the relevant Laws and Regulations.

Social Welfare Development

- Implementation of health insurance schemes for all people.
- Increasing budget for care for the elderly, the handicapped, and children.
- Increase construction and supply of public housing.
- Drafting the 'Overall Land Development Plan' to carry out balanced regional development.
- Increasing construction of means of transportation.

Joining International Societies and Implementing International Duties

Taiwan is currently in a period of transition. The various problems Taiwan is now facing are the same as those of other industrial countries. However, the development of western countries took place over a longer period, allowing more time to solve each problem as it occurred. Taiwan's development, on the other hand, has been so rapid that the problems have accumulated faster than they could be identified or resolved. This rapid development has also been a major factor in the problems of social disorder that the country must now deal with. It is the government's role to forge boldly ahead, to make the right decisions, and to get to the root of these problems. This, coupled with the full cooperation of the public, is the most direct route to establishing a law-abiding, reasonable and harmonious society.

V. CONCLUSION

During the last 40 years, Taiwan has been successfully transformed from an agriculturally-dominated economy to an industrially-dominated one, and is now undergoing transformation from labour-intensive to technologically-intensive industries. The process of transformation may be characterised as follows:

(1) With rapid economic development, the degree of transformation has been substantially reduced and will be substituted by liberalisation.
(2) The share of public enterprise has declined while that of private enterprise has increased correspondingly, and there is a strong trend towards privatisation.
(3) The share of heavy industry in manufacturing has tended to increase while that of light industry has decreased.

(4) The share of the service industry has increased very rapidly, and will replace the position of industry in dominating the economy during the 1990s.

(5) More outward investment and international cooperation in the domestic market will encourage the economy to step out and the government will play a different role in a stage of internationalisation.

All these characteristics imply that the government's role has changed along with the process of economic development. It appears that the best way to accelerate economic growth is to industrialise and expand foreign trade. For a country like the Republic of China in Taiwan, the government, in the early stages of economic development, usually plays a very important part, not only in maintaining a stable social and political environment, but also in guiding and assisting private enterprise to select and develop those industries with the greatest potential. However, with the continuous increase in the level of education and the rapid growth of the private sector, the government may no longer be the wisest master. The most important job of the government is now not to teach private enterprise how to make decisions but to create a favourable climate for investment for all enterprise. The new role of the government will no longer be that of a champion racer but a sponsor of the game, in charge of the game rules and the supervision of all the players.

NOTES

1. According to Liang and Lee's study [1975], the agricultural sector has capital outflow every year between 1950-69. The outflow included land taxes, land rent, interest, fees, and savings into non-agricultural sectors through the bank system. The capital flow was estimated at NT\$ 916,057,000 in 1950-55, NT\$ 1,346,036,000 in 1961-65, and NT\$ 2,078,932,000 in 1966-69.
2. The same study estimated that the agricultural sector labour out-migration was 48,752 persons in 1953, with the number increasing annually to 115,199 persons in 1970. The total estimate of out-migration has been 824,000 which is about 47 per cent of the total labour force in the non-agricultural sector.
3. Yu, T.S., 1988, *The Role of the Government in Industrialisation*, p.11.
4. Republic of China Yearbook, 1989, p.261.
5. Stock price index increased from less than 1,000 (1966=100) in 1986 to 5,000 in 1988, and soared to over 10,000 in September 1985. Real estate price index increased from 100 in 1986 to 141.57 in 1987, and continued increasing to 241,92 in 1988. *The Tenth Medium Term Economy Development Plan*, pp.35-6.

BIBLIOGRAPHY

Council for Economic Planning and Development (CEPD), 1989, *Tenth Medium-Term Economic Development Plan (1990-1993)*, Republic of China: CEPD, Executive Yuan.

Council for Economic Planning and Development (CEPD), 1989, *Economic Yearbook, 1988. The way to Economic Liberalisation.*

Economic Yearbook of the Republic of China, 1989, Taipei: Economic Daily News.

Galenson, W. (ed.), 1979, *Economic Growth and Structural Change in Taiwan*, Ithaca and London: Cornell University Press.

Kuo, Shirley W.Y. 1987, 'Economic Development in the Republic of China' in *The Conference on Economic Development in the Republic of China on Taiwan*, Taipei.

Li, K.T. and T.S. Yu (eds.), *1982, Experiences and Lessons of Economic Development in Taiwan*, Taipei: Academia Sinica.

Li, K.T. and M.T. Chen, 1989, *General Review of Economic Development Strategies in Taiwan, R.O.C.*, Taipei: United Economic Publishing Co.

Li, Y.T. and T.M. Wu, 1990, 'US Aid and the End of Taiwan's Big Inflation', Department of Economics, National Taiwan University.

Liang, K.S. and T.H. Lee, 1975, 'Taiwan: Economic Development', in Shinich, I. (ed.), *The Economic Development of East and Southeast Asia*, East-West Center Publishing for Kyoto Monograph Series, pp.269-346.

Liao, C.H., C.C. Huang and H.H. Hsiao (eds.), 1986, *The Development of Agricultural Policies in Post-War Taiwan: Historical and Sociological Perspectives*, Taipei: Institute of Ethnology, Academia Sinica.

Myers, R.H., 1986, 'The Economic Development of the Republic of China on Taiwan, 1965-1981', in L.J. Lau, (ed.), *Models of Development*, San Francisco: Institute for Contemporary Studies.

Tsiang, S.C., 1984, 'Taiwan's Economic Miracle: Lessons in Economic Development', in A.C. Harberger, (ed.), *World Economic Growth*, San Francisco: Institute for Contemporary Studies, pp.301-327.

Republic of China Yearbook 1989, Taipei, Kwang Hwa Publishing Co.

Yu, T.S., 1985, 'The Relationship Between the Government and the Private Sector in the Process of Economic Development in Taiwan, ROC', *Industry of Free China*, pp.1-16.

Yu, T.S., 1988, 'The Role of Government in Industrialisation', *in Conference on the Economic Development Experience of Taiwan and its New Role in an Emerging Asia-Pacific Area.*

11

Economic Reforms and Transformation of the Role of the State. The Case of Tunisia

SALEM MILADI

During the 1970s Tunisia experienced an economic growth averaging 7.5 per cent per annum, accompanied by an important change in its economic structure. This economic progress, which was largely realised due to a financial equilibrium created by the huge increases in petrol and phosphate prices from 1973, caused a diversification of production and reinforced private industrial enterprise which until then had been dominated by the public sector.

The state continued to play an important role in the economy through public enterprise, which was expanding rapidly. More than half of the economy's gross fixed capital formation at the end of the 1970s came from either the state budget or public enterprise.

However, the Tunisian economy did not maintain this elevated growth during the 1980s due to the unfavourable international economic climate and the limitations of a policy favouring import substitution. The drop in the price of petrol, made worse by a decrease in the amount exported, a deterioration in the exchange rate, unfavourable climatic conditions and a currency devaluation in countries offering similar goods to those of Tunisia on the inter-national market, all ultimately caused a budget deficit of 8.1 per cent in 1983 and an aggravated deficit in the balance of payments by 1984 of 10.8 per cent.

The policy of import substitution had, in fact, favoured production in a protected domestic market which had not encouraged industry to reduce its costs and become competitive. In order to encourage import substitution industries, import duties were created which protected domestic prices, whilst tax exemptions and subsidies reduced prices.

The result of these steps was a progressively deteriorating economic situation, which culminated in 1986 with a heavy overseas debt and complete exhaustion of foreign currency reserves, causing major difficulties in the functioning of the economy.

The crisis of 1986 was therefore the consequence of unfavourable conditions plus an economic system which did not obey the strictness of rationality and economic efficiency. In fact, the Tunisian economy has been shown to comprise a private sector supported through exaggerated protection and subsidies and a public sector whose problems can be summarised in five points:

(1) Too many personnel, combined with a low level of productivity and a rigidity in personnel statutes brings about a lack of flexibility in the mobility of workers plus an excessive number of available workers.
(2) Stocks of equipment due to an incomplete evaluation as to what should be invested and the problems of overproduction without thought to production costs or product quality.
(3) Tariffs, which in the majority of cases do not cover average costs due to the preservation of lower prices for the poorer members of society, and where the true price would cause inflation.
(4) Imperfect management practices and an administrative council which ratifies decisions already taken and which, due to a lack of time, is not able to follow medium and long-term policies of the enterprise.
(5) A debt which is becoming more and more important and an economic structure which favours debts in the short term, made worse by fluctuations in exchange rates.

The crisis is also the result of an income policy which has not taken into consideration the real capacity of the economy, bringing on increases in the level of consumption which are higher than those of the Gross Domestic Product (4.2 per cent per year as opposed to 2.9 per cent during the period 1982-86).

In order to overcome these relatively complex and interdependent problems, a programme of structural adjustment was adopted during the second half of 1986 and confirmed in the Seventh Economic and Social Development Plan for the period 1987 to 1991.

This programme is based on a gradual liberalisation of investment, imports and prices, and limits state intervention to strategic sectors. These reforms aim to improve the market and assure greater efficiency of production.

The liberalisation of investment comprises a suppression of prior agreements granted by the administration, leaving the responsibility of coming to a decision about the realisation of these projects to promoters and financial organisations.

The administration will only examine the acceptance of these projects keeping in mind possible advantages of investment, such investments being limited by priority sectors which favour exportation, regional development, mastery of new techniques and integration.

As for imports, the programme saw a liberalisation in 1991 of 25 per cent on all goods, the only exceptions being those in the category of 'luxury goods'.

A reduction in import duty will decrease the effective interior market protection, a move considered important as import duty in Tunisia is considered excessive. This decrease in protection is designed to reduce the internal market's attraction for producers, to favour a more optimum resource allocation and to improve competition and increase exports.

The liberalisation of prices should encourage competition and improve resource allocation. Both the prices of goods in competitive industries and imported products will be affected.

The final objective will be the liberalisation of nearly 75 per cent on prices of goods used in production and 55 per cent on distributed goods. On the other hand, essential goods - until now subsidised by the state budget - will continue to be controlled by the administration, but will undergo a gradual adjustment towards a more realistic price level in order to decrease both the subsidy level and budget spending.

A change in the type of public sector intervention occurred at the beginning of the 1980s with the creation of development banks that took over the role of direct intervention in productive sectors of the economy from the state. The public sector reformation programme not only aims at a total disengagement of the state in production investment but also the privatisation of competitive enterprises and a restructuration of public enterprise.

The public sector has played a dominant role in the economy. It is responsible for more than a quarter of the GDP and employs 10 per cent of the working population. More than a third of all investments is realised by the public sector and one third of the total amount of salary paid comes from this sector. In addition, the sector is responsible for more than three quarters of the exports and more than half of the imports.

However, public enterprise has created an important financial cost. In fact, during the Sixth Plan (1982-1986), these enterprises received around 1.5 billion dinars (1.6 billion US dollars) in subsidies and budget loans.

The final objective of this programme was to allow transition from an administered economy, where the state fixed credits, prices and exchange rates, to a market-oriented economy where the state intervenes only in strategic activities which are beyond the capacities of private enterprise.

State intervention should stimulate private initiative by assuring a clear and stable political and legislative state. In this context, privatisation must be considered as a reallocation of public participation in the evolution of the strategic character of different sectors.

What are, therefore, the economic, political and social consequences of this programme, and what are the difficulties in carrying it out?

Despite dry climatic conditions during a two-year period, which caused a drop in production, income and the level of seasonal employment in the agricultural sector and related industries, and an increase in the level of agricultural imports, the Tunisian economy has managed to reach an equilibrium with the exterior and achieve industrial growth and restructure of the public sector.

Furthermore, the balance of payments has markedly improved, with the current deficit limited to an average of 1.3 per cent of the Gross National Product during the past three years, as opposed to a level of 8.4 per cent in 1986. Currency reserves now cover the cost of imports for about two and a half months in contrast to just three weeks' cover in 1986. This improved equilibrium with the exterior is principally due to a huge increase in the volume of exports of goods and services (on average 14.7 per cent per year), especially in the textile, mechanic and electrics industries, and also in tourism.

These remarkable results in export activity are a direct consequence of the 1986 currency devaluation and the support of export-oriented industries.

At the same time, the exterior debt is now largely under control, with a decrease in the debt load from about 60 per cent of the GNP in 1986 to 56.8 per cent in 1989. There has also been an amelioration in its structure of long term loans (70 per cent of the total debt) and a relative reduction in the servicing of the debt.

The revival of the economic growth (an average of 3.8 per cent per year) has mainly been experienced in the manufacturing industries (6.6 per cent) and in the services (7.8 per cent), which has helped the growth of the export sector. On the other hand, agricultural growth has been zero, largely because of the past two unusually dry seasons.

The realisation of the public sector restructure programme has necessitated juridical reforms which have permitted a demarcation of protective intervention and have foreseen a reorganisation of the state portfolio. Moreover, the addition of a structure purely responsible for this programme has helped the operations of restructure and privatisation.

At present, there are 25 private enterprises in different competitive industries, of which 14 are in tourism and six in the industrial sector. Nineteen of these 25 enterprises are at an advanced stage of privatisation. The operation has been carried through by either a total or partial sale of the firm, by opening up opportunities for capital to private participants and by a suppression of certain state monopolies.

Programmes were elaborated for certain enterprises in order to help start their restructuration, rationalise their relations with the state and clearly define their objectives while at the same time ensuring management autonomy.

Although appreciable steps have been made in the privatisation programme, certain difficulties have been encountered, in particular concerning the small financial market and overstaffing in most enterprises, made worse by very high salaries compared to the private sector and a restricted schedule of conditions which guarantees employment and social rights.

In addition to these problems in the privatisation programme, there has been little result in the areas of investment, employment, public finance and inflation.

The level of investment, after a long period at low levels, only picked up again in 1989. The reduction in investment during 1986-1988 was mostly due to a decrease in interior demand, different reactions to the policies of reform and the cut-backs in public investment.

Whilst control of investment was one of the essential targets of the policy of adjustment, as much to reduce the deficit in the balance of payments as to improve the budget deficit, this control was stronger than desired and had negative effects on economic growth, incomes and employment.

The employment market has remained with a large imbalance between the offer and the demand for work, and consequently unemployment rates, at present about 15 per cent of the population of working age, is continuing to increase.

Public finance has experienced fairly strong pressure, with on the one hand a moderate increase in revenue following fiscal reform, and on the other hand an even larger increase in expenses due to measures taken to solve the problems caused by the dry climatic conditions.

These pressures originate from a budgetary deficit of about four per cent of the GDP, which is a fairly high level. In fact the two major constraints of the state budget are the reduction in income from petrol and the expenditure required for public enterprise and food subsidies.

Finally, the inflation rate is currently around eight per cent per year, which is quite high considering what was anticipated. This high rate is due to the devaluation of the dinar, the pressure exerted by export demand on the available internal offer, the expansion of the money supply and also the price liberalisation at the production level which effected 60 per cent of agricultural products and manufactured goods in 1989 compared to five per cent in 1986.

To these difficulties must be added a considerable resistance on the part of employers to the lifting of import restrictions on food items, who will require more time to adapt to the different measures of reform, and also an extreme caution exercised by the banks towards the liberalisation of interest rates, a move which has slowed down attempts to maintain deposit account interest rates at a low level.

Furthermore, the wish to control interior demand, especially private consumption, has very much affected salaries. During the past three years, Tunisia has experienced a regular decrease of about six per cent per year in the average real value of salaries. However, at present there is a desire to revive, in a moderate fashion, private consumption in order to stimulate investment, especially in interior demand.

The latest political plan has been to have regular consultations between social partners concerned in the policies of reform, for example between the employers and employees. Although this move has possibly slowed down the progress of reformation, it has, at any rate for the moment, helped maintain social peace and prevent any opposition which could have caused the adjustment policy to fail.

Tunisia must face new problems characterised by economic and political transformations which are occurring throughout the world, particularly in Eastern Europe. Other events which are having a bearing on these problems are the European Community of 1993, the technical revolution, the world economy and the exterior debt situation. In addition there are other problems that Tunisia must cope with, such as the rapid increase in demand for employment - estimated to be in the order of 100,000 per year by the year 2000 and an exhaustion of natural resources, particularly hydrocarbons.

In this context, enterprises must adapt to a different system to that which they are used to, and must create management structures favourable to a policy of development. The public sector, in turn, must disengage itself from activities which are found in the private sector, and concentrate on activities which will help boost the market. From being a producer, the state must start to play the role of someone who encourages and fixes the rules of play whilst respecting the other actors.

The conditions of growth and development therefore become conditioned by a more rational means of managing the competitive economy, by a new reorientation of the public sector and by a reinforced initiative in the private sector.

Such a transition necessitates a political and social pact between the political and economic forces and the unions in order that the actions of these social partners move, with the same goals, in the same direction.

12

Economic Reforms and Changes in the Role of the State in Sub-Saharan Africa: The Senegal Example

ABDEL KADER BOYE

I. INTRODUCTION

Economic Development Ideology during the 1960s: A Time of Established Facts

Most sub-Saharan African countries attained international sovereignty, during the 1960s, which was an era characterised by the emergency of development ideology. A certain number of established facts that soon became dogma were distinguished features in this ideology. For example, only the state could take charge of a country's economic development, and economic planning has to be the key instrument in creating successful state policies. Economic development could not only occur by completely destroying traditional structures and by ruthlessly fighting against archaic conceptions that had been steadfastly observed by traditional African societies.

With only a few rare exceptions, new state leaders faithfully adhered to this vision of their countries' future with unbridled optimism which the euphoria of independence had helped foster. In this way, the state took on all the roles in all spheres of society. In consequence, the state's role began to grow disproportionately, with the creation of state organisations, agricultural development agencies, public establishments and mass programmes of civil service recruitment. In particular, new corps were set up, such as the army, police force, embassies and institutions under regional cooperation.

The relative prosperity that came from cash crops (peanuts, cocoa, coffee beans, bananas, phosphates, iron, etc.), combined with a delay in the infrastructural and industrial spheres and with an almost complete absence of social strata for native entrepreneurs could justify the state role at this time. In an atmosphere of national pride that had been generated by granted or acquired political independence, state leaders thought that economic growth could be assured by them.

Nevertheless, the micro-state's narrow framework, the lack of a managerial elite and the formation of policies that fitted in with the logic of division of labour - figuring prominently in the international economic system - quickly brought a social structuring that had been under the state's control to the harsh realities of international competition. The terms of trade deteriorated. Moreover, a tragic drought and a human population rising exponentially in relation to the available resources, plus the oil crisis, all managed to expose weaknesses which until then had been hidden by international aid programmes and the easy access to international loans. Development ideology, whose followers had once naively believed it was possible to do without social science to carry out development programmes was being challenged.

A Dramatic Turning Point: The 1970s - A Period of Failure

The 1970s marked the end of illusions, when the failure of all development projects reached a crescendo rendering the states completely powerless. As Cl. Freud pointed out:

> The projects are taking the same shape that outside aid intervention programmes have always taken. The idea denotes financing, action and organisation all at once. The goals of these projects are to join these countries to the world economy, to raise farm production and to diversify the economy.

He asked the following question? 'What is a project?' and proceeded to answer it:

> In Europe, we are not familiar with this concept, as development has not been planned. It was first a vague idea that formed after agricultural development took place due to technological progress and growth in productivity. This process stretched over many centuries, which is not the case for the countries that concern us here. In sub-Saharan Africa, development has been voluntarily organised and programmes. It is all-encompassing and its purpose is to control all the technological, economic and special processes. In brief, it is tech-nocratic and comes into fruition only through planning. As it does not have a national base, it can only exist through outside financing. Its first requirement is to look for financing.[1]

Under these conditions, neatly arranging the so-called national economies within the relevant international economic framework could only spark off failures in the development strategies that had been implemented throughout sub-Saharan Africa, despite specialist or liberal political claims. As far as Senegal is concerned, the situation was made worse by the World Bank. In a confidential report World Bank Experts wrote that:

> Senegal is up against unusual obstacles during its development, even for a sub-Saharan African country. When they achieved independence, the people of Senegal inherited a relatively developed material and social infrastructure and a Gross Domestic Product that was then greater than that of the Ivory Coast or Cameroon. This legacy, however, would have been more appropriate to the country in its former role as a very prominent and privileged colony within French West Africa, rather than under the political, administrative and modest economic conditions as a nation which has three-quarters of its territory in the Sahel, and which is periodically subject to devastating droughts. In practice, Senegal has registered the weakest GDP growth rate of all African states (2.3 per cent) that have been spared of war or civilian conflicts. In its very essence, the Senegalese economy has not yet moved out of its dependency which began during the colonial period.[2]

The experts went on to point out that:

> During the 1970s, the government embarked on a number of costly programmes; the Fourth and Fifth Four-Year Development Plans from 1973/74 to 1976/77 and from 1977/78 to 1980/81. The aim of these programmes was to increase farming productivity, develop irrigation and expand the state sector rapidly in order to stimulate new industry and gain control over companies with foreign capital at the national level, and to create a group of highly qualified administrators.

And they note:

> Unfortunately, the impact of these costly endeavours has often been stymied by weaknesses in the institutions and in management, as well as by poor planning in many cases... An excessive portion of public investment has been allocated to public use, either to *preserve urban elite consumption patterns or to extend state control over the economy rather than create new production capacity, although the massive expansion of public and state sectors has no basis for comparison, even with the already existing management capacity* (Author's emphasis).[3]

Numerical results of this policy are as follows: between 1975 and 1980, the income deficit increased from 5.5 per cent to 16 per cent of the GDP. In 1980, the current deficit in the balance of payments rose to 19.3 per cent of the GDP. It decreased by 2.5 per cent but increase again by 2.4 per cent in 1981. National savings became negative between 1975 and 1980. In 1981 the current transactions account, deficit reached around 584 million US dollars, or 23.6 per cent of the GDP. Net situation in Senegal required an immediate structural reform policy.

The Period of Structural Adjustment Policies in the 1980s

Confronted by crisis in all sectors of society and with a lack of liquid assets, made worse by the need to service the debt, the sub-Saharan African states adopted structural adjustment policies which were imposed by their sponsors - mainly the IMF and BIRD. All the policies were the same: reduction of the balance of payments and budget deficits, re-balancing the balance of trade with a new export policy, removing consumer subsidies and liquidating deficit public enterprises, etc.

The first economic and financial reform was introduced, in Senegal, in 1979 through the middle course economic recovery plan (PREF). It was expected to last for a period of five years, with the aims of stabilising the economy, increasing investment in productive sectors, increasing public savings, freeing trade, revising policies in the state's role in the economy and modernising the state sector. The World Bank supported this policy with structural adjustment loans, and in August 1980 the IMF helped by expanding facility mechanisms.

Implementing this policy was the starting point for reducing the state's role in defining, carrying out and monitoring social and economic policies. In other words, the state was advised to operate in this way. The 1984 World Bank report (see above) made four observations:

> First of all, we must look for the roots of the current crises in the overly-ambitious policies (in terms of financial resources and institutional capacity) of the 1970s, and in particular the increased role of the public sector. The crisis was then accentuated by a combination of factors: drought, deterioration in terms of trade, rises in oil prices, a drop in the price of peanuts and an increase in interest rates during the period 1979/81. Secondly, this crisis has been made worse by the fact that we let it go on and did not find a solution quickly. We obviously should have adjusted spending in 1981 rather than wait until 1983 to act on it. Thirdly, it is clear that we cannot keep on ignoring the problems in Senegal; they must be tackled now. Fourthly, the actual situation forces us to admit that not only the choice in political and other types of reform is limited to a narrow field by all sorts of domestic and outside factors, but also that there is no easy or fast solution to what all those concerned now regard as being a profound and persistent development crisis (p.14).

At the end of this diagnosis, World Bank experts drew up policy guidelines for the state to implement, which insisted that the state stay out of certain economic or social sectors so that elements of private enterprise could fulfil the creed of 'less state', which was set up for the sake of efficiency. This led to the state's degeneration that took the shape of the 'best of the state'.

II. THE CREED OF 'LESS STATE' OR THE TIME OF THE STATE'S WITHDRAWAL

The creed of 'less state' comes from the current Liberal economic doctrine which considers state intervention in the sphere of economics, both in southern countries as well as in northern ones, as one of the factors hindering the development of a market economy and economic growth. The basic principle which is taken as the truth is that only free enterprise can assure both economic development and well-being among populations. This principle won support after substandard economic performance in Communist and Socialist system and systems of a socialist nature, and also after crises in capitalist economies.

It is the basis of the reforms that have been proposed or imposed by international financial institutions (IMF and BIRD) on developing countries that have been stifled by unsolved debt problems, and is concretely manifested in the state's economic and social dis-engagement. The situation seems universal, but neither the modes of implementation nor the end results are the same for an under-developed state or a developed state.

In fact, the harsh and dramatic nature of the situation for an under-developed country calls for an analysis that focuses on this last factor because it enables us to not only understand and assess the impact of the reforms that have been undertaken, but also to grasp the dynamics in the international scale of the market economy. In order to do this, we will use the example of Senegal, with the understanding that, all other things being equal, the trends are similar in all countries south of the Sahara (and even beyond). To do this, a series of reforms aiming to reduce the state's role has been set up in the agricultural, industrial and tertiary (public and state) sectors.

Agricultural Reform and Disengagement of the State

Agricultural reform aims at instituting a New Agricultural Policy according to official terminology. A publication from the Ministry of Rural Development entitled 'New Agricultural Policy' states that this new policy:

would involve... creating the conditions to stimulate production in a context that would enable the rural population to participate effectively and would generate their responsibility at every step of the development process and consequently reduce state intervention to a role of a catalyst or impetus.[4]

These two objectives should change the farming sector through bodies of a public or semi-public nature, and diversify farming production with a heavy emphasis on cereal products. The way in which this has been conceived seems very interesting. It has not in any way involved an immediate liquidation of the Rural Development Agencies (ADR), according to World Bank terms, who pushed for this, but rather a restructuration.

In fact, restructuring aims at re-measuring certain ADRs by reducing their missions and personnel, such as at SODEVA. Liquidation has principally applied to those ADRs whose missions have been judged as no longer having any appropriate purpose, such as the Société des Terres Neuves (STN). Programming this whole set of institutional reforms in the rural sector has been delayed for five years (since 1985/86).

Obviously this is a very brief and general idea about the new agricultural policy, and only highlights the institutional reforms that allow the measurement of the extent to which the state has intervened in the rural sector. In this respect one can conclude that states in a disastrous financial situations have made significant steps backwards, but without relinquishing certain missions that were deemed fundamental such as having a command over marketing and instituting a credit support system (Caisse de Crédit National Agricole). Compared to the past situation, this has been a major turning point both for the state and for the farmers who have had to face certain constraints that they were not prepared for, causing deep unrest in the rural areas.

Industrial Reform and Disengagement of the State

As far as the official New Industrial Policy is concerned, the state, under pressure from the World Bank during the past four years, has implemented a reform whose aim was to put industrial enterprises into conditions of international competition. This has called for two measures:

(1) Eliminating legal protection tactics for these enterprises against unbearable competition from more successful foreign firms;
(2) privatising public or semi-public firms.

The plan sketched out for this is to introduce the industrial sector into the international market economy. The 1984 World Bank report casts no doubt about this perspective. In fact, it says that:

> The government's main priority is to create conditions that will allow growth and employment to increase in the industrial sector. This will only be possible on a consistent basis if the firms are efficient and eventually competitive... A more promising approach would involve progressively exposing domestic firms to increasing competition through tariff and quota adjustments, but also liberalising labour legislation to assure producers of price and wage flexibility they need in order to be competitive. Reducing the great number of interventions which were formed to protect large firms will create, in the long run, more possibilities for small and medium-size firms, and will certainly stimulate their development more than will the institutions that have been specially set up to promote light industries, as they have a surplus of personnel, but insufficient funds.[5]

Since state intervention in the industrial sector have been greatly reduced (minimal participation in certain firms through public or semi-public banks) if not completely eliminated, the state's actions have affected private firms. Compliance by these firms with an agreement in the form of a memorandum between the state and the World Bank called SAC II[6] entails the following:

(1) revising the effective protection which firms have been enjoying (i.e. removing previous authorisation for imported products and actual import quotas, and reducing import duties);
(2) supporting exports and broadening the taxation system;
(3) adjusting constraints lying heavily on the firms (stabilising administrative procedures, removing the employment monopoly through the work force service, alleviating rules protecting workers by reforming the labour code now that the possibilities for concluding contracts of an indeterminate length of time have been reduced, etc).

It was not long before the practical effect of applying this New Industrial Policy were felt. For example, a large number of firms unable to withstand industrial competition had to close down, and job loss was considerable. According to official autonomous unions, out of the 40,000 jobs that comprised the industrial sector, there 25,000 jobs were lost as opposed to only 5,000 created thus a job loss of 50 per cent. It can therefore be said that the state no longer plays a regulating role in the industrial sector.

Reform in the Public and Para-Public Sectors

This reform principally affects public and para-public enterprises that mainly intervene in the service industry. The prime incentive behind this reform is to stabilise public financing whilst allowing the state to save substantial amounts of money that until now have been earmarked as money endowments or subsidies for these businesses. Sponsors thus hope that the state will be in a better position to face up to paying off its foreign and domestic debts. As well as declaring a rationalisation of this sector, it also involved closing down a certain number of public or semi-public enterprises in different areas (hotel business, banking, audio-visual business, tourism, distributors, etc), through privatisation. The preamble of the August 1987 Law No. 87-23 concerning privatisation businesses states the goals in offering part of the state's domain for sale and the guidelines for privatisation. Without going into detail, it must be pointed out that privatisation may concern all or part of the state's interest in the enterprises, and that transferring is done through offers. But practice shows otherwise.

In this way, the 26 enterprises initially allowed for increased to more than 40, and certain cases of sales by mutual agreement were developed from the offers procedure. This led to management leasing practices. All this stretching of established rules came from the difficulties the state encountered while trying to find buyers.

According to information currently available, only three businesses were able to be sold to private enterprises: S.P.T., Berliet-Senegal and SENOTEL. Yet, although the state has had its setbacks in privatisation, it is already a well-known fact that it has either partially or totally given up its orienting or regulating role in economic and social policy. The results of this in an environment of deep economic, financial and social crisis are very difficult to assess in the long term. The policy of privatisation could be justified if there was a group of businessmen in a country who could come to the state's aid and if the banking system worked well, which is far from being the case. Strangely, if not logically enough, the policy makers, and outside foreign authorities who have inspired them, thought they had found the creed of the 'best of the state', as a solution to many of the state's problems.

III. THE CREED OF THE 'BEST OF THE STATE' OR THE PERIOD OF REDUCING STATE STRUCTURES

The 'best of the state' creed is the result of the 'less state' creed. Moreover, they have been condensed into one expression, 'Less state, Best of the state', crystalised by modern liberal ideology. But if the 'Best of the state' creed, which liberalist followers of all angles treat in generally the same way, means rationalising in order to make the structures in the state apparatus more efficient in developed countries, it does not seem to have had the same impact in Third World countries. In fact, in these countries it means above all reducing structures in the state apparatus and reducing the number of state officials that go along with it. By taking both of these preliminary steps, we hope we can sort out the problem with efficiency in the state's management of society's problems. Yet beyond this comforting and technical chatter loom more mundane worries which involve no less than alleviating the expenses of public financing.

Reducing Structures in the State's Apparatus

In a widespread crisis situation where the state and its sponsors are mostly worried about the chronic budget and public financing deficit, reducing structures in the central administration seems to be a healthy step forward. The carefully concealed goal of this operation is to allow the state to save up enough resources, and not to rechannel all of them into the productive sector, but to face paying the debt. It is no secret to anyone that increasing and reducing the structures in he state's apparatus had led to an imbalance in public financing in Black Africa.

For this reason the World Bank, in applying this method, has asked all the African countries involved in structural adjustment programmes to reduce structures in their state's apparatus. The Bank has even made this a condition for support in adjustment policies, and thus Senegal has recently removed six ministries and a large number of departments and sections, even if this has not been completely justified. However, it is interesting to note that if certain national departments or sections have been joined to other ministries, many others are disappearing, which means that the state's role in certain economic and social sectors of the country has deeply changed. This change has mainly affected traditional trade sectors (directing price controls, domestic and foreign trade, etc), and social sectors. In other African countries the same phenomenon has been noticed. In fact, removing certain structures in the state's apparatus has resulted in reducing the number of state officers.

Reducing the Number of State Officers

Drastically reducing the number of state employees is an integral part of the plan of action in structural adjustment policies. It worked to lower the number of officers working for public enterprises that have been sold or restructured. The purpose of the official operation is to have a less overcrowded and more efficient administration. It is, however, more correct to say that this operation aims mostly at decreasing the state's financial burden.

The method which has been chosen for Senegal to start reducing the number of state officers is quite original. It involves encouraging people to leave their jobs on a voluntary basis according to the system set out in the December 1989 law. Military personnel, teachers, public health personnel and state workers whose status have been established by a particular law are the only ones who are not encouraged to leave their jobs. For other state workers, the idea behind these measures is for the employee concerned to either agree to retire early (the minimum age required by law is 48) for which he is awarded an early retirement bonus, or to resign (the employee must be aged under 48) for which he is awarded a so-called termination bonus.

Yet, however original and encouraging this chosen method may be, it appears that up to now, there have been only 12 requests from people to leave their jobs, which is considerably below the undeclared goal of weeding out 10,000 officers from the Public Service. This has led may observers to say that the state will have to resort to a disguised method of forcing people to leave their jobs.

Reducing structures in the state's apparatus has already left on the sidelines a considerable number of state employees whose future still remains to be decided. Nevertheless, it is interesting to note the categories of officers who are not legally being encouraged to leave their jobs on a voluntary basis. In so doing, it is possible to draw some lessons for the time being on the trends in the state's role. In fact, if the armed forces, teachers and public health employees are spared by law, it can be concluded that the state will confine its role more or less to the social sectors. However, all this does not mean that the state will significantly increase the budget share for these sectors.

The results of this set of policies are beginning to be felt and are giving rise to social tensions that are difficult to repress, such as a rising informal sector and the number of unemployed, a rural community that is becoming increasingly more impoverished, an economy that is falling apart and educational and health systems that are in dire straits. In short, the state has become more a police state than a state fuelled by economic and social development. This has been seen not only in Senegal, but also in all sub-Saharan African countries.

NOTES

1. Freud, Cl., 'Projets de coopération ou aide aux politiques de développement', in CFACE, 1985, *Paysans, experts et chercheurs en Afrique noire*, Kartala: Sciences Sociales et développement rural, ouvrage collectif, p.201
2. World Bank, *Senegal - Economic Memorandum*, 5 November 1989, p.2
3. *Ibid.*, p.4
4. Dakar, March-April 1984, M.D.R. p.26
5. World Bank, op. cit., p.98
6. A confidential report dated 23 September 1985

PART IV

CHALLENGES FOR RESEARCH AND EDUCATION IN SOCIAL SCIENCES

13

Considerations on the Role of the State in Development Processes in the Light of the OECD Development Centre Research on the Changing Balance between Public and Private Sectors

JEAN BONVIN

I. INTRODUCTION

Whether it be in industrialised, developing or Eastern European countries, policies for altering the balance between the public and private sectors involve redefining relations between the state and the development process. The respective importance of the public and private sectors is not itself a new issue, however. If we look at the economic history of the past 40 years, we can see that two major tendencies have deeply influenced attitudes towards the role of the state and the private sector in the growth and socioeconomic development processes:

(1) on the one hand, the emergence of an interventionist state;
(2) on the other, state disinvolvement in favour of a liberal market system.

In the case of industrialised countries, the former tendency predominated from the end of the World War II until the early 1980s, whereas in the developing countries, it began with independence but also lasted until the beginning of the 1980s. Over this period, the state's role in most cases expanded greatly in terms of direct or indirect intervention: increased government spending, nationalisation, regulation, etc. The trend was even more marked in developing nations as, following independence, everything had to be built or rebuilt. In fact, the state simultaneously became builder, investor, regulator and provider of welfare.

This idea of state pre-eminence was thrown into doubt by both the economic crisis of the late 1970s and the inability of governments to

177

redirect domestic economies back onto the path of growth and development. The second tendency, characterised by state disinvolvement, was tacitly encouraged in developing countries by international organisations charged with the difficult task of correcting trade, monetary and fiscal disequilibria. The implementation of stabilisation and structural adjustment programmes (policies for liberalising the economic environment, and for privatisation) rests on a radically different interpretation of the respective roles of the public and private sectors.

The transfer of responsibility to the private sector signifies something of a victory for microeconomic theories of the allocationary efficiency of the market and the productive efficiency of private management. This change has brought about a reshaping of development strategies and has transformed society, especially in some developing countries. A similar change is now overtaking Eastern European countries.

II. LESSONS FROM THE EXPERIENCE
OF THE DEVELOPING COUNTRIES

The work of the Development Centre has been influenced by these trends. In 1987, research was undertaken on the changing balance between the public and private sectors in the developing countries. It focused on a sample of ten countries: three in Africa (Ghana, Morocco and Tunisia); two in Latin America (Bolivia and Chile); two in Central America (Jamaica and Mexico); and three in Asia (Bangladesh, Malaysia and the Philippines). The research had a double objective:

(1) To evaluate rebalancing policies in the developing countries; and
(2) To formulate reform proposals aimed at achieving more efficient use of domestic and foreign resources.

It may be said that the financial resources of most developing countries are not only limited but inadequate for their future needs. This imbalance, accentuated by indebtedness, is a growing problem which, now more than ever, dictates a better utilisation of resources.

A rebalancing policy, providing for a gradual disinvolvement of the state and a restructuring of the public sector, seeks to achieve two goals: stabilisation and adjustment.

Stabilisation aims at reducing budget deficits by acting on revenues (revenue from sales, increased tax revenues resulting from the healthier financial situation of enterprises, either through tax on profits or transfers) and on expenditure (reducing operating losses), while adjustment seeks to improve allocationary efficiency - by inflecting prices in order to obtain an optimum allocation of resources - and productive efficiency; that is, streamlining costs.

To attain these two goals, rebalancing employs three policies: restructuring, privatisation and liberalisation. However, rebalancing cannot be restricted to any one of these policies, for while their methods may vary, all three are closely linked in terms of their practical application:

(1) In the case of restructuring, the state redirects and modernises government action, while retaining control of capital and management.

(2) Ambitious programmes of privatisation have been launched by nearly all developing countries. A distinction should be made between the transfer of property, involving government enterprise capital, and the transfer of management which only affects the enterprise's decision-making structure. The choice of option depends on the nature of each programme of privatisation, such as how attractive the enterprise is, its strategic importance, etc.

(3) In the case of liberalisation, the essential purpose is to reduce economic distortion and enhance the role of competition. The main policy instruments are lowering tariff barriers, reducing government subsidies and opening up government monopolies to competition. It should be noted that liberalisation only exerts its full effects in terms of economic efficiency if it is preceded by or associated with privatisation.

Redefining the roles of the public and private sectors in the developing countries is more than a matter of simply transposing models derived from the industrialised countries. It has to take into account the history and level of development of each country. The extent to which the public sector's role may be reduced is limited by three main factors:

(1) Some activities, such as community utilities and services which do not fit into the market system, are the natural province of the public sector.

(2) Decreasing the role of the public sector assumes that the factors which led the state to supplant private enterprise no longer exist. This is not always the case. Examples include:

* 'infant industries', unable to withstand international competition without state protection and support for training, research and development and marketing;
* monopolies controlled by private interests (domestic or foreign) to the detriment of the consumer;
* heavy investment and low returns in certain branches of industry and services;
* shortage of able, dynamic and innovative entrepreneurs;
* inadequate private financial channels for directing domestic savings into productive investment.

(3) An embryonic national banking system, narrow or nonexistent financial markets, reduced capital inflows due to the newly-found caution of international banks, stagnant multilateral flows, debt servicing requirements and, in some areas, a non-monetised economy or a return to a barter economy are all factors that tend to slow the development of private enterprise. Private sector growth is an essential condition for successful rebalancing in general, and privatisation in particular.

To what extent can the experience of developing countries with stabilisation and privatisation policies be applied to Eastern European countries? This question is of special importance at a time when countries such as Poland, Hungary and Czechoslovakia are adopting stabilisation and adjustment policies which are not so very different to the ones implemented in the developing countries.

Three main lessons applicable to Eastern European countries may be drawn from the experience of developing countries:

(1) First, it should be recalled that the underdeveloped condition of Third World financial markets and the small number of private domestic buyers place obvious limits on any ambitious programme of privatisation. These two constraints will probably appear to an even greater extent in Eastern European countries.

(2) Second, it must be stressed that economic stabilisation is a necessary prerequisite for structural reform. A difficult macro-economic situation tends to dampen the interest of foreign investors when public enterprises are being offered for sale. This has particular relevance for the Eastern European countries, as they hope to attract Western technology and capital in order to modernise their economic structure.

(3) The third lesson concerns the way structural reforms are sequenced. Probably the best solution is to implement privatisation and liberalisation policies simultaneously. However,

resistance from the heads of public enterprises should not be underrated, as they play a vital role in the success of liberalisation programmes. In fact, where the Eastern European countries are concerned, the attitude of the managers of public undertakings is crucial, in that the public sector generally accounts for over 80 per cent of the economy. Liberalisation policies so far attempted in Eastern European countries, particularly in Hungary, have been frustrated by the omnipresence of public enterprise and central planning. Therefore, it may well be that partial privatisation of the public sector must precede any lasting adaptation of managerial attitudes to the new rules of a market economy.

Altering the public/private sector balance in Eastern European countries is going to take time, and is a question of economic and political realism. Realism does not mean a wait-and-see attitude, nor does it mean opportunism. The major challenge facing the Eastern European countries during the economic transition of the 1990s will be to turn the clock back on forty years of state ownership and invigorate the private sector.

In developing and Eastern European countries alike, these changes and the questions they raise concerning the role of the government in economic development call for a revision of both education and training syllabuses and research programmes.

III. EDUCATION AND TRAINING PROGRAMMES

The change in the relationship between the state and the development process will give rise to new challenges in education and training.

For one thing, state disinvolvement will inevitably contract the job market, reducing employment in government service and public enterprise. At the same time, the reduction in the number of jobs will be matched by new skill requirements. For example, in Ghana, Jamaica and Malaysia, restructuring and privatisation programmes have highlighted the shortage of domestic expertise in the spheres of law, accountancy and finance. For this reason, future schools and universities must train a new breed of administrators capable of ensuring better management of public enterprises, and of government funds in general.

Meanwhile, the private sector will become the main source of jobs for young people leaving school or university. If they are to have a good chance of obtaining work, they must acquire training and technical skills that match the career requirements of the private sector. The specialities most in demand will be, on the one hand, those connected with business, marketing and financial management and, on the other, technical occupations aimed at enhancing the quality of the goods turned out by increasingly productive industries. As in the past, teaching syllabuses must be continually revised according to private sector job market trends and skill requirements.

As regards the working population, retraining and on-the-job training must be undertaken for two groups:

(1) public sector workers made redundant or opting to work in the private sector;
(2) private sector workers, to accustom them to the new situation and the new role of private firms in the economy and society.

From now on, when managers for private and public undertakings are trained, attention must be given to the emergence of a global economy in an interdependent world and the development of new centres of growth. Now that protectionism seems to be on the wane and new information and communications technologies are being developed, leaders, managers, technical and financial staff must be made aware of the strategies used by rival firms all over the world.

In relation to globalisation and regionalisation on the research side, two subjects are already worth exploring:

(1) the interaction between government policy and the strategies of the private sector (which is leading globalisation);
(2) the long-term impact of the homogenisation (a consequence of globalisation) of production methods, products, consumer tastes and, more especially, the cultural homogenisation engendered by new information and communications technologies.

There are many questions which might be raised to widen the discussion. Here are four that are particularly vital in regard to both research and education.

First: In social science research, Marxist theory now seems increasingly irrelevant to the problems of economic transition and liberalisation. How could a portion of social science research be 'de-Marxified' and all researchers be involved in a broad-ranging study of what happens in changing societies (developing countries, those which formerly had centrally planned economies)? This is a major issue for Eastern Europe, Latin America and Africa.

Second: Economic globalisation means that development prospects are less a matter of national development with a strong public sector and more one of international development with a strong private sector. Globalisation, based on increased internationalism, carries with it a whole series of technical, social, economic and cultural inter-actions. Is social science research equipped to identify and understand all these interactions and the issues underlying them?

Third: Relations between state and religious authority are having an increasingly important bearing on education. This is the case particularly, but not solely, in Muslim societies. The question is this: How will education and social science research react to the growing importance of religious considerations in certain developing countries? In some North African countries, when a mathematics teacher defines two parallel straight lines, he says that the two lines will never meet, but adds 'God willing'. How can fundamentalist opinions be reconciled, in certain Islamic countries, with the development of Western-style secondary and higher education?

Fourth: How should the state's new role in the redistribution of wealth be defined? Over the past few decades, the state has played a dominant role in wealth redistribution through public enterprise, government spending and social security. state disinvolvement would curtail its traditional ability to intervene. The resulting vacuum must be filled if social maladjustments are to be avoided.

The redistributive function, which is a vital element in the construction of solid and viable social structures, must on no account be neglected by either the authors of economic modernisation and adjustment programmes or university researchers, whose duty it will be to remind people that lasting economic development is impossible without social progress.

Finally, the period in which we live - even without the upheavals in Eastern Europe - is one of transition for mankind and a turning-point in history. Today, the old strategically bipolar and economically monopolar world is giving way to a multipolar globe with a complex power structure. Such swift change raises any number of problems, of which two may be stressed:

(1) the intelligibility crisis, a cause of perplexity to the elite in every society;
(2) the economic and political organisation of the world prevents globalisation being of equal benefit to different countries.

Is it not high time to revitalise existing world institutions, or to create new ones, in order to ensure at least some degree of consistency in the way the world's affairs - economic, political and social - are handled?

BIBLIOGRAPHY

Akuoko-Frimpong, H., 1990, 'Rebalancing the Public and Private Sectors in Developing Countries: The Case of Ghana', *Development Centre Technical Papers*, No.14.

Bouin, Olivier and Charles-Albert Michalet, 1991, *Rebalancing the Public and Private Sectors in Developing Countries*, Paris: Development Centre Studies, OECD.

Leeds, Roger S., 1989, 'Rebalancing the Public and Private Sectors: The Case of Malaysia', *Development Centre Technical Papers*, No.5.

Michalet, Charles-Albert, 1989, 'Rebalancing the Public and Private Sectors: The Case of Mexico', *Development Centre Technical Papers*, No.4.

14

State and Development into the 1990s: The Issues for Researchers

EMANUEL DE KADT, with ZOE MARS and GORDON WHITE

I. INTRODUCTION: THE STATE IN DEVELOPMENT

Social scientists interpret reality by reference to analytical and theoretical constructions. We do not **see** how the world changes, how resources shift between countries, regions or participants in the productive process, or even how institutions adjust. However, we have to try and understand what is happening around us, to analyse it and to *interpret* it. During times of relative stability our ingenuity is not greatly taxed and we get by using established routines to help our interpretation. But when change accelerates, new approaches are required. New research then needs to answer new sets of questions.

In due course, such new approaches - new questions and new methodologies - have to be passed on to the next generation of researchers. This is when teaching programmes are adjusted. In this chapter we shall concentrate on the issues for research that appear to be emerging as we perceive changes in the role of the state at the start of the 1990s.

In order to make sense of our topic, it is necessary to look briefly at what has been happening in development studies. Most of the work in this area over the past 30 or 40 years has focused on the 'development problems' of 'developing countries'. It has been strongly policy-oriented, asking questions on the one hand about appropriate interventions to create sustainable economic growth and social development, and on the other about structures and processes that have contributed to keeping the majority of the people in most African, Asian or Latin American countries in relative or absolute poverty.

This work has been sustained by a complex network of institutions; from those which handle the resource flows between developed and developing countries, for example the World Bank and bilateral donor ministries, to other kinds of multilateral agencies, NGOs, and specialised research institutes and centres such as those that make up the membership of EADI. In short, development studies is concerned with the special problems of poor countries and with the relationships between North and South; in terms of our particular topic, it examines the special characteristics of the state and its activities in the countries of the Third World.

However, a different view of development studies is emerging to stand side by side with the more conventional approach. It is partly a response to the increasingly visible effects of the differentiation which has occurred over the past decade or so among the countries in the 'South'. One can no longer reasonably speak of the Third World (if one ever could). Between the developed countries of the 'North' and the least developed countries of sub-Saharan Africa there are not only the first generation of NICs (notably the 'Little Tigers' of East Asia and large countries such as Brazil and Mexico), but further layers of countries at different levels of development (with regard to industrialisation, export performance, administrative effectiveness, education and health status and service provision in these areas, etc.). Countries at the same general level of development, even if in different continents, are likely to share certain problems. With respect to the role and structures of the state, the issues for research confronting colleagues in the different regions are increasingly heterogeneous.

This emerging view of our field of study has been given a further impetus by two sets of developments. The first is the acceleration of the pace of recent *political* change in the Soviet Union and the countries of Eastern Europe. The second is the longer term and slower processes of *economic* reform or 'adjustment' in that part of the world, as well as in many African and Asian countries that had defined themselves as 'socialist' (today Romania might be called a NIC, and Czechoslovakia is a relatively advanced economy - neither are sensibly defined as part of the 'Second' World). Together with quite different developments in the 'advanced' section of the world economy - the intensification of regional economic formations in the Pacific, Europe and the Americas - these changes have increasingly drawn attention to 'global processes', understood both as processes that operate at the global level, and as processes that operate globally, i.e. 'everywhere'.

As a result, there are researchers who play down the extent to which development studies can or should be isolated from the study of these broader social processes - a point already made during the 1970s and 1980s, notably by Dudley Seers, the instigator of ICCDA [*Seers 1978*].

Even if we accept that view, conventional development studies continue to have a special contribution to make to the wider issues.

This arises from the considerable and detailed understanding of important aspects of the reality of countries at different levels of poverty, and of their relations both with the 'North' (the richest part of the world) and between themselves. Yet the boundaries of development studies have become more blurred. Greater attention is now being paid to the global changes that are affecting the world as a whole, above all in technology and industrial organisation, in patterns of trade, in financial power and financial flows. To understand these changes it is increasingly necessary to understand what is happening in the countries of the 'North', and to their politics and their states. In parallel, more attention should also be paid to the lessons from development studies that appear relevant to the more developed countries. If the study of structural adjustment in Africa has taught us certain lessons about the way state institutions adjust (or do not adjust!) to policy changes in situations that require a major transform-ation, then those lessons may well be of relevance to what is occurring in Eastern Europe today, and vice versa.

The emergence of this second approach, side by side with conventional development studies, may well be beneficial in various ways. Firstly, it narrows the gap between 'development studies' as practised in Europe and in the countries of the four other regions. After all, people study their own society and economy, which in the North is the study of economics, sociology and political science. Secondly, as - hopefully - more countries escape from the special constraints of the very poor and as more countries become NICs to varying degrees, the field of conventional development studies will shrink, as will the areas thought appropriate for 'development assistance'. The experience gained in decades of work on 'develop-ment' might then be lost, unless it can be integrated more closely with the broader study of change and transformation. One might even argue that development cooperation agencies should begin to prepare for a different role, lest they (and their particular experience and political support) simply wither away as well. The increasing interest of aid agencies in Eastern Europe may not arise from this kind of broad perspective (it is more the result of a political decision to give priority to resource transfers to Eastern Europe), but the experience gained can feed into a longer-term analytical reorientation.

II. TRENDS IN THE ROLE OF THE STATE, AND THEIR EFFECTS

Looking back at recent history, a number of distinct periods can be identified both in terms of the actual role of the state, and of the way in which different analysts have approached the issue.

First, a hesitant process of internationalisation (in production, exchange and finance) has been taking place since early this century. Second, there has been the issue of the relative roles of state and market in the economy. For about 25 years after World War II the role of the state was emphasised in development doctrines, as well as in the reality of institutional development (the 'developmental state'). Since the late 1970s, however, a reaction has set in, both doctrinally (neo-liberalism) and in the actual policies when the importance of the state was de-emphasised compared to that of the market [*Toye 1987*]. We may now be entering yet another phase where the pendulum is swinging back to some extent.

Third, a period of increasing authoritarianism in Latin America, Asia and Africa, starting in the mid-1960s, has been followed by a noticeable easing of the use of the more repressive instruments of state power. From the second half of the 1980s, 'democratisation' has been gathering pace, especially in Latin America and Asia, and in the countries of Eastern Europe [*Lehmann 1990*].

Such changes have produced counterpart effects in other parts of society, as the state has either expanded into and modified existing institutions, or withdrawn from areas of activity. Some of these effects, even if apparently destructive in the short term, have been historically progressive. Also, the new disposition of social forces has often meant that the state has subsequently taken on new functions, so that a new balance has been achieved.

These major changes, which have occurred over the past 50 years or so, have set the context for the problems - and hence the research needs - for the 1990s.

Internationalisation

Here, a number of separate and partly contradictory processes appear to have been at work.

Firstly, there has been the increasing globalisation of the international economy, visible both in long-studied processes of transnationalisation in production (although a number of counter-trends are now visible in the 'international division of labour' changes observed in the 1970s and 1980s), and in the more recent internationalisation of the financial system [*Chen 1983 and Weiss 1990*].

The incorporation of Eastern Europe into the international market economy (helped along by the dramatic decline of East-West tension and confrontation, itself with major implications for the rest of the world) is likely to further strengthen these processes, which have been accelerating under the impact of the rapid introduction of new technologies, especially in the field of communications. Not surprisingly, these processes have manifested themselves beyond production and into the areas of culture (taste, fashion, consumerism) and communications [*IUED 1977; 1983*]. For example, consider the role of television in the Eastern European events of late 1989, as well as in Beijing half a year earlier.

Such developments have important implications for the capacity of national states to limit the extent to which external actors can influence internal political processes; an issue which will become even more significant with the further development of satellite television. It is not clear whether the influence of the metropolitan powers will have a greater effect on the poorer and weaker, or on the more advanced and stronger countries. Although one might expect the weaker countries to be more affected at first, with less autonomous capacity to resist such penetration, yet in the NICs, and emergent NICs, greater numbers of people will have the consumer power to 'latch on' to the latest offerings of metropolitan communication technology, and hence be targets for metropolitan influence.

The outcome of these processes of change might be two-fold. The result could be another form of 'dependent development', with the state losing most of its initiative on development questions (cf. sub-Saharan Africa today). It could also lead to various kinds of nationalist, or even fundamentalist, reactions (cf. Iran). Both could happen simultaneously, creating a basic contradiction for the state. As representative of the 'nation' in a cultural sense, or of the 'national interest' in the economy, it could be sandwiched between accelerating internal pressures on the one side, and a declining capacity to act on the other. This is a fertile area for research.

Secondly, there has been a trend towards the regionalisation of the international economy. The EEC is the clearest example of this process, but one can also see beginnings in East Asia and the Pacific Rim. So far, Africa has remained a by-stander in this type of development, although it is possible that a new regional grouping might emerge in Southern Africa, led by a post-apartheid South Africa. With the notable exception of the EEC, this increased integration at the material level has not been accompanied by growing institutional integration at the regional or global levels. As various failed, or partially failed, efforts at common markets or free trade areas outside Europe have demonstrated, there has not really been an internationalisation of the state (even in its purely economic functions) to parallel the internationalisation of the system of production.

This is also significant from the perspective of future research on the role of the state. The state has always played an important role in the creation, strengthening or control of internal markets, not least when it withdrew from active intervention. Questions need to be asked about comparable processes at the international or regional level: how can international markets develop and operate, and in the absence of institutions, be able to fulfil functions parallel to those of the state on a national basis? In addition, what can be learned from the problems of international organisations, such as the IMF, who have regulatory functions?

Changes in the Relations Between the State and the Market

By the end of the 1970s the international ideological and political environment within which governments in the First, Second and Third Worlds operate had changed radically. The old models of state development - whether based on the Keynesian social-democratic or the socialist central-planning models - had frequently been repudiated in their homelands and had lost much of their appeal. The principles and practice of the new 'market' orthodoxy spread from the major capitalist countries and the agencies of international economic adjustment and discipline, the International Monetary Fund and the World Bank. At the same time, the economic difficulties faced by Third World governments, in particular in the context of global recession, deteriorating terms of trade and a mounting debt burden, reinforced the neo-liberal thesis about the incapacity of states and seemed to render market-oriented 'adjustment' remedies intellectually more cogent.

Thus, by the early 1980s, the intensification of internal and external problems and the apparent absence of alternative visions of economic salvation had virtually universalised the liberalisation paradigm as the only option for Third World governments struggling to extricate themselves from difficult or desperate economic circumstances. The success of the NICs was often paraded as resulting from such neo-liberal praxis (that this was largely wrong [*White 1988*] did not seem to matter in the ideological arguments). The processes of stabilisation, 'structural adjustment' and liberalisation have largely gone hand-in-hand, although in some respects the three are distinct, and raise different sets of research questions. Stabilisation and structural adjustment are respectively short- and medium-term processes. They are a response to an economic crisis, characterised above all by financial austerity and reform in the public sector, and supported by international banks and aid donors. Liberalisation, by contrast, is a more far-reaching and longer-term process involving a more basic change in relations between government and society. It may or may not be a response to an economic crisis and the urgings of external creditors and aid donors.

In the context of debates about both these processes, however, time has brought a reaction against the extreme or purist courses of action originally advocated, even on the part of those actors, such as the IMF and World Bank, who had led the field in terms of explicitly 'neo-liberal' policy recommendations. After the pendulum had first swung wildly from *dirigisme* to free marketeering, there were signs that dominant opinion was moving towards a more 'balanced' approach. Decision-makers are now beginning to ask whether markets work quite in the way suggested by the theories of their economic gurus. Researchers are beginning to examine what diverse forms markets take in the 'real world', and how these compare to the phenomenon described in the textbooks [*Drèze and Sen 1989*]. There is, as one might say, a major job to be done of 'de-construction' and 'de-mystification' of that sacred cow; the market and its magic. There are very serious questions to be asked, too, about the role of the state and its institutions in enabling markets to perform reasonably close to their textbook equivalents. If left to themselves, markets can become oligopolistic, get into self-destruction or, in fact, anywhere.

What is emerging, then, is a recognition among policy-makers of the requirement to 'balance' the greater (theoretical) efficiency of the market in allocating and using resources, with the need to regulate (control) its operation to avoid persistent and long-term malfunctioning in a broader sense, which includes doing harm to those who are economically most vulnerable. UNICEF has waged a persistent campaign on that issue for a number of years [*Cornia et al. 1987*], seeing some of its central points eventually accepted by the International Financial Institutions (see World Bank 1990). Even so, it must be expected that certain institutional forms created or strengthened during the neo-liberal stage, when the state attempted to 'hive off' functions, creating new agencies in some cases, or incorporating other actors (e.g. NGOs) to perform its erstwhile functions, will survive into the future.

A view is emerging of a more managerial state, 'developmental' in a certain sense, with new institutions to fulfil new functions. This state would continue to play a role of strategic guidance, but in a rather indirect way in the context of a market economy and a strong and influential civil society. The Netherlands and South Korea could serve as examples here. However, little work has been done to spell out the details of such a new approach, and the institutional implications demand attention from researchers.

The Decline of Authoritarianism

The transition towards a greater degree of democracy has occurred in various stages. It began slowly in both Latin America and Asia (the Philippines, South Korea and, to a more limited extent, Taiwan), and more recently has had its lightning phase in Eastern Europe. Various issues here demand further investigation.

The first issue is the extent to which such changes in political systems actually reflect (and follow) achievements in the socio-economic sphere. This is an old question which was of primary concern in political science in the United States during the 1960s [*Nelson 1987; Almond 1987*]. This cannot be argued too closely for Latin America, as in most countries in this continent the economic paths during the 1980s have headed downwards rather than in an upwards direction. Nor can the argument be made that the wave of revolution in Eastern Europe has resulted in economic success: if anything, the opposite appears true. However, South Korea and Taiwan both moved down the road of democratisation after their efforts at industrialisation yielded fruits, whilst in other (and less developed) countries of that continent, such as China and Burma, moves towards democracy have been checked.

In Africa the picture is more mixed. A few countries have vigorously maintained democratic institutions (e.g. Botswana and Mauritius), and others are democratising to a greater or lesser extent after spells of harsh repression (Uganda and various countries in Francophone Africa). The political changes now occurring in South Africa are of the greatest significance. Yet elsewhere in Africa the signs, if there are any, have been of the consolidation of authoritarianism. Why is this so? Many states in Africa have been both singularly unsuccessful developmentally, and singularly dictatorial. One-party states survive, quite against the recent trend elsewhere, and the dangers of tribalism are often adduced as explanations, or justifications, for this. But while tribally-based political parties could, indeed, be only limited handmaidens of democracy, one-party states have not been particularly effective in avoiding tribal strife, be it within the one-party state, or on its edges. Alternative views focus on the legacy of the leaders of independence movements and the hero-worship accorded them, which has faded over time. There is a considerable body of literature on the state in Africa [*see e.g. Clapham 1982; Chabal 1986*].

In the 1970s and early 1980s Latin American analysts were taxed by the claims of dictators that development and democracy were incompatible, and much of their work addressed that issue [*Lehmann, 1990*]. By the beginning of the 1990s those issues have assumed a new relevance, as the arguments over the effects of rapid democratisation have become more passionate. Democratisation may strengthen the state and the government by increasing consent or support, yet it may weaken its capacity to provide a coherent, longer-term development strategy which may demand politically difficult decisions: Elections, and the chance to be ousted from power, make governments (overly?) concerned about the short and medium-term effects of their actions and policies, and unwilling to take a really long-term view. This is an argument which was used for 16 years to justify dictatorship in Chile, but it also figured (even if in not so many words) in the justifications of the Tiananmen Square repression, and its aftermath, in China. How far such arguments really do hold water is a subject weighed down by emotions, on which, however, serious and 'objective' research is essential.

Finally, the regime changes brought about by democratisation, and the attendant constitutional modifications, change the rules of the game for the policy process. This often involves the emergence of new relationships between the state and civil society, which grant the latter a greater role and make the policy process more 'mediated' than before - a subject on which research is only beginning. Although the new visibility of NGOs have probably primarily resulted from the shifts from the state to the market and back, these changes at the level of regime and constitution have also helped their emergence into prominence. Once NGOs were playing a greater development-related role, they became more significant recipients of development assistance - hitherto almost exclusively a 'state to state' affair. The longer term implications of this shift, both for the recipient state and for development cooperation agencies, need to be assessed.

III. NEW ROLES FOR THE STATE?

Internationalisation

Globalisation and regionalisation will, on the whole, make national states weaker and more vulnerable, although this will clearly vary as one moves outward from the central (metropolitan) states. In response to the new interdependence and interpenetration, various forms of integration are likely to emerge- some functional (i.e. more related to specific issues and the fulfilment of particular functions), and others of a broader, more all-encompassing nature (such as the EEC). There are important issues for research here: Is there anything left to say today about the ideas that seemed able to move mountains only a short while ago, ideas such as the New International Economic Order, collective self-reliance, or even economic nationalism?

Eventually, states or regional political organisations are likely to come face to face with the logic of some form of world government. Without this, international markets in goods and money may spin out of control, with devastating consequences. These would not only be economic, such as persistent instability, or maldistribution even more unmanageable than it is now, but also environmental, as the absence of rules that were enforceable and binding on all producers would encourage shifts of production to areas with the least restrictive regulation, and hence the lowest costs to the producer. This is the problem of 'externalities' with globally damaging effects, such as issues like acid rain, waste disposal, the destruction of tropical forests and damage to the ozone layer [*Brundtland Commission 1987*].

Changes in the Relations Between the State and the Market

Wherever the pendulum comes to rest, for the time being, at *dirigisme* or free marketeering, it will be necessary to monitor and scrutinise the efficacy of the instruments available to the state for (economic) policy management: existing institutional forms will almost certainly require adjustments if they are to be effective in the new circumstances.

Policy management institutions comprise in the first place the public administration. In recent years there has been much emphasis on the fact that the public administration, in many places, requires rehabilitation or reform, and also with respect to mechanisms of accountability [*World Bank 1983*]. In addition, new functions have to be fulfilled, for which existing agencies have to be transformed or new ones set up to deal with issues such as market promotion, market regulation, or the revision of legal frameworks.

Such innovations are not confined to the central administration. New developmental roles have been emerging for the public administration at regional or local levels, both in some of the more successfully innovative developed countries (e.g. Italy) and in certain developing countries - notably China [*White 1991*]. Studying the lessons of those experiences for wider application in developing countries should be of considerable interest to policy makers.

The public administration has not been the sole area of attention, however. Under the influence of neo-liberal ideology, the private sector has been promoted as an alternative (and more effective) delivery mechanism in many areas; the result has been widespread privatisation and divestiture of activities hitherto undertaken by the state. Yet our understanding remains quite limited of the extent to which transfers of such institutional forms can be undertaken without difficulty from more developed to less developed settings. Where institutional development in the private sector is very rudimentary (banking and credit, legal framework and institutions, consumer protection, etc) such as in much of sub-Saharan Africa, there may be major problems, here. Furthermore, in certain circumstances privatisation may involve little more than *largesse* to the friends of those in power, with minimal (or even negative) efficiency benefits. Research on the experience of different kinds of countries is required.

In addition, and partly in reaction to this emphasis on market mechanisms, NGOs have of late been given a role in the implementation of certain areas of public policy, especially in connection with poverty alleviation [*Drabek 1987*]. Hence, research on future forms of policy management needs to deal not only with the state bureaucracy, but also with a whole range of semi-public and private organisations, to which the task of ensuring the implementation of certain public policies may be 'delegated'.

Comparative research has yielded a number of suggestive findings, which can be seen as starting points for theory-building on institutional effectiveness in public policy - for example Arturo Israel's finding of the importance of 'specificity' and 'competition' [*Israel 1987*]. Nevertheless, a major World Bank conference on this subject recently concluded that there is, as yet, not much 'theory' in this field, nor even a coherent conceptual framework [*World Bank 1990*]. Moreover, it was found that policy interventions stimulated by the Bank have not been very successful; its 'accomplishments on institutional development are relatively few and declining' [*ibid: 1*].

Two matters stand out from the discussions at that conference. First, the time-frame for effective institutional development is much longer than that of the usual donor-supported 'project' - more like 10 to 15, or even 25 years, rather than three to five. Second, only detailed analysis, taking account of circumstances that vary from country to country, can hope to lead to the identification of feasible options for induced change. This has consequences for operational interventions in the field of policy management, but also for research.

As it takes many years to achieve successful institutional develop-ment, it is almost certain that significant aspects of the problem are likely to be missed by snapshot 'surveys', or even by a comparative and synchronic analysis. In this problem area an in-depth historical analysis appears to be almost a *conditio sine qua non*.

An analysis needs to address not only the strictly organisational characteristics of the institutions of economic policy management, but also contextual factors which might set limits to them (e.g. prevailing political ideologies, socio-cultural attitudes and behaviour patterns, the 'texture' of civil society, and dominant economic interests), or the lack of particular resources (financial, technological and human) which could create serious obstacles to change. Such factors change over time.

The Decline of Authoritarianism

In many countries authoritarian regimes have recently been replaced. The dynamic of change has ranged from extremely violent (Romania) to relatively peaceful (Hungary, Czechoslovakia and Chile). The existing institutions of policy management have, in most cases, been built up over long periods of time prior to the recent transitions. They are usually ill-adapted to the tasks that need to be carried out in the new circumstances - especially in terms of the wider mechanisms of citizen participation and accountability of the state, which are demanded by democratisation, but also, in many cases, in terms of the newly emerging economic policies. In most countries that have experienced such transitions, understanding the obstacles that linger from the earlier regime, as well as tracing feasible paths of insti-tutional change, are major challenges for research in the early 1990s.

Three areas are likely to need considerable attention in the newly emergent democratic states.

First, there is the issue of property rights - their definition and guarantee. This is a matter of particular importance to countries that are moving away from a centrally planned command economy. It also has relevance to those developing countries where the role of the state in the economy has been overwhelming, without the system having been formally defined as socialist or centrally planned. Both the particular modality of the transfer of property rights from the state to the private sector, and the legal framework under which private property will operate in the future are at issue here. Different modes of transfer have different distributional effects (who can acquire such privatised assets), and different legal frameworks affect the future control of the property once it is acquired. The fierce debate in the countries of Eastern Europe over the modalities of privatisation suggest that this is a major area for research.

Second, democratisation involves a re-ordering of political space, and a re-arranging of the relations between the state and civil society. It often requires, or leads to, the strengthening of the latter: the emergence of new organisations, new interest groups and new institutional forms in the political and socioeconomic spheres. How such organisations acquire access to the policy process is an issue of major importance. The new democratic structures, or the organs of public administration that support them, may in fact become 'colonised' by civil society, with different interest groups developing special relations of mutual support with different government depart-ments, ministries, and so on. A process of this sort has occurred in the few years since the demise of the military government in Brazil, and has been analysed under the label of neo-corporatism [*Lehmann 1990*]. It suggests important questions for research elsewhere.

Third, democratisation often generates pressures for decentralisation and participation. These have become leading concepts in discussions of development paradigms in recent years, and are being promoted on the international scene (especially by various UN organisations), almost as a panacea for a more effective policy implementation.

However, both concepts make assumptions about the workings of the state and its relations with civil society that are neither justified nor even properly examined. Their promotion also discounts certain inherent and unresolvable dilemmas between 'bottom-up' and 'top-down' approaches. Both draw attention to the undesirability and drawbacks of control from the centre to the exclusion of the 'ordinary people'.

There is, indeed, much evidence of innovativeness and creativity, as well as technical capacity, away from the centre, and of the centre's control being often rightly experienced as a 'heavy hand' - for example, the role of generalised rules in the domain of public finance, budgeting, and financial control on the one hand, and of civil service employment and appointment on the other, both of which stifle sectoral initiatives [*SIDA 1990*]. In various countries, notably Italy and China, local government has provided an effective arena for fostering development. Yet there is also much evidence of divergence between 'projects' promoted from the grassroots and the priorities derived from nationally agreed policies, and of the tension between decision-making at the periphery (or by 'the people') and control over resources from the centre (to ensure standards of equity or the allocation of resources to those most in need). Decentralisation (and even 'participation') can result in local squabbling and the pursuit of sectional interests, especially where local elites have a chance to take control of local decision-making.

The uncertainties and dilemmas set out above suggest that much research will be required on the extent to which decentralisation and participation are appropriate mechanisms in the context of a changing role for the state in the 1990s.

IV. CONCLUSIONS

While these observations have emphasised a number of generally observable trends and tendencies, specifically towards globalisation, there is no doubt that specificities, at both the national and regional levels, will remain highly important and will be significant candidates for research. The identification and explanation of such variations is a task for which the member organisations of ICCDA will be well qualified. At the same time, the effects on the home country or region of developments elsewhere need to be followed closely. For example, the growth of democracy in Eastern Europe and Latin America may have an unsettling and destabilising effect on one-party states in Africa. Alternatively, the notion that African politics are *sui generis* may well remain persuasive.

One conclusion that can be drawn from the evidence of convergence and globalisation is that the world 'two party system' is showing signs of disintegration. This has important military implications, which were not considered above. There is hope that the 'Garrison states' of the East, West and South, with their associated military-industrial complexes, will be less defensive, and that this will feed through into the behaviour and dispositions of states, possibly affecting such factors as the pattern of international arms trading and the incidence and intensity of regional wars.

Of the other major globalisation trends, probably the most dramatic are the increasing visibility of the impact of technology, and the accelerating pace of environmental degradation. The latter, especially,

198

is a source of alarm. There is a feeling that control is being lost and that external events are dominating mankind. The short term effects are likely to be unevenly distributed, with the poor suffering the most immediate impact of resource depletion. But in the longer run, the wealthier and more developed nations are equally at risk. This presents a major challenge for nation states, and for their capacity to cooperate in developing the institutional structures needed to engineer new solutions.

In terms of the specific political structures of nation states, some would discern a widely generalised drift towards social democracy. Clearly there are major exceptions to this. The growth of social democracy is paralleled by an intensification in some places of old fashioned nationalism and newer fundamentalism, Iran being an outstanding, but by no means an isolated, example. While research cannot give definitive answers to such questions, it is nevertheless worth asking whether we are to see such phenomena as the last dying embers of old solidarities, or as a new and robust reaction to the cultural and political homogenisation; the transnational levelling, which produces a MacDonalds in Moscow and Levis throughout the consumer world.

Finally, it is up to us to ensure that development studies gets the new vigour it needs to plausibly restate the claim that it is uniquely well placed to contribute to this analysis of the modified roles of the states, and to come to terms with the new era, along with its inter-dependencies and contradictions. Development studies, as it has been practised in its full diversity, has much to offer because its focus is intrinsically broad and its approach is both comparative and interdisciplinary. In these times when all eyes appear to be on Eastern Europe and on those developing countries that were wont to regard themselves as 'socialist', it may be able to make a special contribution to bridging the analytical frameworks employed to examine what used to be called the 'Second' and the 'Third' Worlds. This involves above all the construction of new theory, based on sound empirical research, but in due course should also give rise to a fundamental reorientation of our teaching.

REFERENCES

Almond, Gabriel A. and James S. Coleman, 1960, *The Politics of Developing Areas,* Princeton: Princeton University Press.
Almond, Gabriel A., 1987, 'The Development of Political Development' in M. Weiner and S Huntington, eds, *Understanding Political Development,* Boston: Little, Brown, pp 437-490.

Emanuel de Kadt, with Zoe Mars and Gordon White

Brundtland Commission (World Commission on Environment and Development), 1987, *Our Common Future*, Oxford: Oxford University Press.

Chabal, Patrick, (ed.), 1986, *Political Damnation in Africa*, Cambridge: Cambridge University Press.

Chen, E.K., 1983, *Multinational Corporations, Technology and Employment*, London: Macmillan.

Clapham, Christopher (ed.), 1982, *Private Patronage and Public Power*, London: Francis Pinter.

Drabek, Anne Gordon (ed.), 1987, 'Development Alternatives: The Challenge for NGOs', *World Development*, Vol. 15, Supplement, Autumn.

Drèze, Jean and Amartya Sen, 1989, *Hunger and Public Action*, Oxford: Clarendon Press.

Israel, Arturo, 1987, *Institutional Development. Incentives to Performance*, published for The World Bank, Baltimore and London: Johns Hopkins.

IUED, 1977, *La Fin des Outils: Technologie et domination*, Paris and Geneva: PUF and IUED.

IUED, 1983, *Les Nouvelles Chaînes. Techniques modernes de la télécommunication et le tiers monde: pièges et promesses*, Paris and Geneva: PUF and IUED.

Lehmann, David, 1990, *Democracy and Development in Latin America. Economics, Politics and Religion in the Postwar Period*, Oxford: Polity Press.

Nelson, Joan M., 1987, 'Political Participation' in M Weiner and S Huntington, eds, *Understanding Political Development*, Boston: Little, Brown, pp 103-59.

Seers, Dudley, 1978, 'Concluding Remarks' in *Europe's Role in the World*, Proceedings of the EADI Conference in Milan, Finafrica, Milan.

Swedish International Development Authority (SIDA), 1990, *Central Authority Blocks Local Autonomy*, SIDA Evaluation Report, Local Government Development, Zimbabwe, 1990/2, Stockholm: SIDA.

Toye, John, 1987, *Dilemmas of Development. Reflections on the Counter-Revolution in Development Theory and Policy*, Oxford: Basil Blackwell.

Weiss, J., 1990, *Industry in Developing Countries: Theory, Policy and Evidence*, London: Routledge.

White, Gordon, (ed.), 1988, *Developmental States in East Asia*, London: Macmillan.

White, Gordon, (ed.), 1991, *The Chinese State in the Era of Economic Reform: the Road to Crisis*, London: Macmillan.

World Bank, 1983, *World Development Report*, New York: Oxford University Press.

World Bank, 1990, 'Conference on Institutional Development and the World Bank: Summary', *mimeo*, CECPS, World Bank, Washington DC, 16 January.

15

Autonomy and Stability.
The Challenge for Latin American
Social Science

FERNANDO CALDERON and
PATRICIA PROVOSTE

I. OPENING THE DEBATE

During the past two decades, the institutional life of social sciences in Latin America has become more complex in several ways. It has grown irregularly in its institutions and disciplines and with different rhythms and intensities in various countries. It has also diversified its institutional models, activities, orientations, themes and theoretical and methodological approaches. In addition there are now different institutional sizes, incomes, influential power and prestige and a more complex insertion of social sciences in society: the target audiences, types of activity and the results of research activity have changed.

In short, diversification seems to be the main trend in the institutional world of social sciences in the region, a world which is much more complex than it was 20 or 30 years ago. It is therefore impossible to advance a simple explanation for such a heterogeneous situation, as the analysis will inevitably reflect a corresponding degree of complexity.

Changes in social sciences do not take place haphazardly. They are not only a part and a reflection of social and cultural transformations in different countries, but they also originate from scholarly tradition, the production of knowledge, various theoretical models and cultural frameworks for professional and institutional performance. In addition, they are cumulative and represent projections of past achievements, constraints and conflicts, as well as prefigurations of the future.

In order to better appreciate the continuity of the process of change in social sciences, we should bear in mind that they preserve a certain basic identity which has been observed during the second half of this century, and may also be found - in the most dissimilar ways - in its obvious preference, both thematic and theoretical, for the problem of the transformation of national societies and of the limits and possibilities of progressive transformation.

Thus, one of the main axes of professional practice in the social sciences in the Latin American region is the construction of a more equitable society with a greater freedom of space. It is this area that most theory and research since the end of the Second World War has concentrated on: modernisation, marginalisation, centre-periphery relationships, dependency, dependent capitalism, social classes, the state, authoritarianism, social movements, democracy and modernity-postmodernity issues.

The relations between the 'vocation' and its outcome, the adequacy of its questions and answers to each historical moment, the links it has established with society and politics, the kind of intellectuals it has generated, and even the accuracy of this characterisation, constitute a set of interrelated issues which determine the scope of this chapter, despite the fact that the large analytical universe which is being opened cannot be encompassed as a whole.

On the other hand, the reference to continuity within change allows us to note the extent to which the central questions which have been posed by some of the founders of 'modern' social science of the region, for example Germani and Medina Echavarria, are still in force, in particular those referred to in the central orientations of socio-cultural transformation and to the actors able to command it.

The founders have also stated some problems which remain central to the professional and institutional profile of the social sciences. Germani pointed out the need to complement the great tradition for a global analysis of Latin American intellectuals along with a higher precision and an interest in details.[1] In this sense, it would seem that the tension and displacements between empirical and 'large theory', when observed in perspective, have been constant in social sciences in Latin America. At another level, we should also remember how Medina Echavarria has similarly stated the issue of institutional diversity when, in his comments on the university and development, he explored what he calls 'extramural research' and the roles which could eventually be assumed by the different types of research, national states and other entities.[2]

However, even if there is a long-standing nucleus of central questions and issues, the situation in which these arise is constantly changing. Changes in different countries, the growth and diversification of social science activities and institutions and the transformation of social conditions in which they operate, have forced us to look for new answers and reformulate the questions.

The aim of this chapter is to address some of these problems from the perspective of both consolidation and development of the social science institutions of the Latin American region, in particular those in which research takes place. Nevertheless, rather than emphasise the achievement of definite answers or assertions, we hope to identify problems, state questions and suggest some hypotheses to open the debate.[3]

In order to do so, we have organised our work as follows: First, we ask the question 'What has changed in the social sciences and for the social sciences in Latin America?' A brief, descriptive and non-hierarchical revision of the changes in the different areas is given. Second, we address the central issue of relations among the three most important actors - the research centres, national states and the external institutions which collaborate in research founding - and finally, comment upon the two crucial problems - the build-up of institutional stability and institutional autonomy.

It is important to note that this chapter is supposed to provide a regional vision of the problem, and therefore excessive generalisation cannot always be avoided.

II. CHANGE

Uneven Expansion

The changes which should be highlighted have been caused by a process of accelerated quantitative growth of the social sciences in the Latin American region during the 1960s and 1970s. Spectacular growth has been witnessed in the number of graduates - from 6,400 at the beginning of the 1960s to 59,000 by the mid-1970s[4] - in the number of undergraduate and postgraduate programmes and in the number of research centres.[5]

The quantitative expansion of social sciences also includes the increase in research activity. Furthermore, there is a qualitative correlation, as evidenced in the diversity of countries and individuals which are now the compulsory reference for many issues. This could be compared to the 1960s, when a few names from three or four geographical areas dominated the scene. Although there were persisting limitations and differences in the quality and extension in each country's scholarly training, during these decades the possibility emerged of training professionals in the region itself, thus developing a significant variety of careers and special programmes and courses.

This description applies in general terms to the region as a whole, but should not conceal the heterogeneity and diversity in the rhythm of this process. Not all the countries or disciplines show the same growth rate, and within each country and discipline important differences may be observed.[6] Furthermore, the rhythm of quantitative expansion seems to register downward movements in several countries. This can be seen in the decreasing numbers of enrolment in some disciplines since the late 1970s. Nevertheless, during the two decades under analysis, the 'younger' social sciences, particularly sociology and political science, were institutionalised as university disciplines in almost every country.

In addition, and in contrast to the trend of 20 years ago, there are almost no 'small' countries outside the general framework of quantitative expansion. They all have more or less significant centres, publications and research teams whose scholarly quality is acknowledged both within and outside the region.

The internationalisation of the social sciences is another important change. Factors such as exiles and the Latin American postgraduate programmes (FLACSO, CLACSO and ILPES) have increased the regional circulation of people and ideas which had been limited until the late 1960s. The number of regional meetings now taking place is a good indicator of such change.[7] On the other hand, it is interesting to note the inflection undergone by certain patterns of scholarly recognition through links with other geographical areas: whereas until the 1960s these links were almost exclusively located in the United States and in European universities, nowadays there is a trend towards mutual acknowledgement within the Latin American region.

Internationalisation also encompasses the other continents, although it is greater concerning the United States and Europe than the Third World, and this preference has restricted the development process in this area. However, the growing relevance of Latin American problems in worldwide processes is of utmost importance, as well as the flourishing of Latin American groups in developed countries[8] and the intensity of personal and institutional scholarly exchanges among the regions.[9] Nevertheless, the circulation of scientific information among the regions, and even within the region, is limited.

As in the other cases, the process of change has been uneven. The flux of contacts has increased between centres and researchers, although not by the scientific community as a whole. In fact, the capacity for international contact is one way in which scholarly differentiation is expressed. On the other hand, there is a progressive build-up of a set of formal or informal networks which follow some adherence criterion, often thematic, but which may also refer to disciplines, geography or subregions. Thus, for instance, in Latin America there are important circuits which operate within the Andean Area, Central America, the Caribbean and the Southern Cone, as well as regional groups such as CLACSO. These circuits link groups of researchers belonging to centres mostly located in the largest cities. Other cities and many researchers remain outside, confined to a certain locality either due to a lack of opportunity or to a work-style inertia.

This situation has been fostered by the limited use of computers in the social sciences and by the consequent lack of regular access to data from other countries, and this problem has arisen from the high degree of centralism prevailing in the Latin American region.

Theoretical and Empirical Research

During the period under analysis, intellectual production changed dramatically. What was called the 'crisis of the paradigms' - more cautiously defined as the revision of the theoretical models in force in the region between the 1950s and 1970s - could be considered as one of the most relevant developments.[10] On the one hand, it is true that the explicatory capacity of the 'total' theoretical models such as modernisation, dependency and class struggle, which developed between the 1950s and the beginning of the 1970s, became insufficient for the production of knowledge vis à vis the mutations undergone by Latin American society.

The different opinions regarding this statement range from those which refute it to those which affirm that it is a recognition of the fragmentary character of reality which cannot be reduced to global explanations. In between, there are those who aspire to build up new explanatory models, or to update the former ones. Moreover, these interpretations are linked to the diversity of explanations of the 'paradigmatic (or theoretical) crisis'. According to these explanations, this crisis arises from changes in reality which cannot be framed within those models, or which could only be framed with some difficulty.

The crisis could also be due to the social and political processes entailing a revalorisation of the idea of democracy and the conception of change and its actors, or else simply due to the accumulation of knowledge and the introduction of debates external to the region. However, the prevalent perception appears to be that, for the moment, no general accepted model exists which could perform this globalising function. Thus, the uncertainty about the future in the region mirrors the uncertainty in the build-up of scientific social knowledge.

On the other hand, it would be difficult to deny that these revisions and questioning of the theoretical models can be associated with an increase in the number of new approaches which form the process of theoretical research and renewal. In fact, they appear to be theoretical constructions of a more restricted scope and to offer a more complex view of reality.

The process of thematic diversification which has taken place in the region cannot be separated from the process of theoretical renewal. Thematic diversification, both induced and produced by the former, has developed simultaneously and, during the past two decades, has generated a remarkable proliferation of studies on a variety of issues. These have included both new and recovered empirical fields (for example the 1970s debate on the national question, the study of social movements in the 1980s and also rural, ethnic and population issues) as well as different dimensions and temporalities of reality such as cultural dimensions and sociopolitical change. On another level, this thematic diversification confirms what appears to be a sustained trend in the region towards defining the research areas as problematic fields rather than disciplines, giving way to a trend towards interdisciplinary compositions of many research centres.[11]

An important portion of the research recently undertaken in the Latin American region on the processes of theoretical change and thematic diversification appear to have more of an empirical character than the research produced a couple of decades ago, which tended more towards essayist and generalisation. In spite of series of conceptual-methodological and technical limitations which have been detected, research has been generating an important empirical foundation. However, theoretical 'uncertainty', and other factors such as the slow transfer of the research experience to the classroom and the rest of the scientific community, have contributed to limitations in the building, interpretation and comparability of the data. The dividing line between empiricism and the empirical basis of research is often diffuse, making the tension between empirical and theory, and between theoretical and technical research, appear more complex than in the past.

Social Insertion of Research

Another relevant aspect of the changes which have occurred in the social sciences in the Latin American region concerns its links with the extra-scholarly sphere. Analytical approaches and outcomes in the social sciences have often transcended the public and been taken up by parties and governments, but this phenomenon now appears even more widespread. The audience to which scientific activity is oriented has expanded, and there is a diversity in the research-related activities.

Target audiences today range from the national state to different sectors of civil society, including a variety of social organisations and political parties. The activities cover, among others, the publication of research findings, public debate, counselling within government organisations or agencies, training and the support of specific social or economic development programmes.

Within the region, there is a wide variety of intensity, character and orientation of these activities, as well as of the types of target audiences. However, a CLACSO centre survey has shown that in almost every country there is some kind of institutional or personal presence of the researchers in the media and in public opinion oriented activities. In several countries, the centre carries out technical and professional activities which channel research findings towards practical uses by non-scholarly users. These users may be popular sectors such as peasants, trade unions, women, ethnic groups or youth, but also the national state at different levels (ministries or local government agencies).[12]

There is also a wide diversification of target audiences and activities within the research centres, including university centres, which indicates a diversification of scholarly professional practice. Beyond the expansion of the fields for professional practice as a whole (such as teams engaged in techno-bureaucratic, counselling, marketing or community work activities), different work-styles have developed within scholarly practice. Their common feature is an attempt to increase the social impact of the research activity and to establish a more active communication with different social and political actors. This communication should be understood as a two-way flux between the centres and society, or certain actors within society, who demand the explanation and application of the social scientific production.

The relation of the centres with society and politics appears to be more complex. There has been a displacement from the type of professional practice in force during the 1970s to a type of practice that, in the 1980s, recognises bases which are more professional and autonomous vis à vis the political identities of the researchers. This orientation, however, does not imply an estrangement from political or social issues which refer to an exchange between society and the state. The same applies to the active participation of social scientists in the political contingencies, as in revolutionary processes such as Nicaragua, pacification processes such as Central America and

Colombia or in political debates and campaigns such as Bolivia, Chile and Ecuador.

The difference lies in the fact that the relation emerges from the field of professional competitiveness, or from the social scientists' self-determination as 'critics of the praxis'. It is probable that this change of emphasis is related to other processes such as theoretical revision, and the social processes themselves which have generated a more complex vision of social changes, of the actors and factors of changes, and a revalorisation of democracy and the social issue.

The Diversification of the Research Institutions

At the institutional level, the number of institutes and centres has increased remarkably. During the 1960s and 1970s, university institutes and centres of sociology or of social science appeared and expanded in size. This growth was ostensibly limited by the end of the 1970s due to a combination of factors, including political repression, the saturation of employment markets, the decrease in state funding and even through conflicts within the universities themselves.

However, also during the 1970s, a sector of independent, mainly private, centres grew in several countries and has since expanded, both within the countries and throughout the region.[13] This sector is mainly formed of private centres, but includes some centres that, although featuring scholarly autonomy and independent management, rely heavily on state funding.

The expansion of this sector has been heterogeneous. There have not only been differences regarding the relative weight of the sector between countries and disciplines, but also among the sizes, resources, prestige and international links of the centres within each country. Such differences are also present within the centres themselves, which often appear like small stratified universes with their scholarly personnel having different levels of prestige, links and access to funds.

The type of activity prevailing in the independent sector of scholarly centres also varies. Although they all carry out research activities, and most also provide professional training, a significant portion perform activities which could be grouped under the term 'community work', meaning supportive action to specific social groups.

It must also be remembered that the sub-group of centres combining research and action represents an intersection between the universe of scholarly agencies and the much wider universe of non-governmental organisations (NGOs).[14] This analysis focuses only on those institutions that can be considered as research centres due to the weight of their scholarly component.

The extension and scholarly relevance of the private sector of research centres, as well as the relative weight of its two sub-sectors in each country, varies a great deal depending on the combination of several factors, including the degree of development and numeric growth of the universe of social scientists, the absorption capacity of the traditional employment markets, the impact of the economic crisis on national research resources, the policies concerning scientific development, the availability of external financing and the orientations of the financing agencies, and finally the individual traditions of the scholarly communities and their political and social links.

The situation in Mexico and Venezuela, until a few years ago, shows how the differential weight of these factors can have a bearing on the overall social science development. In these two countries, the amount of resources available and the highly developed university system, which absorbed a vast number of social scientists, meant that independent scholarly centres developed much less than in other countries of the region. In contrast, the experiences of 'community development' and 'rural integral development' in Central America and the Andean area shows the importance of joint action with popular sectors.

Finally, the authoritarian regimes that triggered the development of a relevant sector of private centres in countries with a large professional community have had different effects in Argentina, Chile and Uruguay. In these countries, exclusive or repressive policies have been applied to the social sciences, thus expanding the private sector. On the other hand, in Brazil, where scientific and university development policies have been sustained, the displacement of social scientists towards an independent sector has been reduced.

However, overall the general aspect of the Latin American region shows that the university is still the strongest scholarly sphere in countries with institutional continuity and state funding, such as Brazil, Mexico, Venezuela and Colombia. Cuba is a special case, for there is recent development in the non-economic social sciences within the state framework. At the other end there are countries such as Argentina and Chile whose independent centres form a relatively large sector with a large proportion of the production. In between, there are a number of countries such as Paraguay with very little research carried out almost exclusively independently, or Ecuador with an important and productive independent sector which does not exclude the participation of the university in research.

Growth of External Financing

One of the most remarkable changes in the institutional life of social science was the growing weight of the financing agencies external to the region, and the central role they have played in the process of expansion of the independent centres. The participation of external agencies - mainly from Europe and North America - dates from the end of the Second World War, but since the 1970s it has flourished in all Latin American countries.

During this period, the wider presence of such agencies was not limited to increasing the funds available. It also involved a diversification in the modalities of support and in the type of agencies participating in this process. During the 1960s, funds were mostly granted individually to researchers by scholarly agencies. At another level, research was linked to local development programmes such as the one carried out in Peru during the 1950s by Cornell University, and involved Peruvian university researchers.

During the 1980s, considerable funds were granted to independent and university institutions covering a variety of types of research, training and community work programmes. These funds came from both scholarly agencies and other organisms such as governments, state-funded autonomous entities, international organisms and the church. There was a wide variety of types of criteria in the operation of these agencies, which ranged from institutional support for specific projects to scholarly or practical activities. This diversity shows how difficult it is to analyse the agencies as a whole, for they are complex entities with highly dissimilar origins and orientations.

The weight and importance of each kind of agency varies according to each national circumstance and the relative weight of the types of centres. In addition, there are internal factors such as the constitution of the professional field and the economic and political-institutional context. For example, research centres in the Andean and Central American countries have a priority of action, whilst in contrast, Mexico supports scholarly activities.

However, the factors derived from international politics, and from the agencies' policies, determine their presence in each country and the activities they support. For example, Puerto Rican centres, being considered as part of the United States system, find it difficult to obtain external support. Cuban centres also have problems as many countries consider Cuba as being outside their field of relations. In another sense, due to its thematic policies, the Ford Foundation has become relevant, even in countries with a significant amount of state funding.

Among the factors determining the presence of these agencies in the Latin American region during the past two decades, the domestic ones must be remembered, as they represent fields of potential demand. In addition, the offer of external resources has had a strong impact on these domestic factors as it has provided alternatives for social scientists who could not find funding either within the national sphere or through institutional channels.

The dynamics of the developed countries which have led to the expansion of government and non-government cooperation with Latin American societies should also be considered. The most remarkable face concerning these agencies is the central role they have acquired in several countries, thus becoming an alternative to domestic resources and sometimes even providing a larger funding then the one provided by the national state.

A rough assessment of the external contribution to research, which excludes scholarly teaching, shows that in a large group of countries (Bolivia, Peru, Chile, Paraguay, Uruguay, Guatemala, Honduras, Nicaragua and the Dominican Republic), more than 75 per cent of the funding comes from external agencies. In Costa Rica, the figure is over 50 per cent, and in Argentina and Colombia it is between 25 and 50 per cent, whilst in Mexico, Venezuela and Brazil external funding represents less than 25 per cent of the overall amount.[15]

These agencies play a vital role in the social science sphere, and some have been key elements in the survival or reconstitution of scientific communities in countries where, at critical times, the social sciences were persecuted or expelled, particularly in Argentina, Chile, Uruguay and in Central America. They have helped develop research capacity in almost every country, and their contribution has been specially evident in those countries where the development of social science research occurred later or in strict correlation with the availability of this kind of funding, such as in Bolivia and Paraguay. They have provided alternative and complementary funding to the funds offered by national sources, and have allowed the development of 'non-traditional' activities, particularly in independent centres, for which support is not easily found within universities. Furthermore, they have stimulated the internationalisation of social science within the region through the support of conferences and meetings, networks of scientific information (especially IDRC) and the publication of research. Finally, these agencies have extended the practice of competition through projects, thus raising the general level of professional capacity.

Nevertheless, the relation with the agencies has created a number of problems connected to the incorporation of the project market in scientific life, which in practice has implied new rules and new conditions of production. The development of a 'managerial capacity' within scholarly activity is an interesting product of this type of institutional existence. Certain constraints have been witnessed: the permanent management of projects, the need to adapt to relatively fixed deadlines and the uncertainty regarding the continuity of funding.

Problems have arisen at another level, such as agency priorities which have not always coincided with those of the centres and the researchers, and also the preference for action as opposed to pure research. Centres in general have devised strategies to guarantee the continuity of the institution through the diversification of sources to cover both areas.

The National Context

To conclude this overview of changes, those which have occurred in the national context where research is undertaken must also be mentioned. Most of the changes have already been touched on, but two in particular should be considered in greater depth: the changes in society, including political and economic change, and the role of the state concerning scientific development in general and the social sciences in particular.

First, all change which has been registered in the social sciences has had its roots in changes in the society. We could cite, for example, the impact of the authoritarian regimes on the process of theoretical renewal and thematic diversification, as well as on the development of independent institutions, the transformation of the social structure and the economic crisis. This latter is also important because of its restrictive effects on nationally financed scientific development which has established the need for alternative sources of funding.

Within the political-institutional context, during the past two decades we have witnessed political coups, democratic restorations and long-term military conflicts such as those in Central America, Colombia and in Peru, which have had complex effects on the social sciences. However, it is worth noting that in Nicaragua research has not been interrupted (although it has been severely curtailed), whilst in Argentina and Uruguay the democracy has not been able to consolidate research, although some new opportunities have been presented. In fact, if the status of the social sciences was to be observed from the viewpoint of the conditions for political-institutional stability, for example peace, continuity of the institutional system and a standard-ised and institutional framework for social science, only a few countries have had a relatively acceptable level of these conditions during the past two decades, namely Costa Rica, Cuba, Puerto Rico and Brazil.

The role of the state concerning the production of spaces and resources for the social sciences concern at least two different kinds of policies: university policies and those of a scientific-technological development nature.

In fact, the state has an historical role in the development of the universities, and their expansion is the starting point of all the dynamics of development of the social sciences, whose trends and changes, as related to the political regimes, are key elements in the history of these disciplines. In this way, the differences in the development of the social sciences in each country can only be explained through the analysis, for instance, of the long-standing performance of some of these disciplines in Brazil which, together with a high degree of stability in the university system, account for the relevant Brazilian production of knowledge in social sciences.

At another level, the relevance of the CSUCA in Central America during the past decade must be stressed, particularly the crucial roles played by its General Secretariat in San Jose in the generation of institutional and scholarly conditions for the sub-region as a whole, notwithstanding the political convulsions of the period. Costa Rica's international policy and democratic tradition have had central roles here. In contrast, the closure of universities for non-economic social sciences by the Stroessner regime explains why research has been concentrated in a small independent sector since the 1960s. In Mexico, the social sciences closely follow the evolution of universities, and the state has provided a space for alternative institutional models of scholarly research and training (mainly post-graduate), thus supporting large autonomous scholarly institutions such as el Colegio de Mexico, CIDE and INAH.

It must be remembered that by the beginning of the 1980s, Latin America, with eight per cent of the world's population and seven per cent of the world's GDP, had contributed only 1.3 per cent of the total world expenditure in research and development. In 1980, while developed countries devoted 2.24 per cent of their GDP to research and development, Latin America spent only 0.49 per cent.[16] Moreover, Brazil probably contributes more than half of this.

The proportions of funding from the state and external sources differ from country to country. For example, in Chile most research is undertaken with external financing, whilst in Cuba the state supplies almost all the funds.

It is interesting to note that in national scientific and technological development agencies, which are important in countries such as Brazil, Mexico, Venezuela, Colombia and Argentina since 1984,[17] a tension exists between the polar models of open competition (Brazil) an thematic-disciplinary priorities (Mexico). In fact, the first model created important spaces for social sciences,[18] while the second has almost excluded them in recent years.[19] There is a need for further progress in the discussion of alternative models of scientific policies. Nevertheless, rather than choosing one or the other, it would be useful to stress the differences in the economic, state and scholarly contexts which render each model more or less effective, and the need to meet the modalities and the degree of participation of the scientific social community in each of them. Thus, for example, the Brazilian case cannot be understood merely through the effect of a scientific policy based on important funding, but also through the social sciences' own capacity in exerting pressure on the quantity and quality of the projects, and in institutionalised scholarly participation of the social scientists.

Finally, it must be indicated that several states have established a users relationship with the centres, in particular at the secretariat, regional offices or local government levels. This phenomenon should be considered part of the process of social insertion of the social sciences institutions into the society.

In short, there is a process of diversification of institutional models, orientations and activities, and this diversification also encompasses the financial sources and modalities of scholarly activity. This process has been described by Brunner and Barrios [op. cit.] as part of a process of intra and inter-institutional differentiation related to the role of the state both in the pre-crisis period and during the expansion of the universities, and also related to market factors. This would explain the higher or lower degree of development of the independent centres in different countries, as well as their relative weight when compared to the universities.

Furthermore, what appears to be a process of redefinition of professional practice needs to be considered. This is not only following a market logic, but is also taking place within the framework of the position of professional activity within the society; this is suggested by the growing trend of research towards non-scholarly, socially or politically relevant audiences, the search for a social or political impact of scholarly activities through the participation in community work programmes or in state activities, technical-professional counselling in social organisations and the presence in the media.

214

This widening of the types of target audiences, objectives, activities and results seem to indicate a process of redefinition of the social insertion of the centres, and possibly also new forms of expression of the basic identity of the social sciences.

III. THE INSTITUTIONAL SCENARIO

We would now like to highlight, from the set of changes mentioned above, some problems referred to in the transformation of the institutional scenario in which research institutions operate. There are three main types of actors: the centres, the national states and the financing agencies.

The Centres

The diversification of the models of institutional build-up is the key factor. If the independent centres emerged, at a given moment, as a conjunctural response to political, institutional or market limitations, it would now seem that the different models have achieved legitimacy. However, all models will possibly continue to exist within a pluralistic scenario.

As has already been mentioned, the universe of the centres is formed from a variety of models with different orientations, activities, specialisations and financial bases. CLACSO's network represents this diversity, including university centres, autonomous centres depending on fiscal support, independent centres devoted to research and post-graduate training, and also research and community work. Of course, the extension and relative weight of these centres varies from country to country, and a heterogeneous and differentiated universe is formed where professional practice, theoretical and thematic orientations and the relations with society have diversified. We wish to point out, in a very general way, the more relevant difficulties and problems faced by each type of institution.

The university centres, and particularly those belonging to public universities, are naturally branded by the current limitations of state resources. However, their insertion into an institutional context (which is complex and difficult nowadays) is nevertheless relevant. The central problem now appears to be the maintenance and consolidation of the space won for research and tutoring, as the university institution itself is in a crisis and salaries are falling. In addition, difficulties are being experienced in the updating of libraries and equipment, and in obtaining funds for research projects.

The survey of directors of CLACSO centres shows how answers to these problems have been generated during the past five years, mainly through the search for complementary funding from external sources. But it must be remembered that the extent of these problems differs; for example in Brazil the crisis, whilst having some impact, has an important pre-existing infrastructure of scholarly and financial development, whilst Ecuador's infrastructure is much smaller.

In general terms, these difficulties at university level concern the whole scientific system, as it affects the training of the researchers who, in the near future, will replace those currently working. Moreover, the university is often the place where theoretical reflection takes place, a role not normally available to private centres. Thus, the roles, features and perspectives of university research, and the training social scientists, in diversified national systems of scientific production must be discussed further.

Independent centres presently face a number of difficulties largely related to their dependence on the project market, including the stability of their personnel and the reproduction of a scholarly institutional project within a financial framework favouring short-term projects and practical results. There are also internal tensions derived from the tendency to conform 'inner rings', as noted by Brunner and Barrios, and the difficulty to guarantee, while operating on a project basis, the conditions for its scholarly reproduction in terms of scholarly training, equipment and services. In fact, the independent centres must devise several complementary strategies in order to ensure the renewal of resources, sustain institutional operations independently from the projects, and establish reproduction conditions. Therefore it is essential to obtain stable institutional support, either from the state or from external financing agencies.

The situation is still more complex for those centres which undertake community work activities as well as research. Although they have more access to external funding, these funds generally allow little space for theoretical reflection or for research programmes.

In addition, many centres face the tension between their research teams and their action counterparts. This is expressed in two ways: as a difficulty concerning an effective integration of both areas within the centre, and sometimes as an ideological tension between the people working in each area (*basismo* - work with grassroot organisations - versus 'scientificism').

The case of the Associaçaõ Nacional de Pesquisa e Posgraduaçaõ em Ciencias Sociais (ANPOCS) in Brazil shows the relevant role that may be played by an associative agency. It promotes the circulation of scientific information, organises joint activities and, on the basis of its scholarly prestige, advises the state and other institutions of action to take for the development of standards for the evaluation of social science production. The success of ANPOCS possibly lies in the high degree of consolidation and development of the universities in Brazil, and within them the social sciences, as well as an open scientific policy which has allowed access to large amounts of funding. But there is a stress on scholarly quality and on activities based on specific interests, such as the ANPOCS working-groups. Other than some modest attempts in the creation of a national social science council (for example in Ecuador and Mexico) and some informal associations with the CLACSO centres in some countries (Chile, Ecuador, Peru and Uruguay), it would seem that, in general, the possibilities for this type of organisation have not been explored.

The State

Two main aspects should be noted concerning the link between social sciences and the state: the state as the generator of a stable normative-institutional framework, and the state as the provider of research funds. Both aspects are connected, and different regimes, institutional stability and resources have different impacts on them.

In many countries, including democratic ones, the lack of a stable national and university institutional framework persists, and the economic crisis imposes a reduction of resources for scientific development in the whole Latin American region. Nevertheless, it is in this climate that the centres have developed and will continue to operate, and it is difficult to foresee a different framework in the short term, or a reconstitution of a development of the social sciences sustained exclusively be the state and based on complete scholarly autonomy.[20]

The crisis may also represent a retrogression in other issues, such as in scientific policy, which is less urgent today than other social problems. In addition, the character of scientific policy is a controversial issue: it is debatable, from the institutions' point of view, whether a priorities system is better than an open competition system, and whether priorities should be thematic or scholarly, and so on. Each country will probably have a different opinion, but for the social sciences this is a pending problem which should be considered in terms of disciplines as well as of global scientific policies. However, discussions, especially in democratic contexts, could be established which, while not generating financial resources, could make way for the creation of normative and political conditions to facilitate the tasks of the centres.

But it must be remembered that generally national states officially consider scholarly activity as being exclusively the concern of universities, and their relations with private centres is often highly ambiguous. In other words, an official acknowledgement of the current plurality of the research system is still pending. On the other hand, if the trend of searching for a greater social impact of research persists, it is possible that in some countries the position of these centres may be strengthened on the basis of their technical-professional contributions (as institutions) to the state. However, these possibilities depend not so much on the state as on the initiative of the centres and the researchers themselves.

In short, rather than the solution to the financial problem, which will probably still require external cooperation, the issues that nowadays seem more immediate regarding the state are the normative aspects, the technical and professional role of research institutions and the conditions of assignment and maximisation of scarce funding.

The Agencies and the Project Market

It is difficult to imagine a stable and sufficiently funded scenario due to the limitations imposed by adjustment policies, as well as the slower rhythm in the growth of external resources. Nevertheless, it appears that in the near future the agencies will still be a central actor in the institutional scenario of social sciences. On the other hand, as shown by the centre survey results, the trend seems to be for university centres to increasingly look for support from external financing sources.

There are two problems concerning the perspectives of the agencies: funding continuity and the conditions of support. There is a degree of uncertainty due to the fact that the conditions generating the resources are external to the Latin American region, thus establishing a degree of dependence which, whilst still allowing the development of research, still subordinates an important volume of scientific production to conditions that are not under the region's control. However, local resources hardly offer better guarantees. Some centres have devised noteworthy strategies aimed at financial autonomy on the basis of the generation of their own resources, but such strategies cannot be reproduced by the majority of the centres. But even if the situation is generally unstable, a general stability of external funding has been observed.

The modality and conditions of contributions constitute the rules of a game the centres must play. However, this does not imply an impossibility of negotiation, but it seems that the centres have not developed their full capacity to do so, possibly due to the pressures of individual negotiation, or to the difficulties of setting up a common front with a higher bargaining capacity. Nevertheless, at this level the strategies for the diversification of sources and for securing stable support will apparently still play a key role in the future.

IV. THE HORIZONS AND THE UNCERTAINTIES

The institutional scenario described shows a constant but unfinished process of institutional build-up, with different institutional modalities and actors, and different projects and profiles linked to historical features as well as to new challenges faced today by the different actors in the development of social science. The main features of the registered changes are a complex dynamism of institutional diversification and of growing thematic and interdisciplinary specialisation. These are a part, but also a product, of the mutations undergone by the Latin American societies as well as by the contemporary modernisation processes. The different institutional orientations are naturally interrelated with society and politics, but also with the limits and progress of the social sciences themselves. Not only is there a process of political and cultural conditioning of knowledge and its institutions, but also of their effects on society. Account must therefore be taken of the fact that the different institutional and knowledge orientations in the region are not alien to either the processes of crisis and the reconstitution of the relations of dominance, or to the challenges posed, in theory and in practice, by the modernity crisis.

The possibilities for an historical projection of the social sciences in the near future depend on the capacity to understand and meet the changes undergone within society through innovative theoretical-methodological orientations and institutional profiles, and on the capacity to creatively redefine institutional space within the national societies of the Latin American region.

Given the current modalities of institutional development, two related issues constitute the main tensions faced by social science institutions today: the search for stability and the building of institutional autonomy.

Institutional stability and instability are two aspects of the same historical process, and are directly related to the capacity of the different institutions to adapt to the changes imposed by different national and regional realities. It would therefore be a matter of institutional capacity to maximise resources (financial, organisational, personnel, political and scholarly) within the context of sociohistorical and knowledge change.

The process of institutional building of the social sciences in Latin America may be characterised as 'precariously stable'. The constant and persistent instability of the political system has conditioned the presence of a scholarly community strongly submitted to the pressures and limits set by these processes. On the one hand, the scholarly system itself, particularly within the university sphere, has shown a series of limits and tensions of a different kind which affect the consolidation of the institutions. On the other hand, it is evident that the scholarly system has a capacity to adapt to such circumstances, allowing for the permanence, the innovation and the diversification of the institutions.

This capacity for adaptation involves, at the same time, strategies where the financial and institutional resources are located, for example in the agencies, the state and in the university system, and adequate organisational modalities or institutional functioning 'styles' as regards the resources, the social orientations and the professional concerns of its components. Thus, the search for institutional stability, under the pressure of a variety of tensions and interests, constitutes in itself a problematic nucleus for the institutions, insofar as the strategies they devise solve certain problems and pose new ones which sometimes, paradoxically, threaten stability from other angles. We could consider, for example, the difficulties presented by the logic of 'inner rings', which tends to be found in private centres, or the often unresolved tension between community work and research in the centres carrying out both types of activity.

In this sense, many university centres show a permanence whose strong points would be (although not always) the continuity of their personnel and basic infrastructure. This does not, however, guarantee the resources needed to carry out projects or to update the scholarly services indispensable for the continuity of a scholarly project. In addition, private centres, generally under the pressure of current financing modalities, neglect training, theoretical research activities or studies relevant to the continuity of a scholarly project.

The examples noted above show that this scenario of 'precarious stability' differs according to each national and institutional situation, and that situations in which successful stability strategies exist can be found.

At present, three phenomena are relevant to the future development of social science research institutions, and tend to influence the type of stability achieved: the orientation of relations between the three types of institutional actors, the dynamic of differentiation of the centres and the scholarly community, and the insertion of the centres in national society and their search for social legitimacy.

Within the first phenomenon, the function of the project market and its control is especially relevant. This control is mainly exerted by the offer generated during the constitution of interests and orientations of the agencies, and secondarily by the centres' demands for finance. Despite growing interdependency, from the centres' points of view the basic problem is probably in the degree of their passivity in the changing orientations and in the competition within the market.

In relation to the state, we can foresee the persistence of cuts in funding and of difficulties within the public university system. Both are factors that will affect the stability of the institutions, and of the whole scholarly system in general. However, several countries could develop their institutional and normative sphere to recognise the plurality of institutional models and practices, and perhaps the mechanisms for the assignment of sparse funds will be multiplied within the system of competition. But in order to be effective, this multiplication must include an active participation from the scholarly community (for example in Brazil).

The second relevant phenomenon concerning institutional stability refers to the processes of differentiation of the centres and the scholarly community. The character and functioning of the elites, both in the market and in relations with the society and politics, as well as their effect on the shaping of the features of reproduction of institutional stability are particularly outstanding. This is perhaps why there is a tendency for the elites to become relatively close in their capacity to expand the scholarly community. On the other hand, in many cases the systems of rational competition are in conflict with ascriptitious or clientelistic interrelation patterns. Paradoxically, both phenomena are elements of the build-up of a relatively stable institutional system.

In the third place, the different processes of social legitimation and institutionalisation of action are also relevant. It seems that a redefinition of professional practice is presently taking place, which is partially related to the incorporation of social scientific activity into the market system, but is also a sign of a redefinition of the social insertion of the centres, and is related to the build-up of a social legitimacy whose sense and modalities are linked to the stability of institutions.

This redefinition, including a plurality of options for scientific activity, will perhaps be one of the key elements of the institutional landscape during the next few years, and which will still be variegated and diversified. This process is also apparently defining new forms of identity of the social sciences in the Latin American region in order to create progressive transformations of society. Perhaps the fact that this 'vocation' is now mainly defined from professional practice rather than from an ascriptitious relation to the state, the parties or particular social groups, may help the institutions to take root in civil society, thus ensuring their long-term stability.

In fact, the build-up of institutional autonomy, understood as the institutions' capacity to define policies, goals and activities, has an uneven record in Latin America. It has been affected, on the one hand, by the ups and downs of the political system which has excluded, persecuted or censored scientific practice. This problem also affects the wider issue of institutional autonomy vis à vis the political context and the relation of institutions to the state. On the other hand, there are problems of autonomy which are derived from the options taken by the researchers and the institutions themselves, particularly concerning the insertion of the centres within a market system, and their social insertion and social impact.

In authoritarian regimes, researchers have tended to devise strategies for the establishment of autonomous spaces, particularly in independent centres. In these countries, mechanisms of adaptation exist, ranging from self-censorship to production and circulation within a greater or lesser margin of limitation, including the ascription to officialism. War, conflicts and terrorism which have affected a group of countries in the region, notably Nicaragua, Guatemala, El Salvador, Peru and Colombia, have shown evidence of restrictions to scientific autonomy.

The definition of autonomy within a context of relative stability or democratic rule should also be analysed. During the 1960s and 1970s, the trend was absolute autonomy in the scholarly universe, with no state participation whatsoever. This trend has continued in several countries. But at the same time, there was an attempt to establish a university which could be the 'critical conscience of society'. In fact, state interference during democratic periods seems to have less affected intellectual autonomy than the production of knowledge. How can autonomy today be conceived vis à vis the state? Brunner's observation on the perspective of a higher degree of public responsibility on the part of research carried out with national funding should be kept in mind, and should be examined in the light of the historical and contextual significance of the idea of autonomy.

222

There are often a series of related issues attached to the links between autonomy and the insertion of the centres in a market system, such as the induction of themes and the pressure towards action on the part of the financing agencies. In fact, this sphere has a certain bargaining capacity, where in practice a process of adjustment of interests between each centre and agency is registered. On the other hand, part of the centres' strategies consists of attempting to carry out those activities which interest them, within the scope of the available resources. In this sense, the strategies towards diversification and towards obtaining stable funds are also strategies of autonomy build-up. The centres have different internal capacities for ensuring the achievement of their goals, including a pressure on action, but it must be remembered that this pressure is often exerted on a scholarly sphere interested in widening its social insertion. The problem here would be the capacity of the centres to legitimise, vis à vis the sources of finance, patterns of social impact based on their own criteria and on a particular national dynamic which accords different significance to the purpose of social impact.

This applies to the individual links between centres and agencies. However, in a more general perspective, it should be noted that the whole scholarly system faces, in practice, an effective degree of limitation, as shown by the existing difficulties, due to the reconstruction of domestic and external resources, which hinder the production of knowledge in certain areas, or the undertaking of ambitious or theoretical projects. This limitation may occur at the level of an individual centre, but it strongly affects the scholarly system as a whole. The scholarly community's capacity of action on the definition of criteria and orientations of the financing agencies is highly relevant.

Finally, the autonomy of institutions vis à vis society and politics appears to be a process of autonomination of professional activity in relation to political or social ascriptions. This even applies to groups of social scientists linked to revolutionary processes such as those of Cuba or El Salvador where, although there exist activist definitions of scientific practice, there is also a strong participation of social scientists who, without abandoning their activism, make a more critical and professional contribution. The social insertion of the centres, particularly those combining action and research, have given way to other mechanisms of questioning autonomy, and the 'rank and file' ideology existing in some of them has operated in a similar way to the activist identity. In addition, the problem has concerned the institutions' capacity to recognise this tension and to define the kind of contribution which, starting from social or ideological objectives and appraisals, may have proved more professionally acceptable.

We may therefore conclude that the build-up of autonomy, as the build-up of stability, is a permanent process with no pre-established pattern, and that it is present as a problem for every institution facing tensions between the production of knowledge and political conjuncture, social orientations or the market.

NOTES

1. See the preface in Wright Mills, C., *La imaginación sociológica*.
1. Medina Echavarria, José, 1967, *Filosofía, educación y desarrollo*, Siglo XXI, Mexico.
3. This analysis is mainly based on experiences and research being currently carried out by CLACSO, entitled 'Perspectives of institutional development of the social sciences in Latin America', aiming at a scholarly and institutional characterisation of the member centres of CLACSO and its links with national states, financing agencies and society. This research began in 1988 and is sponsored by the Ford Foundation, COTESU in La Paz, CIID in Bogota and CEDEAL in Madrid. The project is coordinated by the Joint Committee for Latin American Studies of the Social Science Research Council (JCLAS-SSRC) of the United States: 'Intellectual trends and international scholarly relations in Latin American studies'. In particular, information from a group of preliminary reports on the general situation of social sciences in each country has been used to prepare this chapter. These reports were written by Jorge Balán (Argentina), José Joaquin Brunner (Chile), Mario Lombardi and Marta Licio (Uruguay), Tomas Palau (Paraguay), Sergio Miceli (Brazil), Carlos Carafa and Carlos Guzmán (Bolivia), Mariano Valderrama (Peru), Luis Verdesoto (Ecuador), Gabriel Murillo (Colombia), Isabel Licha (Venezuela), Gabriel Aguilera (Costa Rica and Guatemala), Edelberto Torres Rivas (Nicaragua), Marcos Carias (Honduras), Giovanna Valenti (Mexico), Luis Suarez (Cuba), Magaly Pineda (Dominican Republic), Carman Gautier (Puerto Rico). In addition, the preliminary results of the survey to the directors of the 110 centre members of CLACSO have been available, but the bulk of this information, currently being processed, will be analysed in a future document.
4. Brunner, J.J. and Alicia Barrios, 1987, *Inquisición, mercado y filantropía. Ciencias sociales y autoritarismo en Argentina, Brasil, Chile y Uruguay*, Chile: FLACSO, pp.21-22. The authors also point out the uneven regional distribution of these figures. In the 1970s, Brazil had 57 per cent of the graduates, with another 40 per cent concentrated in Mexico, Colombia, Venezuela, Argentina, Chile and Peru.
5. The current number of social science graduates is around 450. The Coordenadora de Aperfeiçoamento de Pessoal a Nivel Superior (CAPES) is registered only in Brazil: in 1987 there were 252 graduates in social sciences, namely 189 masters and 63 doctorates. In Venezuela in 1984 there were 96, namely 84 masters and 12 doctorates, whilst in Mexico the figure was 47 in 1985. Sources: (Brazil) 'Postgraduaçaõ. A avaliaçaõ dos cursos de mestrado e doutorado fita pela CAPES', *Guía do Estudiantes 87*, pp.274-79, Saõ Paulo; (Venezuela), Castro,

Gregorio, 1988, *Sociólogos y sociología en Venezuela*, Caracas: UNESCO, Tropycos; (Mexico), Valenti, Giovanna, 1988, 'Ethos académico y calidad de la formación de postrado', Mexico. These figures contrast with the 96 graduate programmes registered by CLACSO in 1977, even considering that this did not include all existing graduate programmes. See *Programas docentes de postgrado vigentes en América Latina*, 1977, Buenos Aires: CLACSO, Serie Postrado. Concerning the increase in the number of research centres, CLACSO itself offers a good example. Created in 1967 with 25 member centres, by 1989 it had 120 associates, with 62 per cent created after 1971, and another 20 per cent created between 1961 and 1970.

6. Inter-country heterogenity in social sciences follows fairly approximately the socioeconomic distribution among 'large', 'medium' and 'small' countries.

7. From 1983 through 1987, CLACSO organised 108 regional meetings with an approximate total attendance of 3,200 people.

8. In the United States alone, there are more than 5,000 registered Latin Americanists, which is equivalent to the total number of scholars within all the CLACSO centres.

9. The CLACSO survey has registered 172 guest researchers sent by the centres in 1986 and 1987, and 198 guest researchers hosted by the centres during the same period. This figure includes interchanges within and outside the region.

10. For a more thorough analysis of this issue, see, for example, Touraine, Alain, *El retorno del actor*, and Lechner, Norbert, 1988, 'De la revolución a la democracia', *Los patios interiores de la democracia*, Santiago: FLACSO, pp.21-45, or Sonntag, Heinz, 'Los retos internos de las ciencias sociales en América Latina y el Caribe', paper delivered at the UNESCO meeting 'América Latina y el mundo hacia el año 2000', Quito, 1989.

11. The survey mentioned shows that 71 per cent of the directors prefer to classify their centres by their thematic specialisations and 23 per cent by their disciplinary specialisations.

12. The answers to the different questions are as follows (each centre was allowed to choose more than one option):

    (1) Different types of audience to which the research outcomes are directed: scholarly, 88 per cent of the centres, state agencies, 64 per cent, popular organisations, 47 per cent.

    (2) Participation of the centres' researchers in the following activities directed at public opinion: public fora, 89 per cent, TV or radio shows, 67 per cent, press, 81 per cent.

    (3) Different kinds of users of short studies, advice, counselling and analyses: state agencies, 52 per cent, international agencies, 49.5 per cent, non-government and non-political organisations, 51 per cent, political parties, 12.4 per cent.

13. For a thorough analysis of the build-up process of private centres and the institutional development of social sciences in the Southern Cone, see Brunner and Barrios, op. cit.

14. This analysis does not include the kind of centre which carries out 'community work' (NGO), whose expansion has undoubtedly been much larger than that of the scholarly centres, with a different intensity in each country of the Latin American region. It is probable that this sector is absorbing a larger amount of social scientists than the scholarly centres. In this analysis, some centres that combine community work and research which, due to the weight of the latter

225

component, may be considered as scholarly centres, have been taken into account. Within CLACSO's network, 40 per cent of its members share this feature.

15. Rough estimates provided by the authors of the CLACSO project's national reports.

16. Figures from Brunner, J.J., 'Desarrollo de los recursos humanos para la investigación en América Latina', paper submitted to the Seminario Regional sobre Desarrollo de los Recursos humanos para la Investigación en América Latina (IDRC), Salvador de Bahía, April 1987.

17. The study carried out by CLACSO includes a series of interviews with social science coordinators in the main agencies for the scientific and technological development of the region, to be analysed in a future document.

18. As pointed out by Giovanna Valenti in the research on Mexico carried out for the CLACSO project, CONACYT has redefined its priorities for the 1984-88 period, establishing 11 main areas for study. One of these areas is social sciences, identified as 'nature and society'.

19. Paper by CNPq's Social Sciences Director, presented at the meeting 'Políticas gubernamentales de desarrollo de las ciencias sociales en América Latina', CNPq-CLACSO-FLACSO, Brasilia, May 2-5, 1989.

20. See the paper presented by J.J. Brunner at the May 1989 meeting, for the perspectives for the relations between the state and social sciences. It examines the possibility of a tendency towards the formation of a system of competition for the assignment of state resources, on the basis of the Brasilian and (more recently) the Argentinian and Chilean experiences.

BIBLIOGRAPHY

Ansaldi, Waldo and Fernando Calderón, 'La búsqueda de América Latina: entre el ansia de encontrarla y el temor de no reconocerla. Teorias e instituciones en la construcción de las ciencias sociales en América Latina', report presented at the CLACSO-SSRC meeting on 'Relaciones Académicas Internacionales y Desarrollo Institucional de las Ciencias Sociales en América Latina', Montevideo, August 17-19, 1989.

Arahuetes, Alfredo, 'La consideración que reciben los centros de investigación en ciencias sociales de América Latina en las estrategias de las instituciones europeas de cooperación', document presented at the CLACSO-SSRC meeting on 'Relaciones Académicas Internacionales y Desarrollo Institucional de las Ciencias Sociales en América Latina', Montevideo, August 17-19, 1989.

Balán, Jorge, 'El impacto de la asistencia externa en la institucionalización de las ciencias sociales: el caso argentino', report presented at the CLACSO-SSRC meeting on 'Relaciones Académicas Internacionales y Desarrollo Institucional de las Ciencias Sociales en América Latina', Montevideo, August 17-19, 1989.

Barrios, Alicia and José Joaquin Brunner, 1987, *Inquisición, mercado y filantropía. Ciencias sociales y autoritarismo en Argentina, Brasil, Chile y Uruguay*, Chile: FLACSO.

Brunner, José Joaquìn, 'Desarrollo de los recursos humanos para la investigación en América Latina', document presented to the Regional Seminar on 'Desarrollo de los Recursos Humanos para la Investigación en América Latina', organised by the IDRC, Bahia, April 1987.

Brunner, José Joaquin, 1989, *Ciencias Sociales y Estado. Reflexiones en voz alta*, Santiago: FLACSO.

The Challenge for Latin American Social Science

Calderón, Fernando and Patricia Provoste, 1989, 'La construcción institucional de las ciencias sociales en América Latina', *David y Goliath, CLACSO's Magazine*, No.55.

CAPES, 1987, 'Postgraduaçaõ. A availiaçaõ dos cursos de mestrado e doutorado fita pela CAPES', *Guía do Estudiantes 87*, Sao Paulo: pp.274-79.

Castro, Gregorio, 1988, *Sociólogos y Sociología en Venezuela*, Caracas: UNESCO/Tropycos.

CEPAL, 1988, *1987 Yearbook*, Santiago: CEPAL.

CLACSO, 1977, *Programas docentes de postgrado vigentes en América Latina 1977*, Buenos Aires: CLACSO, Postgraduation Series.

CLACSO, 1987, *Memoria de actividades 1983-1987*, Buenos Aires: CLACSO.

Coatsworth, John H, 'International Collaboration in the Social Sciences: the ACLS/SSRC Joint Committee on Latin American Studies', report presented at the CLACSO-SSRC meeting on 'Relaciones Académicas Internacionales y Desarrollo Institucional de las Ciencias Sociales en América Latina', Montevideo, August 17-19, 1989.

Cotler, Julio, Romeo Grompone and Fernando Rospigliosi, 1988, *El desarrollo Institucional de las Ciencias Sociales en el Perú*, Lima: Instituto de Estudios Peruanos.

Drake, Paul W, 'From Retrogression to Resurgence: International Scholarly Relations with Latin America in U.S. Universities, 1970s-1980s', document presented at the CLACSO-SSRC meeting on 'Relaciones Académicas Internacionales y Desarrollo Institucional de las Ciencias Sociales en América Latina', Montevideo, August 17-19, 1989.

Garretón, Manuel Antonio, 1982, *Las ciencias sociales en Chile. Situación, problemas, perspectivas*, Santiago: Academia de Humanismo Cristiano.

Germani, Gino, preface to the Spanish version of 'La imaginación sociológica', from Charles Wright Mills.

Goodman, Louis W, 'Trends in North American Funding for Social Science Research on Latin America', document presented at the CLACSO-SSRC meeting on 'Relaciones Académicas Internacionales y Desarrollo Institucional de las Ciancias Sociales en América Latina', Montevideo, August 17-19, 1989.

Klubitschko, Doris, 1986, *Postgrado en América Latina. Investigación comparativa: Brasil-Colombia-México-Venezuela*, Caracas: CRESALC-UNESCO.

Lechner, Norbert, 1988, 'De la revolución a la democracia', *Los patios interiores de la democracia*, Santiago: FLACSO, pp.21-41.

Lombardi, Mario and Olga Beltrand, 'Estado y ciencias sociales en América Latina', report presented at the CLACSO-SSRC meeting on 'Relaciones Académicas Internacionales y Desarrollo Institucional de las Ciencias Sociales en América Latina', Montevideo, August 17-19, 1989.

16

Development Models and Culture Identities in Asia

D.G.P. SENEVIRATNE

The parameters within which the present discussion is to take place show that the debate on the role of the state is far from being resolved. The legitimate criticism of the inefficiencies and the dampening of enterprise associated with 'big government' has been countered, at least in industrialised societies, by the working man's fear that the withdrawal of the state from its regulatory functions would remove the only institution that is capable of standing up to the corporate putsch. Carey has argued that among the techniques employed in the corporate endeavour to identify interventionist governments with oppression, and the free enterprise system with every cherished value, has been 'economic education'.[1]

This certainly is the case in Third World countries, where the state has a direction-giving role with respect to the management of the economy and also a primary responsibility for maintaining minimum standards of nutrition and other living conditions, from which it cannot easily absolve itself.

In Asian countries, where historically the so-called Asiatic mode of production has prevailed, the state continues to carry the burden of authority and responsibility which the people are accustomed to investing in it.

On the question of participation and the new relationship between the state and civil society, once again the Asian region displays a broad spectrum of experience within which there is a strong military presence in many countries.

There is considerable literature concerning what has been described as military-bureaucratic regimes in Asia.[2] It has been argued that the military has only intervened in societies where extra-state forces were perceived by its leaders as a threat to the state, or where the state has lacked the legitimacy of an established legal order, the economic resources of an efficient and independent extractive capacity, and the stability which comes from the emotional allegiance of its people.

Whatever the genesis of such military regimes, it is undeniable that they have led to the marginalisation of the institutions of civil society. If we were to measure 'development' in terms of the degree to which people have control over the forces which shape their lives,[3] the relationship between such regimes and development would become clear. If such regimes do deliver that minimal degree of autonomy of action essential to human life, one would have to regard them as protectors of that fundamental prerequisite for development.

In fact, it has been observed that the actions of such regimes - those which exercise state power - obviously depend on how they interpret the nature of their society and its economic structure, their concepts of justice and equity and on the legitimacy derived from international recognition. Given that these regimes come into being by the elimination of all plausible threats to their claims to state power, it would appear that they have tended to ignore the long-term political and social implications of the policies they pursue. Since such policies relate to how national resources are harnessed or exploited, and how external resources are secured, the choices made would reflect on the relative sovereignty and stability of their societies. As a Reuter report on Zimbabwe phrased it, 'liberalisation of "the market" would seem to have gone hand in hand with "deliberalising" politics'.

Under these regimes, the military and the bureaucracy are seen to act in concert with the dominant metropolitan bourgeoisie in formulating economic policy. For convenience it shall be taken that the nations of South and South-East Asia are post-colonial states, although in the case of Thailand, for instance, the dependent relationship is of more recent origin.

In most cases the ex-colonial powers continued to remain the dominant class within these states until, in more recent years, they have come to be largely replaced by a consortium of the dominant economies of the world. The ruling classes of these countries continued to be the metropolitan bourgeoisie acting with or through a native class of dependent bourgeoisie. In its task of gaining dominance over the indigenous social classes, and subordinating precapitalist social formations in colonial capitalism, the colonial state had established bureaucracies which have since come to diversify the links of the post-colonial state to include bourgeois factions from countries other than that of the ex-colonial power.

In fact, a parallel development has occurred in the social sciences; changes in the balance of power among the metropolitan countries have been reflected through changes in the perspectives adopted by the national intelligentsia with respect to the social sciences.

If the economic task of the colonial state was to make inroads into pre-colonial economies opening them up for mercantile accumulation by metropolitan capital, the current discussion would appear to centre on whether social science research and training is being called upon to perform a similar role today. Even nowadays, Edmund Burke's horror at the dismantling, on speculative principles, of society's immemorial systems is being echoed. The communications revolution is in the process of completing the subversion of even those elements of traditional societies which have survived the phase of direct colonial rule.

Therefore, the social sciences in Asia confront, on the one hand, the task of functioning within a context in which the state has surrendered its autonomy to the forces of external economic pressure, with often a strong military presence in the management of its internal affairs. On the other hand, they are confronted by the real problems of food, clothing and shelter of the people who constitute their societies. The dialogue at that level has increasingly taken the form of a contemptuous and cowed silence on either side.

The resulting instability, of which anti-intellectualism is a symptom, has led to an exponential growth of social scientists who are willing to pay for the celebrated free lunch and are able to do so - perhaps in the short term. Their prescriptions are addressed not to their own societies but directed outward to various agencies in the metropolitan capital. For this purpose the adoption of a view of man as homo-economicus provides a facade of value-neutrality which helps anaesthetise whatever intellectual aspirations they may have started off with. As Michael Edwards has shown, the politics of development studies have run up against attempts to orient the social sciences towards policy recommendations that would enlarge the capacity of the people to promote their own interests rather than to push them down in the other direction.[4]

For most people in the Third World, and elsewhere, the road prescribed for development, if it is pursued throughout the 1990s, could well become the primrose path to damnation. The dehumanising of the objects of economic management is perhaps reflected in the terms employed for the measurement of the output of development: in academic treatises and in World Bank analyses, people have ceased to exist. The alliance of mercantile capitalism and Christian missionary-dom defined labour as 'souls'; now we have measurements made in terms of 'per capita', as if people were so many head of cattle.

The term 'development' first entered the English vocabulary from the French some 400 years ago and substantially means 'to unfold, unroll, flatten out, disclose, unveil, bring out all that is contained in, open gradually, bring forth from a latent or elementary condition, bring out and render visible, cause to grow, evolve, and grow into a fuller, higher, or maturer condition'.[5]

It is a truism now that the fundamental paradigm of western development theory is econocentric and quantitative, and that it has tended to devalue the other social sciences, while at the same time evoking nativistic responses that emphasise the positive virtues of traditional cultures as outweighing the temporal (and often temporary) benefits to be gained from market-based economic policies.

Concepts of 'cultural comparative advantage', as constituting a primary explanation for the rapid industrialisation of some east Asian countries, are being explored by the Institute of East Asian Philosophies in Singapore. The notion of a 'Confucian East Asia'[6] has given rise to the question of whether certain attitudes and values are universally associated with socio-economic development and attempts are being made to identify cultural values that are functional to development and to distinguish them from those which are dysfunctional. Therefore, the assumption that the adoption of modern technology is the essential pre-requisite for development, rejects, perhaps in a very real sense, the notion of the latecomer advantage.

It follows then, as Asian examples show, that the economic consequences of the national development strategy chosen - whether it was protectionist and conservationist as it was in Sri Lanka up to a decade ago, or perhaps the rapid exploitation of internal resources towards export-led growth, (of which there are many examples) - the strategy chosen has had a direct impact on the strength of the state and on its ability to govern. Broadly speaking, in one case countervailing forces within the state have grown in strength as the state has been exposed to strong external economic pressures, while in the other, oppositional forces have been delegitimised with the tacit concurrence of the external world.

The foundations of the push for development lie in a perception of the disparities in wealth between the 'developing', or newly independent countries of 30 years ago and 'developed' countries which were also among the colonial powers. The response to that perception has been an attempt to accelerate economic development in order to catch up with the western model of development.

This western model increased the aspirations of the ruling elite in the newly independent countries. One consequence of this has been that indigenous social and economic assets have tended to be largely discounted or ignored and an alternative future based on them has been barely contemplated. Independence was accompanied by a strong left-wing/Marxist presence in many countries and the 'Western educated intelligentsia' came to be almost synonymous with a commitment to the Marxist view of the world. As is well known, Marx believed not only that the industrially developed countries showed the less developed countries the image of their own future, he also foresaw that the 'Western bourgeoisie' by the vastly improved means of communication would draw, as he put it, 'even the most barbarian nation into civilisation'.[7]

With the rise to dominance of the United States which developed as an immigrant society, the view that traditional forms of society were irrelevant came to be widely disseminated. What is currently under discussion here is partly related to the world view outlined above. Even if we assume that the forces which are driving the world in this particular direction have become irresistible, it is obvious that developing countries in general are being called upon to embark on programmes of economic development based on export markets at a time when economic space in the international market is shrinking.[8] The pressure exerted by funding agencies to accelerate the pace of growth and to undertake a major restructuring of the economies of developing countries in the service of growth must necessarily be evaluated against this background.

Attempts by Asian countries to engage in the management of the economy on a macro level through planning have been challenged in terms of the economic efficiency and administrative viability of such exercises. Recent developments in the socialist economies have also strengthened and given legitimacy to 'the market' as an instrument of efficient economic development.

We all know that the impersonal autonomy of the markets is a myth, that the markets are most frequently characterised by market failure and that 'the market' is essentially an abstract paradigmatic construction of theory.

The challenge facing the social sciences in Asian countries arises from the fact that England's experience in the transformation of its economy from being agriculturally-based to industrial capitalism has been taken as a model, especially by Marx. 'Development' has come to be associated with the proletarianisation of agricultural labour to serve as a rapid expansion of the industrial sector. This diagnosis has been disseminated through orientations provided by the curricula of universities in the West which train social science teachers for developing country universities. At the most elementary level, hundreds of such people have returned with the message:

This is how it was done in England; industrialisation, not agriculture, is the road to development; take people off the land; develop and utilise such human resources because you have that one asset above all, an abundance of cheap labour, in which it would be laughable for the developed world to try to compete with you.

The task facing the social sciences in South and South East Asia is to address the problem of development as defined above, within the context of the continuing importance, if not dominance, of the agriculture sector despite a variety of strategies adopted to induce industrialisation. The following figures provide an index to the nature of the problem:

TABLE 1
AGRICULTURE SHARE IN GROSS NATIONAL PRODUCT

Countries	Agriculture share in GNP %		Average Annual Growth 1965-1985 %	
	1965	1985	1965	1985
Bangladesh	53.0	50.0	1.80	2.70
India	4.0	31.0	2.80	4.20
Indonesia	55.0	24.0	4.00	6.80
Malaysia	56.0	21.a	4.4 b	6.80
Pakistan	57.0	25.0	3.00	5.40
Philippines	58.0	27.0	3.90	4.30
Sri Lanka	59.0	27.0	3.00	4.30
Thailand	60.0	17.0	4.50	6.80

Source: World Bank[9] - a. for 1983; b. for 1970-1985

Whilst each of those figures have a specific explanation in their support, they are broadly indicative of historical changes in the economic structure of each country.

The response to the belief that industrialisation and economic development were virtually synonymous has led to policies intended to support industry at the expense of agriculture.

Import-substitution, or import-competing production, has competed with 'export-led growth' as a strategy for industrialisation, the first due to a desire for economic independence and the second, more optimistic, favoured by the existence, at a particular time, of the requisite opportunities abroad. 'Import-substitution' strategies appear to have foundered due to the limitations imposed by the size of domestic markets, - a problem that has been compounded by the concomitant depression of farm-based incomes. The so-called 'mini-tigers' of East Asia entered the world market at a time when the rapid expansion of the economies of the industrialised countries was accompanied by a decline in industrial protectionism among them.[10] Today their prospects for economic growth remain bright as the ideologies of 'the market' find their efforts to capture markets hampered by domestic production inefficiencies.

Whichever strategy was adopted, it implied a discounting of agriculture as a basis for 'development', both in the meaning generally assigned to it, and in the larger sense. Industrialisation has been attempted on the shoulders of the farmer on whom direct and indirect taxes have fallen under both strategies for modernisation. This process, which has involved the institutionalisation of the consumer surplus, the pauperisation of the producer, the proletarianisation of the farmer and the creation of a surplus of labour for appropriation by the service and manufacturing sectors, has been well documented. What the social sciences need to address are the dynamics of an agriculture-based development strategy which also focuses on the primary need for food security at household and at national level.

In this endeavour, the social sciences are being called upon to orient themselves towards the social impacts of agricultural research. The Indian experience has shown that while technological change has virtually eliminated country-wide shortages of food, rural poverty has increased and that, so far, the social sciences have failed to develop solutions to problems that are being created by the changing structure of agriculture.[11] The problems encountered in crop science research would seem to mirror those faced by the social sciences: the externally-stimulated (and, to a significant degree, externally-funded) agricultural research in India appears to have belatedly discovered the need to develop technologies that are region-specific. A significant aspect of the current status of modern agricultural technology in India is that it has failed to develop alternatives which 'surpass the stability of indigenous farming system'.[12]

Given the disorientation of the ruling intelligentsia in Asian countries caused by its largely uncritical adoption of the Marxist construction of history; the visible failure of its attempts to capture and manage 'the commanding heights of the economy' through state institutions; and the capacity of external agencies and economic forces to cripple the economy and destabilise the political systems of developing countries, the ideological message of the free market is being extended world-wide. The primary challenge faced by the social sciences in Asia arises from the fact that in this process the social scientists themselves have often been subverted. Self-interest alone would show that those who promote the dissemination of the free-market ideology are in practice engaged in subsidising both agriculture and industry, and in protecting them through state-imposed quotas on domestic production and/or on foreign imports.

The present discussion assumes that a certain transformation of the relationship between the state and the development processes is in motion and that research and training in the social sciences should orient themselves, perhaps in a supportive way, towards such a transformation. What we have here, however, is not a spontaneous process of indigenous origin nor one that has been set in motion primarily in response to the needs of the Asian societies, but rather a top-down exercise in socio-economic engineering at a global level.

The awareness and concern of the intelligentsia, where they exist, of the dangers of such developments, have given rise in Asia to a renewed examination of the relationship between culture and development. Like all attempts at social engineering, the present exercise has been confounded by the diversity of the strategies that need to be adopted towards achieving geopolitical objectives in real situations that are not uniform in terms of the relative autonomy of the target groups. The contemporary search for the recovery of national identities, whether they are based on the historical record or on more or less fictitious claims to territory, have implications for the management of the resources of the world. Conceivably we might soon have a host of tribal entities secure in their pre-colonial identities and ready for the table of big bad wolves equipped with an appetite that appears beyond appeasement.

In 1969, a path-breaking paper on 'The implantation of Sociology in Asia' by Ralph Pieris reviewed the genesis of the social sciences in the West, their orientation, the process of dissemination adopted and the socio-political interests which they sought to serve.

This subject was once more recently addressed by Takashi Onami in a paper on 'Area Studies in the Global Multi-Cultural Society.' What they have in common is an appreciation of the diversity of Asian societies in the economic foundations of the cultural matrix within which development takes place. The social sciences, in research and training which are symbiotically related, need to address the problems of each specific universe without referring to the forces which demand conformity to a 'value-free global culture'.

236

NOTES

1. Carey, Alex, 'Managing Public Opinion', 1987, in S.F. Frankel (ed.), *Union Strategy and Industrial Change*, Australia: University of New South Wales Press.
2. Riggs, Fred W., 1966, *Thailand: The Modernisation of a Bureaucratic Polity*, Honolulu: East-West Center Press.
3. Edwards, Michael, 1989. 'The Irrelevance of Development Studies', *Third World Quarterly*, Vol. 11(1).
4. *Ibid.*
5. The Oxford Universal Dictionary on Historical Principles, 1955.
6. Wei-ming, Tu, 1989, 'The Confucian Dimension in the East Asian Development Model', paper presented at the Chinese Institute for Economic Research, Taipei.
7. Marx, Karl, Preface to *Capital*.
8. Petras, James, 1990, 'The World Market: Battleground for 1990s'. *Economic & Political Weekly*, January 27.
9. Adapted from Bautista, Fomeo, 1990, 'Development Strategies, Foreign Trade Regimes, and Agricultural Incentives in Asia'. *Journal of Asian Economics*, Vol.1., No. 1.
10. *Ibid.*
11. Easter, K. Williams, *et al.*, 1989, 'The State Agricultural Universities in India Face New Challenges', *American Journal of Agricultural Economics*, Vol. 71., No. 5.
12. *Ibid.*

17

The Crisis of the State in Africa

PAULIN J. HOUNTONDJI

I. INTRODUCTION

The current situation in Africa appears to be marked by the acceleration and the gigantic progress of what has been rightly called 'the long march towards democracy'.[1] To comprehensively evaluate and bring out the main features of the current situation, we shall elect the political criterion as it takes into account the relations of power within society. We shall not choose, from among the many parameters which are generally called upon to define a particular situation, the economic parameters which is often the case when faced with a severe 'economic crisis'. Nor shall we choose other possible parameters such as the level of cultural activity or of scientific and technological development. We shall favour political parameters.

The economic crisis has not developed spontaneously, nor is it the mechanical result of 'blind forces' whether market rules or any other laws. On the contrary. it has evolved from serious mistakes in management decisions, at least in Africa and probably in other areas also. In fact, at the beginning of the crisis, in the African version at least, there has not only been a deterioration in the terms of trade and other adverse effects due to the international economic crisis, but also some unforgivable management mistakes and a deliberate policy of spoils and plundering which a democratic revolution should be able to prevent and correct. Finally all the other parameters, all the other facets of our collective future, are directly or indirectly dependent on the political dimension, that is to say on the nature and evolution of the relations of power in our society.

Acknowledging the progress of democratisation does not necessarily mean that the difficulties attached to the process are underestimated, nor is it pretending that everything goes well and will be fine. Actually, nothing is definitely won in Africa. Over the past 16 months we have witnessed the sustained victory of the democratic movement in Benin - a small country with a population of four million. But, though a 'National Conference' was able to bring a 17-year old dictatorship which called itself Marxist-Leninist to an end and was able to establish an interim government whose responsibility is the transition to a lawful state within a year, the situation could still change for the worse, like in the Chile of Salvador Allende. It is, therefore, too soon to crow over victory.

Likewise in Gabon, Zaire, Ivory Coast and other similar countries where the political situation has rapidly matured over the recent months and where the multiparty idea has been impressed on everyone, even on the most authoritarian heads of State, the die is not yet cast. Despite the 'granted' democracy, the promises to establish a multiparty system and some timid cabinet reshuffling - mere patching up, which allows the regimes in place to gain time - there are no institutional guarantees that the pendulum will not swing back again.

Therefore, it is necessary to be cautious when speaking of democratic progress. However, one thing is certain. People have become bolder and are no longer afraid of proclaiming their demand for liberty to the autocrats who, only a short while ago, were still redoubtable and a cause for fear. The days when criticisms and demands had to be kept to a whisper among small or even clandestine groups are over.

In some countries at least, the time has come for the supporters of democracy to lead the struggle openly and thereby deny the dictators the satisfaction of still feeling redoubtable. The constraints of a clandestine struggle have been rejected as 'clandestinity' itself is an undeserved concession made to dictators. In the present circumstances, this new courage is an essential element of what must be called the crisis of the state in Africa today. This new determination has fostered hope and made any relapse in the democratisation process difficult, at least for the time being.

Thus, the crisis of the state is firstly a crisis of confidence: The people no longer believe the official statements. The damaging effects of corruption have made the general population wary of and suspicious towards great declarations of intent, generous programmes and long-winded ideologies. Civil society has no longer any faith in the state; it knows that the state lies, steals, plunders, stupefies, as much from inclination as from necessity. The state can only assure its survival as an apparatus of coercion, by means of lies and mediocrity.

To be better understood, the new economic policies which are characterised by a readjustment of the public and private sectors, a privatisation and liberalisation drive and the decline of the state in both the Third World and in Eastern Europe have to be put in the context described above. The structural adjustment programmes miss their aim as long as they are felt as a constraint imposed by outside creditors, notably the World Bank and the International Monetary Fund. They will only have a chance of success if supported by internal political will and a national programme of economic recovery. Of course external aid will have to be called upon but not in a lazy and automatic way as if the destiny of the country was to be condemned to international begging. On the contrary, it will be considered in an intelligent and methodical way, as a transitional step in a strategy aiming at other horizons.

Thus understood and reinterpreted, the so-called adjustment programmes imply democracy and that civil society itself takes over its collective destiny, beyond the excesses and encroachments of the parasitic state.

II. THE CONFLICT OF PARADIGMS

Two explanatory models - two paradigms - have always competed in the social science studies of the Third World, and in particular of Africa. The first one explains the crisis by endogenous causes, whilst the second model favours above all explained external forces. The theory of underdevelopment proposed by Rostow is an illustration of the first paradigm.[2] It shows economic backwardness as a consequence of traditions, in other words of cultural backwardness, and the society concerned as solely responsible for its underdevelopment. Today, no-one really believes this explanation which seems to have been supplanted by neo-marxist theories, such as those of André Gunder Franck,[3] Celso Furtado[4] or Samir Amin,[5] who see underdevelopment not as an indication of traditional backwardness, but as the historical result of the integration of subsistence economies in the world capitalist market.

By drawing attention to certain phenomena in the Third World such as corruption and the misappropriation of public funds, or autocratic and dictatorial power, the current crisis might induce a return to the endogenous explanatory model, at least in the short term. Then, all the problems of the Third World will appear as having been brought about by the Third World itself. Internal parameters, internal causes, forms and modes of social dysfunction will be insisted upon, and will be isolated from the larger context of the world geopolitics and economic crisis.

In fact, a good understanding of the crisis requires both an internal and an external analysis which take into consideration endogenous and exogenous factors as well as their interactions. One of the theoretical challenges that social sciences in Africa is confronted with today is to conciliate these apparently contradictory paradigms. This cannot be achieved by weakening both approaches, but by going further in the analysis of each, driving them both to maximum fecundity. It is necessary to get to the end of the analysis of the dependence theory, of the obvious or more subtle means of exploitation. But it is also necessary to critically examine and understand the internal mechanisms of the oppression and dictatorship. At this depth of study, the complementarity of the two approaches would become evident, whereas it would stay hidden stopping half way through the theoretical analysis.

In order to illustrate this complementarity, we will use the example of science and technology in Africa. The relevance of the neo-marxist paradigm, which the author has stressed elsewhere,[6] has been little acknowledged up to now. Generally, this paradigm is applied to the analysis of economic underdevelopment, however in this case we will try to apply it to scientific and technological dependence.

In the worldwide production of knowledge, the peripheral countries have, for a long time, functioned, and still continue functioning, as immense reservoirs of primary data and information which have been collected and selected for the need of scientists and economic researchers in the industrialised countries. Thus they were immediately drained and exported to outside laboratories to undergo appropriate theoretical treatment. In this sense, the scientific and technological 'underdevelopment' of Africa, and perhaps of the Third World at large, cannot be understood without reference to the system which has generated and carried it: the world system of production of knowledge. This system is managed and controlled at the centre of the world capitalist market.

However, this explanation is not sufficient. The criticism of the imperialist exploitation would become partial and unilateral if the internal mechanisms which daily increase the subservience to the world capital were not mentioned. It can even run the risk of degenerating into a lazy discourse or being trapped into easy recrimination and good conscience.

Therefore, any worldwide critical approach to underdevelopment must necessarily be completed by a critical examination of the local mechanisms of underdevelopment reproduction. In addition, a criticism of science extroversion, such as the one being promoted here, must lead on to a critical appraisal of the internal mechanisms of the reproduction of mediocrity. We are not only subject to mediocrity, we have also accepted it, internalised it and have even enhanced its value.

242

We have made ourselves the active accomplices in the destiny that is overburdening us. A thorough analysis must also take this fact into account and not merely push the responsibility for our misfortune onto others.

If the external explanation leads us to take internal factors into account, the internal explanation inversely needs to take the international environment into account. For example, corruption and dictatorship must not be solely analysed as internal phenomena because this restricted vision of reality would then only consider their African specificity and could eventually lead to racist conclusions. Although it is important to understand the internal mechanisms of autocracy, we must not forget to question its (conscious or unconscious) real function in relation to the logic of capital, in relation to the diverse forces fighting in the region or the sub-region and also in relation to world geopolitics. This is the only way which can enable us to understand why, for example, a country like socialist France helped during such a long time, and perhaps continues helping, some of the most abject dictatorships from behind a smoke screen of human rights rhetoric.

III. NEW TASKS FOR THE SOCIAL SCIENCES

Faced with the complex crisis experienced by our societies (and the state crisis is only its most visible expression), the historical task of the social sciences in Africa is to contribute, with the power of their own intellectual possibilities, to the definition of credible alternatives. The various disciplines must cooperate in a true interdisciplinary spirit, methodically and rigorously overcoming departmentalisation and rivalries. From sociology to law, from economy to political science and philosophy, the circulation of information and concepts should help to solve new problems by proposing original and constructive solutions.

Two fields are particularly concerned: politics and economics. Social sciences must echo the democratic movement in today's Africa. They should further and promote it by explaining the mechanisms of oppression, by analysing and exposing the dysfunction of previous political systems so as to facilitate their dismantling. This task will also include the construction of democracy which is a form of management where civilian society holds or has control over power, which allows transparency and moral honesty and which guarantees the respect of human rights and encourages the progress of intelligence. Social

243

sciences must also help in finding clear and constructive alternatives to the current economical crisis.

If, as some people think, the structural adjustment programmes currently implemented in our countries are incompatible with social and economic progress, the social sciences must go beyond mere politics and rhetoric to suggest reasonable options, based on a rigourous analysis of the true particulars of the problem.

A third field which should also have our attention: is political science. The deep-down rooted extroversion and the persistent dependence of our scientific and technological activities requires, on the one hand, a systematic analysis of this facet of the dependence system - too often neglected - and, on the other hand, the proposition of practical alternative solutions.

This is where a relatively young discipline, sociology of science, becomes useful. Its objective is to study the relations between science and society, but until now the slant has been on the examination of the relationship within industrial societies, whilst neglecting societies on the periphery and therefore evading the essential question of the relationship of scientific and technological production on an international scale. We will have to use the conceptual tools inherited from this traditional science sociology and apply them to countries in the periphery while taking into account the specificity of knowledge production in a context of underdevelopment. Once the diagnosis is established, we will have to propose a new orientation, likely to lead us onto a more promising path, for our national scientific and technological policies.

The 'Inter African Philosophical Council', has tried to review and assess philosophical studies in Africa. This was done through a descriptive directory of books, articles, theses and papers by African authors or on Africa since the very beginning up to nowadays. The first two volumes were published in 1987 and 1988 respectively and covered the period from 1900 to 1985. The third volume will be an addendum to that period, whilst the fourth will cover the previous period i.e. from the origins until the end of the nineteenth century. The goal of this project is to enable researchers to make better use of what exists to avoid unnecessary duplication of already available information and to ensure real complementarity.

A small team, called 'the National CODESRIA Working Group', has been created at the National University of Benin. This group is currently working on a collective volume concerning endogenous knowledge with the view of exploring how to revalue the so-called traditional knowledge and know-how in the context of modern science.

244

In relation to these two bodies (the Interafrican Philosophical Council and the CODESRIA group), an attempt is being made to launch a wider programme of research on sociology of science in Africa. The ultimate goal of this programme is to offer a better understanding of the current mechanisms of scientific and technological dependency, in order to draw up possible axes for a new research policy.

Finally, we must consider Jean Bonvin's following question: 'Faced with the collapse of the socialist regimes, would it not be good to 'demarxicise' social sciences?' This question is essential. In the Benin context,[7] the historical failure of a regime that had claimed to be Marxist-Leninist could only fuel primitive and passionate anti-Marxism. Under these conditions the answer is simple. The real problem, overshadowed by the cascade of events in Eastern Europe and in the South, is not to know which ideology we support but the relation we have with it - either catechismal, therefore servile, or critical and free-thinking. In fact, what the current political crisis compels us to question is not Marxism itself, but its mode of historical appropriation in the East as well as in the South and even in the West through political parties. The current collapse shows that there have been some errors of judgement. Wrong answers were given to badly-put questions and the dogmatic approach, which saw in Marxism a closed system with potential solutions to every problem was doomed to lead to the collapse we are now witnessing.

For social scientists, Marxism is still the most appropriate theoretical tool for the understanding of inequality in its genesis and its complexity. As Bogumil Jewsiewicki[8] points out Marxism is today, as yesterday, the tool which cannot be disregarded when setting the problem of inequality, but it can no longer be useful to solve it.

To transfer the failure of social practices on the doctrine itself could lead to the destruction of the only coherent - and not yet replaced - theory of inequality currently at our disposal. But social sciences should not only state the failure worldwide of the Marxist policies, they should also accurately and intelligently report on it and explain it. In conclusion we could say that this is a task which has been underestimated until now, and which should be given much more importance.

NOTES

1. Anyang Nyongo, Peter (ed.), 1988, *Afrique: La Longue Marche vers la Démocratie*, Paris, Publi-Sud.
2. Rostow, W.W., 1960, *The Stages of Economic Growth*, Cambridge: Cambridge University Press.
3. Gunder Franck, André, 1966, 'The Development of Underdevelopment', *Monthly Review*, No.4.
4. Furtado, Celso, 1976, *Théorie du développement économique*, 2nd Ed., Paris: P.U.F.
5. Amin, Samir, 1970, *L'accumulation à l'échelle mondiale*, Paris: Anthropos.
6. Hountondji, P., 1988, 'L'appropriation collective du savoir: tâches nouvelles pour une politique scientifique', *Genève-Afrique*, Vol.XXVI, No.1, pp.49-66.
7. Hountondji, P., 1990, 'La démocratie aujourd'hui', *Afrique 2000* (revue de l'Institut Panafricain des Relations Internationales), No.1.
8 In a paper at the annual congress of the African Studies Association at Atlanta, USA, in November 1989. Bogumil Jewsiewicki is an African specialist from the department of history at Laval University in Quebec.

18

The Transformations in the Role of the State and their Impact on Higher Education - A Latin American Perspective on Research and Graduate Training

ISABEL LICHA

I. INTRODUCTION

In this chapter, I shall attempt to balance the main problems that feature in Latin American societies today, and the challenges they pose, particularly for social scientists in the region. An analysis will be made of the changes that are taking place between the state and the social sciences in Latin America, which seem to point to a new role for the university as an institution, particularly concerning the function of research and postgraduate teaching.

Current Problems and Challenges in the Latin American Society

It is trite to maintain that the countries of the region are experiencing an extremely difficult situation due to external debts and the imposition of programmes set by the International Monetary Fund (IMF), which disturb the development of the continent. In an attempt to balance this situation, Cardoso [*1988: 18-19*] puts it this way: '...we have clear signs of crisis, which indicate a Latin American economy totally weakened by a large debt, the scarce capacity of investment and the disorganisation and incapacity of the Public Sector to continue investing'.

The current situation in Latin America, including its insertion into the international system, the new social division of work, external conditioning and technological issues, is once more focusing the debate around the 'new dependence' problem [*Castells y Laserna 1989*] and the 'economic and social stagnation and disarticulation' [*Fajnzylber 1989*] that characterise the countries of the region.

Facing this situation, Latin American societies are trying to respond through action and pressure that express their social and

247

political demands, summed up by their expectations for a more equitable society and the improvement of democratic life in both social and economic terms. These 'new demands', pressures and institutional conflicts in the continent [*Calderón 1989: 58*] will become more critical during the next few decades, and will imply the creation of new socio-political and cultural spaces for a more pluralistic and substantial democracy. However, Calderón states as a warning that in spite of positive action by the proper social actors, it is impossible to foresee if they will really be able to oppose the new dominant forms of power which have resulted from the current capitalist restructuring and power accumulation in the central countries [*Calderón 1989: 61-62*]

The importance of the Latin American intellectuals' commitment (the 'commitment ethics', as Cardoso calls it), and the new role of Latin American universities to produce knowledge and create values during the next decades should be emphasised when searching for a solution to these problems.

The Challenges of Social Sciences Facing the Latin American Situation

The so-called 'crisis of paradigms' in social science, understood as the revision of theoretical models, was in force in Latin America between 1950 and 1970. It has been explained in terms of 'societal' crisis of the world system including both Latin America and the Caribbean. This crisis could have interdicted the inherited approaches, thus generating the crisis of its proper explanatory models [*Sonntag 1989: 16*].

Nevertheless, when producing knowledge and facing social change in Latin America, it is necessary to keep in mind that the inadequate explanatory capacity of the theoretical models, developed between 1950 and the beginning of 1970, is possibly due either to changes not considered by those models, or to social and political processes that have led to the revaluation of the idea of democracy and the concept of change and its actors [*Calderón 1989: 68-69*].

In the process of theoretical renovation, the need to re-think the epistemological foundation, the process of conceptualising, the theoretical construction and the way to approach reality, in social science, has been emphasised. This implies both the analysis of new topics and the reconsideration of old ones [*Sonntag 1989: 17*].

Attempting to analyse the challenges that Latin America and the Caribbean pose to social sciences, Sonntag differentiates between real social challenges and internal ones. He considers that the big

248

challenges to social sciences in the region emerge as a result of the processes of change experienced in the real-social ones. These changes are related to the following topics:

(1) The power problem, being the political problem concerning the new structural heterogeneity (that is, the accelerating differentiation and diversification of Latin-American societies), and its effects on the insertion of collective actors into society;
(2) The social movements and their organisations;
(3) The state reform (rethought and reformed as a collective institution);
(4) The democracy issue (to know it in social and economic terms).

As far as the renovation of topics in the Latin American social sciences is concerned, Sonntag poses the political problem first, and second, refers to other relevant topics, such as the cultural pluralism and the problem of heterogeneity and homogeneity, the transnationalisation processes and the integration of Latin America and the Caribbean (with emphasis on the macro-cultural aspects), and the accelerated technical change and its impact in terms of opportunities and risks.

Sonntag maintains that the internal challenges cannot be focused separately, since the theories, concepts and methods of social sciences are closely linked to the objects of study. He suggests the need to review the interdisciplinarity that has characterised social sciences in the region, and proposes that it should be given new epistemological contents together with new conceptualisations and methods, so that it can visualise the economic, political and ideological-cultural activities, from an integral analytical scope [*Sonntag 1989: 13-25*].

In this way, new theoretical challenges (paradigms and methodologies) are posed, which compel the introduction of changes in the systems of scientific education and the setting-up of new research programmes. This, in turn, leads us to consider a new institutional development frame (for research and teaching) permitting a renewal, a consolidation and an extension to academic activity. Such new conditions of institutional development for social science are seriously threatened and constrained by an increasingly precarious situation suffered by academic activity.

Social Sciences and the State in Latin America

During the 1960s and 1970s, social sciences experienced accelerated growth in Latin America. This growth was illustrated by the surge of

249

important offers of careers and specialities at university and post-graduate degree level, in increased research activity and in the number of research centres or institutes.

By the end of the 1970s, a downfall in the number of research centres or institutes for social sciences began, probably due to a combination of factors such as political repression, the saturation of occupational markets, the decrease in state resources and conflicts within universities. These circumstances favoured the growth of private centres in different Latin American countries, and this independent sector prevailed in terms of academic work in some countries, such as Argentina, Chile and Uruguay, and reached a certain relevance in others, such as Brazil, Colombia and Ecuador, while Mexico and Venezuela registered a minor development.

Latin American research still prevails at university level, mainly where there has been an institutional continuity more or less linked to resource availability provided by the state, such as in Brazil, Mexico, Venezuela and Colombia.

In the Latin American region, the role played by the state in the development of universities, and particularly in scientific activities, is fundamental. The extension of universities is considered as the starting point of the dynamics of science development in the region. Brunner [*1989*], points out that social sciences could not have developed in Latin America if they had not been incorporated as modern disciplines into universities. At the same time, he states that universities themselves could have neither existed nor reached their targets without financial support from the states and, consequently, social sciences could not have developed in Latin America without public support canalised through university budgets.

University centres, however, are afflicted by the current restrictions in state resources, where the main problem today is to maintain and consolidate the places for research and teaching. Given the crisis affecting the university as an institution, and the increasing precariousness of research in terms of deteriorated wage rates and difficult working conditions, a dismantling process in research capacities is taking place at universities.

The crisis affecting the activities of research centres and the transformation suffered by the state itself in Latin America are two factors significantly influencing institutional development and the academic system. This influence could mean a serious backward movement in the scientific policy of these countries.

As for the state, continuous budget-cuts and difficulties within the public university system, are foreseeable. Generally speaking, the difficulties within universities concern both the preparation of researchers, and the need to maintain and develop important places for typically academic theoretical reflection. For this reason, it is important to discuss the role, characteristics and prospects of university research, and the preparation of social scientists.

Towards a New Role of Universities?

In Latin America, universities are an important part of the national scientific and technical infrastructure, and the greatest portion of national scientific research is undertaken in them. But while they have been experiencing strong growth during the last few decades, they have also suffered a chronic scarcity of financial resources, which has severely restricted their research possibilities. Since university research in underdeveloped countries is closely linked to the expectations of contributing to a more equitable and autonomous society, and since a great portion of scientific effort is made through the preparation of human resources and research activities at university level, their participation obviously becomes essential.

The prime objective should be to build and preserve a consistent and balanced scientific and cultural system which is able to create new possibilities, and prepare highly qualified personnel capable of developing the universities. Today, however, we are witnessing a process of increasing loss of influence by the public university which could be considered as one of the main obstacles to the achievement of these social development objectives.

In this period of crisis, different governments are trying to create a transition based on strategies for modernisation and restructuring, through industrial restructuring policies, labour productivity improvement, real salary decreases, the introduction of new products and service technology, etc. All of these have serious consequences on employment, decentralisation activities, services and so on. This context also introduces changes in the state-science relationship, since it provides new outlines to scientific activity, marked by a short-run conception and immediate benefits, and biased by the 'helpful research' notion, according to the techno-economic imperativeness. This compels us to re-think the relationships between science-university-society, so that universities can carry out their social and cultural missions.

Academic research plays a fundamental role in the total effort to produce balanced knowledge. In this sense, it carries out educational, economic, social and cultural functions. The degradation of the academic research system would have serious repercussions. The budget-cuts imposed on universities during the 1980s, together with new ways of distributing state resources for research and the pressures (from the state and the market) for doing research considered 'especially helpful', forced universities to seek new ways of organising research activity. But there is a risk of having academic researchers work on short-run objectives, giving up the more social and cultural ones linked to a strategic research activity. On the other hand, it could restrict the places assigned to academic research and, consequently, reduce the university capacity to develop research activities.

How can we face the crisis experienced by universities and particularly by research activities linked to them?

The case of research

During the past decade, we have witnessed an increasing reduction in resources from governments to university level research activities. This trend can imply a progressive reduction or the collapse of many research units. As Dagnino [*nd: 140*] points out, the causes of this reduction are not merely the result of certain circumstances, for they are closely related to the way the development of Latin American economies is being carried out, particularly in state participation. As long as the pattern of a dependent and excluding development, characterised by an internationalisation of the economy, keeps wide sectors of the population out of the development process, it is impossible to overcome such a situation.

Should these trends continue during the next few decades, Latin American universities will certainly play an increasingly passive role in the preparation of both new researchers and research activities. They will have more restricted functions than ever, and will rely on financial organisations and on the productive sector.

A better scenario would be an equitable, autonomous and democratic society where the university could play a new, active and broader role related to the development of new skills demanded by the society in terms of producing knowledge, preparing researchers and servicing the community. However, it seems at this moment that the intervention of the Latin American scientific community is required to rescue and consolidate the historically-created academic spaces.

These trends are best appreciated in the case of social sciences. It should be recalled here that at the beginning of 1990, there was a real 'explosion of numbers' [*Brunner*] - institutions, researchers, students, resources and projects - and a real 'multiplication of disciplines'

[*Brunner*], as shown in the explosive increase of the 'matricula', the proliferation of courses at university and postgraduate levels, the continual flowing of resources (at least until the beginning of the 1980s) from the states and international cooperation. Thus, according to Brunner, the social sciences sector (and in general all sciences) has reached such a level of complexity, proliferation and institutional differentiation in Latin America that the sciences-state relationship needs to be rethought. Brunner points out that in the case of social sciences, these relationships will imply that the state - together with the so-called 'academic oligarchy' (or the 'high clergy' of the social sciences community) - will become the driving force in the new guidelines for the distribution of public subsidies, which are meant for the market mechanisms. We will therefore witness new relationships between the sciences and the state, in which state resources will be assigned with the participation of the 'high clergy', who as expert judges will choose among projects. What Brunner points out in the particular case of social sciences seems to be the rule for all sciences.

Postgraduate research training dilemmas and deadlocks

Even postgraduate training in Latin America is developed thanks to an explicit official policy for the improvement of higher education in the different countries of the region. This was due to the modernisation of the higher education system undertaken by different states and reflected in the different attempts to reform the university and to make new laws for higher education.

We think that postgraduate training is implemented in Latin America with this new vision of the university as a research centre producing knowledge.

The main reasons underlying the rise of postgraduate training in Latin America refer to several needs; the need to expand the higher education system and to improve the quality of teaching through the preparation of competent professors, the need to prepare researchers in order to stimulate the development of scientific research, and the need to prepare technical and intellectual workers who are highly qualified and capable of meeting the needs for national development.

In this sense, the research-postgraduate training relationship arises basically with the aim of getting an effective contribution from the postgraduate studies to prepare excellent professors, researchers and highly qualified professionals. In spite of the distorted relationship often established between research and postgraduate education, which will not be considered in detail here, during the past few decades there has been considerable development in postgraduate studies, but its structure needs to be consolidated.

The basic weakness of the Latin American postgraduate system, as expressed by the institutional, administrative and financial instability of most postgraduate courses, as well as their uncertain continuity which is basically threatened by the perspective of more budget-cuts, is highly preoccupying. Given the changes that have been taking place in the role of the state in scientific development, the question is whether the conditions are right for the master and doctorate programmes to develop further. Taking into account that master and doctorate programmes are introduced into universities, and that investment in research done by Latin American universities is decreasing, it could be concluded that research activity will be increasingly missing in these programmes. These trends are related to postgraduate studies, together with those observed in research activities, and comprise the major challenges that Latin American universities have to face in the future.

The future of research and postgraduate education structures at universities should be carefully studied through analysis and understanding of the mechanisms that simultaneously determine their efficiency or non-efficiency [*Durham 1986*]. This obliges us to investigate the future of research activities and postgraduate studies done by universities in our respective countries. We should also ask why the development of research activities apparently rely on the creation of relatively autonomous niches within universities; why it is difficult to link research activity to university degrees, or to consolidate it at master and doctorate levels; and why this has been concentrated at a small number of institutions. This will certainly lead to a better understanding of the level of development reached by the university as an institution, its limits and potentialities, in order to re-think and change it, so that it can play an active role in the transformation of the society.

II. CONCLUSIONS

Several conclusions can be drawn:

(1) Latin America is moving towards a new kind of dependence and new ways of development, which emphasise its economic and social disorganisation and/or stagnation.

(2) Even though a period of new demands, pressures and institutional

254

conflicts is predicted as social organisations struggle for greater well-being and a better democratic life, they will not have enough strength to deal with the new ways of domination.

(3) The future development of Latin America will inevitably be dependent on the new configuration of the world system. There could be little development without any equitable access and distribution of benefits, which would increase social conflict and tension.

(4) This situation poses big challenges to social sciences and intellectual workers for the new topics which focus on the economic, political, social and cultural problems that affect Latin American societies, implying a theoretical and epistemological renovation of social sciences. Meanwhile, there is also a great need for renewing the ethical commitment of intellectual workers and universities with the demands of well-being and democracy in Latin American societies.

(5) One of the most important consequences of the changes produced in the role of the state in Latin America influences the relationships between the state and social sciences, which, in turn, implies the assignment of a new role to universities. This is illustrated by a progressive process of resource reduction from the governments to research activities done at universities, and by the surge of a new pattern for the distribution of public funds for research activities.

(6) The new role of universities is justified by conjunctural reasons, and, most importantly, conceptual ones. It is closely related to the pattern of dependent and excluding development governing the Latin American economies. This forces universities to play a passive role, submitting themselves to the guidelines and directions given by financial and productive organisations.

(7) A process of 're-arrangement' of social sciences facing the state is taking place, marked by an increasing 'mercantilisation' of the research function.

(8) As for the master and doctorate programmes, they are marked by the same fate imposed on university research, as their continuity and consolidation are menaced.

(9) Since the university crisis is manifested simultaneously in the creation of autonomous or state centres, which tend to become the new research locus, this problem should be given first priority due to its complementary versus competitive relation with universities and for what it implies as a mechanism of intra-academic classification.

(10) The situation analysed here poses the need for undertaking a profound study on the future of research and postgraduate training at universities, as well as the need for re-thinking the role that the university as an institution should play under the current Latin American conditions, so that it can effectively contribute to the social transformation of the continent.

REFERENCES

Brunner, Jose J., 1989, *Ciencias Sociales y Estado. Reflexiones en voz alta*, Chile: FLACSO, Mimeo, p.23.

Calderón, Fernando and Patricia Provoste, 1989, 'La Construcción Institucional de las Ciencias Sociales en América Latina', Buenos Aires: *David y Goliath* 55, pp.66-79.

Castells, Manuel and Roberto Laserna, 1989, 'La Nueva Dependencia. Cambio Tecnológico y Reestructuración Socioeconómica en Latinoamerica', *David y Goliath* 55, pp.2-16.

Cardoso, Fernando H., 1988, 'Olas Chocando Contra los Arrecifes. El Estado ante la Perplejidad Social', *David y Goliath* 53, pp.16-24.

Dagnino, Renato, (s.f.): 'A Universidade e a pesquisa científica e tecnológica', *Ciencia e Cultura* 37(7): pp.33-154.

Durham, Eunice, 1986, 'A Política de Pos-Graduçaõ e as Ciencias Sociais', Rio de Janeiro: *BIB*, pp.41-55.

Fajnzylber, Fernando, 1989, 'La Reestructuración Industrial y Tecnológica Internacional: La Caja Negra del Progreso Técnico', *David y Goliath* 55, pp.25-33.

Sonntag, Heinz R., 1989, 'Los desafíos de las sociedades y de las ciencias sociales de America Latina y el Caribe hacia el proximo milenario'. in SONNTAG, Heinz (ed.), *Nuevos Temas, Nuevos Contenidos. Las ciencias sociales de America Latina y El Caribe ante el nuevo siglo*, Caracas: UNESCO-Editorial Nueva Sociedad.

19

Social Sciences in the Arab World

BASSEM SERHAN

The overall condition and performance of the social sciences in the Arab world could be described as poor or marginal, as it has several crippling handicaps, at both the theoretical and the research levels.

Most Arab social scientists have been trained in the Occident, especially in the United States and in Western Europe. This training has prepared them to deal with problems in industrial societies rather than in their own countries, and has therefore set the priorities of issues and social concerns to be addressed by Arab social scientists, priorities which do not generally coincide with those in their own societies. Moreover, Arab social scientists, by virtue of their training, have been equipped with theoretical tools - theories and concepts - which fail to explain social interaction and social development in their own countries. This problem exists in areas ranging from family relations to social change and modernisation.

For this reason, some Arab social scientists have been, during the past decade, calling for a build up in indigenous Arab social sciences which would have conceptual relevance to Arab culture and historical development. Whilst a few efforts have already taken place, it still appears difficult to break though the Western social science shell which has been acquired by Arabs. It could take another two or more decades to improve the indigenous resource base. However, the universality of science does not appear to contradict the contention that social sciences are conceptually historically based and directed or geared.

Arab social scientists work either in universities or in research institutions, most of which are government controlled and financed. Due to the fact that most Arab states, if not all of them, are politically repressive and oppressive, freedom of thought and the avenues of research open to Arab social scientists are highly curtailed by various open and subtle mechanisms.

The above conditions have created three groups of Arab social scientists:

257

(1) Those who stick to teaching and avoid carrying out any controversial research work;
(2) Those who consider themselves as technocrats or experts whose job is to rationalise government policies and the state system if reform is adopted by the state;
(3) Those who consider themselves as having the duty to understand their own societies and to carry out research work that will raise the consciousness of the masses and accelerate the Arab social movement towards democracy and to create a better society.

Five areas of social research are frowned upon in some Arab countries and are considered taboo in others. These areas are:

(i)   The political system and political corruption;
(ii) Religion and religious conflicts;
(iii) Ethnic relations and conflicts;
(iv) Income distribution;
(v)   Gender issues.

Since most research is government financed, and any field research must receive government approval, Arab social scientists mostly find themselves working on micro issues and problems, for example relations, media, educational problems, social work, women's work, etc.

The other major area for Arab social scientists is development studies and research. This is mostly done by social scientists employed by various Arab development centres and by Ministries of Planning. However, since most Arab countries lack the institutions that can make use of the findings of these micro studies, and to some extent of development studies, the real return of such research is minimal. Moreover, pertaining to development studies, little benefit arises from them, as social and developmental policies in the Arab countries are set a-priori by the ruler and his consultants, or by a small clique of the ruling elite. One major example concerns manpower development and labour migration studies which several Arab governments commissioned social scientists in development centres and universities to study during the course of the past 12 years. Huge sums have been spent on these studies, of which most revealed fascinating findings, recommendations and planning alternatives. However, the actual policies of Arab governments have run contrary to all that was expressed or recommended by these studies.

This leads to the point that the gap is still wide in the Arab countries between social science research and social policy. Arab policy makers are still suspicious of Arab social scientists, as it seems that they require research for 'decorative purposes' or because it is a phenomenon of 'modern states'.

As for the prevalent schools of thought amongst Arab scientists, one could speak of the classical division of left and right or Marxist and capitalist. An emerging school of thought is the Islamic social, which is basically returning to Islamic teachings and heritage to extract its concepts and definitions of socio-economic phenomena. The future of this school is not clear.

Finally, there are the positivist social scientists who believe that they should carry on a 'scientific' study of society and of social phenomena without any ideological attachments.

Despite the gloomy picture described above of the lot of social sciences in the Arab world, many Arab social scientists are struggling to establish their field and to enhance the role of the social sciences in societal change and social progress.

CONTRIBUTORS

AFSHAR, Farhad
Institut für Soziologie, Fachgebiet Entwicklungssoziologie
Bern - SWITZERLAND

AL-NASSAR, Ali
Institut Arabe de planification
Safat - KUWAIT

AUROI, Claude
IUED - Institut universitaire d'études du développement
Geneva - SWITZERLAND

BEAUD, Michel
GEMDEV et Paris VIII
Paris - FRANCE

BENACHENHOU, Abdellatif
UNESCO
Paris - FRANCE

BONVIN, Jean
OECD - Development Centre
Paris - FRANCE

BOYE, Abdel Kader
Université de Dakar
Dakar - SENEGAL

CALDERON, Fernando
CLACSO
Buenos Aires - ARGENTINA

De KADT, Emanuel
IDS - Institute of Development Studies
Brighton, Sussex - U.K.

Dos SANTOS, Mario
CLACSO
Buenos Aires - ARGENTINA

HOUNTONDJI, Paulin J.
Université Nationale du Bénin
Cotonou - BENIN

JAIN, R.B.
Department of Political Science, University of Delhi
Delhi - INDIA

LICHA, Isabel
CENDES
Caracas - VENEZUELA

MAMDANI, Mahmood
Centre for Basic Research
Kampala - UGANDA

MARS, Zoe
IDS - Institute of Development Studies
Brighton, Sussex - U.K.

MILADI, Salem
Ministère du plan & du développement régional
Tunis - TUNISIA

PROVOSTE, Patricia
CLACSO
Buenos Aires - ARGENTINA

SCHVARZER, Jorge
Centro de Investigaciones Sociales Sobre el Estado y la Administración
Buenos Aires - ARGENTINA

SENEVIRATNE, D.G.P.
Agrarian Research & Training Institute
Colombo - SRI LANKA

SERHAN, Bassem
Department of Sociology - Kuwait University
Kuwait City - KUWAIT

SØRENSEN, Georg
Institute of Political Science
Aarhus - DENMARK

FOH TSRANG TANG
Institute of Economics
Nankang - TAIWAN

WHITE, Gordon
IDS - Institute of Development Studies
Brighton, Sussex - U.K.